10/02

Crisis on Campus

Crisis on Campus
Confronting Academic Misconduct

Wilfried Decoo
with a contribution by Jozef Colpaert

The MIT Press
Cambridge, Massachusetts
London, England

The book was set in Sabon in '3B2' by Asco Typesetters, Hong Kong
Printed and bound in the United States of America.

Library of Congress Cataloging-in-Publication Data

Decoo, Wilfried, 1946–
   Crisis on campus : confronting academic misconduct / Wilfried Decoo with a
contribution by Jozef Colpaert.
      p.   cm.
   Includes bibliographical references and index.
   ISBN 0-262-04201-0 (hc. : alk. paper)
   1. College discipline. 2. Plagiarism. I. Colpaert, Jozef. II. Title.
LB2344 .D43   2002
378.1′958—dc21   2001044477

The single most important component in an institutional culture of research integrity is institutional leadership committed to ethical conduct. If the institution's leaders are committed to integrity in research and act on that commitment, the campus will follow that lead; conversely, if the perception develops that the leaders pay only lip service to ethical conduct, the campus will adopt the same attitude.

—C. Kristina Gunsalus

Contents

Preface

Persons who become involved in the discovery, investigation, and reporting of alleged academic misconduct seldom do so voluntarily or because of a natural scientific interest in the matter. One day without warning the subject is forced on them, much as they may become the victims of an accident, an assault, or a burglary. The first reaction is often bewilderment, anger, or fear. Nothing has prepared them to assess the situation calmly and objectively, or to decide on a judicious course of action.

My own involvement with the subject came about in just this way. In 1996 I was asked to review for an American journal a book written by a professor whom I will call X1. In the course of my analysis, I found passages that had been taken verbatim or nearly verbatim from other authors without, in my opinion, adequate citation. Fortunately, the responsibility of assessing and eventually reporting the matter was not mine alone. An Australian colleague of mine had discovered that some of her work had also been reused by X1, in her opinion also without proper identification of the sources. For several months we struggled with the excruciating question of how to handle this distressing discovery, in the process learning a lot about the challenges and variables associated with such a quandary. My Australian colleague contacted X1 privately, but his response was not deemed satisfactory. We finally consulted with the review editor of the journal concerned, who happened to work at the same American university as X1. From that point on, the matter was out of our hands and was handled by X1's department chair, by his university administration, and by the executive committee of the journal. Both the university and the journal conducted independent evaluations, which led to the conclusion that plagiarism had occurred. With the agreement of X1, the journal published the case in detail, including a confession and genuine apologies by X1, who showed meekness as well as courage in facing the charges.

The case of X1 showed remarkable contrasts. On the one hand there were extenuating circumstances. All who knew X1 agreed that he was not a dishonest person and that there was no intent to deceive. The reasons for the plagiarism were understandable, even ordinary: a book that evolved from a course syllabus that had been put together hastily using various sources; a tradition of free sharing of information; enthusiasm to produce; time pressures; and, yes, slovenliness in referencing. X1 was probably not the first person in his field to indulge in this kind of behavior. In view of these circumstances, the assessors could have handled the charge quietly, minimizing the infringements and avoiding public disclosure. On the other hand, the university where X1 worked is known for its high moral standards and its strict honor code. It had to handle the case as seriously as possible, though it was obvious that the administrators involved struggled with the determination of an appropriate sanction in view of the extenuating circumstances and X1's otherwise good character. But a sanction was applied. The journal that published the case devoted much space to an analysis of the facts. Though it was done in agreement with X1, the public handling left him with deep scars.

In 1998 I was confronted with a second case, this time in Europe. As a member of an academic committee, I was asked to evaluate a recently defended and accepted doctoral dissertation for a supplemental research award. I will call the writer of the dissertation X2. After a thorough analysis, I concluded that X2 had not conducted any original research, nor indeed any of the announced research, and that nearly all of the material had been copied or paraphrased from other sources without, in my opinion, adequate citation. I submitted my report confidentially to the committee chair, who was also the president of that university. I expected a process similar to that followed by the U.S. university. I witnessed instead the distressing but, I have discovered, more common process of minimizing the alleged academic misconduct and invalidating the investigating process: a primary institutional concern with damage control, immediate containment of the matter, a limited internal investigation within a closed circle, ambiguous conclusions, and a forced closure of the dossier without further consequences for the academic in question.

The irony of the two cases is that X1's plagiarism was relatively minor, explainable in terms of time pressures and a defective methodology. Still his university, to its credit, did not hesitate to act appropriately, make a finding, and apply proper punishment. In the case of X2, the weight of identical offenses was tenfold, a whole doctoral committee was involved, and the yield obtained (a doctoral degree) was incomparably higher. The key players at that university, however, preferred a different approach and came to a different assessment.

After the first case was concluded, I received praise for my contribution to the advancement of professional standards. Even X1 thanked my Australian colleague and me publicly for having discovered the improprieties and for having helped resolve his problem. In the second case, my report, though requested, was clearly viewed as an unwelcome and even inappropriate intrusion. The message I got was that I had taken my assignment too seriously and should have closed my eyes as a matter of "collegiality."

Those disparate experiences, the effort involved, and my ensuing interest in the subject encouraged me to further investigate aspects of the detection, analysis, assessment, reporting, and prevention of alleged academic misconduct. In the course of this book I will continue to refer to the cases of X1 and X2—in particular the latter, because it provides numerous instructive examples. An "X3" and an "X4", in whose cases I was also involved, appear later in this study (see sections 2.3.3 and 2.5.2). And we may one day, regretfully, need to add more X-numbers. I felt no need to identify any of these persons—and attributed to all the masculine gender—though insiders aware of the cases may of course remember them. I did my duty in reporting the findings discreetly to the appropriate superiors; the responsibility from that point belonged to those who handled the cases. X1 was found guilty, X2 was exonerated, X3 and X4 never faced an investigation. This book does not tell their accounts as the usual "case studies". It is not a document filled with anecdotes about misconduct. There are no unsavory revelations. The details of how to detect and analyze alleged academic misconduct is a lengthy and strenuous—and even tedious—process.

Objectives

There are already numerous publications on academic misconduct. The bibliography at the end of this book represents only a small part of the estimated five to six thousand books and articles that have already been devoted to the subject during the past few decades. As I studied this literature, it was clear that the authors have struggled to find an acceptable balance between general features describing the phenomenon of academic misconduct as such, and characteristics typical of a certain discipline, a certain aspect, or a certain case. A book focusing on misconduct in medical research or on plagiarism will almost always discuss the broader perspective as well, whereas publications meant to sketch the entirety of misconduct actually tend to concentrate on just one discipline—for example, biochemical research—or on the codification of rules for avoiding misconduct, or on consequences for the whistle-blower. I also struggled to find a balance as this book grew from an analysis of alleged plagiarism to a broader-based investigation. I must now stake out its territory.

This book, mainly intended for faculty, institutional decision makers, and graduate students who have only scant knowledge of the realm of academic misconduct, has five goals:

• Against a short historical background, it presents a concise view of contemporary circumstances and developments that seem to affect the nature and frequency of academic misconduct.

• It presents a brief, but still comprehensive view of what can be seen as phases in academic misconduct: detection, analysis, assessment, reporting, handling, and prevention. Some publications are meant to deal with only one or two of these phases and/or with detailed histories of famous cases. Some authors make a thorough investigation of only one particular aspect, an approach that is very valuable for specialists. This book aims at giving a more general overview of the realm of academic misconduct. I have avoided writing in detail on items that have already been treated exhaustively elsewhere, referring the reader instead to earlier studies for more specific information. However, I have probed aspects that seemed to deserve greater attention more deeply.

• It applies this methodology to a detailed case study—a doctoral dissertation—to show the complexities and ambiguities of a specific case in the humanities and to provide concrete information on related facets. Particular attention goes to techniques of academic "make-believe," to the (electronic) detection of possible plagiarism, to the analysis of textual similarities, to the mutual collusion that can occur within a doctoral committee, and to the challenges associated with correct assessment. The case study forms a thread throughout the rest of the book, providing both the testimony of personal experience and an empirical basis. Some of these elements may be useful for subsequent comparative research on misconduct.

• It gives practical and sensible advice both to whistle-blowers and to those accused of academic misconduct. My hope is that this book will be useful to those who will one day be confronted with the unexpected.

• Finally, this book is rather short and clearly structured for easy reference, so that it can serve as a handy guide, particularly at the graduate-student level.

As acknowledged above, on a number of aspects of academic misconduct, I am less specialized than researchers who have studied these topics for a much longer time and from highly qualified perspectives. I commend these studies to those who need further information on a relevant point. My point of entry is somewhat different from the usual specialties that deal with misconduct. My discipline is in the humanities. I have academic experience in both Belgium and the United States. My linguistic expertise is useful in studying and identifying textual plagiarism, and my focus is on practical matters. I hope that this combination introduces elements that will meet with the interest and indulgence of those whom I consider major researchers into facets of misconduct. Whatever the weaknesses of this book, I am sure specialized researchers will concur on this point: every new publication on misconduct helps to raise the awareness of a phenomenon that deserves much more attention within academia.

Structure

The chapters of this book deal systematically with major phases of the subject. It is important to carefully separate each phase from the others if academic misconduct is to be handled with prudence, dignity, and respect of the rights of each side. Indeed, the history of academic misconduct shows that it is an area where hasty judgments, generalizations, outrage, and irrationality have set the tone and influenced the consequences.

After an introductory chapter, which deals with context and general concepts necessary for understanding academic misconduct, the next two chapters handle "Detection" and "Analysis" of alleged misconduct. Both chapters often refer to each other, for the data of an analysis are necessary in understanding the rationale of detection techniques. Space limitations do not allow a thorough description of all detection procedures and analysis techniques, as they apply to diverse forms of misconduct. I will concentrate on some more than on others but will try to touch on most, referring the interested reader to more detailed approaches to certain forms of misconduct.

Detection and analysis focus only on gathering and studying the facts. The fourth chapter, "Assessment," deals with appraisal: to what extent do the facts support a diagnosis of actual academic misconduct? What valid criteria can be applied to build a case? How should traditions and regulations in one field that differ from those in another field be taken into consideration? Can we obtain evaluations from respected academics to corroborate the seriousness of the findings?

The fifth chapter, "Reporting and handling," discusses whether and how to take the next step. Should we report misconduct? In view of all the misery it can provoke for the whistle-blower, the accused, the institution, and individuals associated with all three—what considerations should compel this step? What reporting procedures can be used both to protect the whistle-blower and to respect the rights of the accused? What are the options for institutional response? If they chose to minimize and neutralize the allegations, what prompts such decisions? What are the options for the whistle-blower and for the accused at that stage? What can go wrong at the institutional level and what are the consequences?

Finally, the whole matter requires a more constructive perspective than sometimes ad hoc and unsatisfactory reactions to alleged misconduct. What can we do to help prevent academic misconduct?

This book refers to a number of examples of alleged academic misconduct. Most of them have been reported in professional journals or in the press. Although I indicate my sources, I avoid using the names of the whistle-blowers, the defendants, and the arbitrators. These cases have indeed been traumatic for the people involved, and I want my readers to concentrate on the cases, rather than the individuals, although the sources that I cite do contain such information. Because an important part of the discussion deals with X2's doctoral dissertation, which is meant as a case study of specific problems, I opted for a strictly anonymous approach.

For the sake of delineating responsibilities for what is written in this book, Wilfried Decoo is the author of all the material, with the exception of sections 2.3.1 and 2.3.2 and the Appendix on Cerberus, which were written by Jozef Colpaert.

Acknowledgments

I am indebted to my colleague and friend Jozef Colpaert of the University of Antwerp, who contributed to a few valuable sections. My deep gratitude goes to Ruth H. Sanders of Miami University at Oxford, Ohio, who read the manuscript as it grew and who provided many suggestions and corrections. Other very beneficial and effective readers included Randall H. Jones of Brigham Young University (U.S.A.), and Michael Levy of the University of Queensland (Australia). Thanks go to Elizabeth Judd for her editorial fine-tuning.

1

Introduction

1.1 Finding the right balance

Since the 1980s, professional journals in many fields and numerous books have delineated cases of academic misconduct and discussed the phenomenon. An online search of any well-known journal with keywords such as *misconduct, plagiarism, falsification*, and *fraud* will yield a perhaps surprising harvest. At the same time, major groups and institutions in various parts of the world, such as the U.S. Office of Research Integrity, the American Association of University Professors, the European Committee on Publication Ethics, the German Max-Planck-Gesellschaft and Deutsche Forschungsgemeinschaft, the French Centre National de la Recherche Scientifique, and the Dutch Koninklijke Nederlandse Akademie van Wetenschappen, have acted to raise the academic community's awareness of academic misconduct. Their new or renewed policies and regulations encourage reporting of cases of alleged misconduct and suggest procedures for handling them, for combating misconduct more efficiently, and for protecting the whistle-blower.

When dealing with a delicate subject like academic misconduct, it is important to avoid two extremes. One is the tendency to minimize the seriousness of the offense. Some feel that the academic community receives undeserved and disproportionately negative attention when cases of alleged academic misconduct are discussed and handled publicly. Aren't the cases very rare? Aren't they best resolved easily and locally, without publicity? This approach, however, risks underrating the extent of the problem, of encouraging inaction, and of undermining academic credibility in the long run. At the other extreme is moral indignation and rancor about such cases, which may quickly become highly adversarial and legalistic. This negative response can infuse our collegial relations with fundamental distrust, breed witch hunts, and defame our profession.

Thus, finding the right balance is crucial. One way to do this is to make the issue discussible in an atmosphere of probity and objectivity. Academic misconduct is an inescapable reality that deserves to be researched like any other subject, even if such research presents major challenges, as Anderson (1999), for example, has pointed out. Any scientific field with the ethical courage to look at its own realm, identify areas of risk, analyze and assess troubling data, suggest ways to avoid deviation, and work to raise standards is an honor to its discipline and to the larger academic endeavor.

1.2   Entering the realm of academic misconduct

A few preliminary considerations are in order to introduce the topic as such. How old are controversies about academic misconduct? How do we define the terms *academic* and *misconduct*? Do characteristics of hard sciences versus soft sciences influence the perception of improprieties? Does such perception depend on the status of offenders?

1.2.1   A historical perspective

Recognition of academic misconduct dates back to at least the seventeenth century, when disputes about authorship and invention rights were taken before the newly created royal scientific societies in England and France. Gradually concepts such as intellectual property, copyright, patent, and trademark became accepted in the Western world and backed up by its legal systems. The history of research and discovery is replete with dramatic controversies over "who was first?", with accompanying accusations of stolen concepts, falsified data, plagiarized texts, sabotage of research work, and even more repulsive deeds.

In 1830 Charles Babbage, known as "the father of computing," described most of the fraudulent practices that still occur today. He identified them as "hoaxing," "forging," "trimming," and "cooking." He could not have foreseen how ineffective his intention to "deter future offenders" by simply exposing them would be:

Scientific inquiries are more exposed than most others to the inroads of pretenders; and I feel that I shall deserve the thanks of all who really value truth, by stating some of the methods of deceiving practised by unworthy claimants for its honours, whilst the mere circumstance of their arts being known may deter future offenders. (Babbage 1830)

Publications on various forms of academic misconduct appeared throughout the twentieth century, showing that the phenomenon is far from recent (Hering 1924; Salzman 1931; Edwards 1933; Bennington 1952; Lindey 1952; Weiner 1955; Harrison 1958; Arnau 1961). Since the mid-1970s, and particularly during the 1980s, a number of well-publicized cases have drawn the attention of the American public and of politicians to the phenomenon of misconduct at universities and research institutes (see, for example, Hixson 1976; Broad and Wade 1982; Savan 1988; Bell 1992). These cases led to new considerations and procedures for investigating and handling misconduct—in other words, to the "regulatory response," which LaFollette (1999) has described very well. Meanwhile the literature on misconduct has exploded. As early as 1992, a report by the National Academy of Sciences on research misconduct listed over 1,100 bibliographical entries, mainly from the United States (National Academy of Sciences 1992).

No academic today can deny that academic misconduct is, at the very least, potentially present in all disciplines, in all parts of the world and that it involves both students and academic personnel. It not only produces unreliable scientific data but also leads to major conflicts between individuals and groups, undermines the credibility of institutions, and has a major negative impact on lives and careers of both whistle-blowers and defendants.

1.2.2 Defining academic misconduct
A brief discussion of definitions may be helpful.

About terms
The basic substantives vary: *misconduct, fraud, deceit, wrongdoing, impropriety*, and so on. Often these terms are used as synonyms, meeting the writer's need for stylistic variety, while specialists may give or request precise definitions for each. I use them interchangeably, but my preference is for the word *misconduct*.

However, *academic* misconduct, *research* misconduct, and *scientific* misconduct communicate shades of meaning that deserve some explication. *Scientific*, as used in Anglo-American institutional settings, usually refers to the hard or natural sciences, excluding soft disciplines such as the arts, humanities, and social sciences. In other languages and cultures, *science* usually includes all academic disciplines. Most of the literature dealing with research misconduct draws its examples from the natural sciences and hence uses the phrase "scientific misconduct." But since misconduct is not limited to the natural sciences, this book makes no distinction between "scientific misconduct" and "research misconduct" even though it recognizes that the nature of misconduct may differ between hard and soft sciences (see section 1.2.3).

Academic is a broader term than *research*. Strictly speaking, *research* misconduct applies only to the infringement of rules dealing with actual research (for example, experiments, data gathering, calculation, and publication of results). Most reported misconduct has to do with those activities. But other forms of wrongdoing in academia are not directly related to research per se. These include falsifying a curriculum vitae, misusing project funds for unrelated purposes, embezzling grant money, purposely giving students either higher or lower grades than they earned, giving bogus course credit to winning athletes, using one's office and position to conduct private business, granting an undeserved diploma in return for certain favors, omitting the name of a coauthor, either in publishing the article or in citing it later, rating a project proposal dishonestly or without having read the dossier, and so on. Since this book touches occasionally on such practices, the broader title "academic misconduct" seemed more suitable, though the core issues deal with research improprieties. Furthermore, within this broad focus, I concentrate on possible plagiarism as a case study.

In the United States

For research misconduct as a general phenomenon, it is common to refer to the definitions of two major American institutions, the National Science Foundation (NSF), with its Office of the Inspector General, and the Department of Health and Human Services (DHHS), with its Office of Research Integrity (ORI). NSF defined scientific misconduct as "fabrication, falsification, plagiarism, or other serious deviation from accepted practices in proposing, carrying out, or reporting results from activities funded by NSF" (NSF, Code of Federal Regulations, no. 45.689). The ORI published a similar definition: "Misconduct or misconduct in science means fabrication, falsification, plagiarism, or other practices that seriously deviate from those that are commonly accepted within the scientific community for proposing, conducting, or reporting research. It does not include honest error or honest differences in interpretations or judgments of data" (ORI, Scientific Misconduct Regulations, no. 50.102).

Faced with heterogeneous cases of alleged research misconduct, many felt that these definitions were too narrow and therefore inadequate. The U.S. Federal Commission on Research Integrity, created by Congress in 1993, held fifteen months of public hearings, studied thousands of pages of case histories, and found that a third of the reported cases of misconduct involved activities other than fabrication, falsification, and plagiarism. The commission proposed a broader definition: "significant misbehavior that fails to respect the intellectual contributions or property of others, that intentionally impedes the progress of research, or that risks corrupting the scientific record or compromising the integrity of scientific practices." It added subdefinitions of each type of misconduct (cited in Burd 1995; see also Kaiser 1996; Price 1994a; Parrish 1996; Ryan 1996).

Scientists and organizations such as the Council of the National Academy of Sciences critiqued this proposed definition. Among the grounds cited were that the need for such a wide definition was exaggerated or that it might come to encompass accepted scientific practices, such as critical reviews that could be seen as a "failure to respect the contributions of others." Holton and Grinnell (1996:I) warned that "to remain healthy, scientific research must be protected not only from misconduct but also from the undue zealotry in expanding the grounds for charging misconduct." C. K. Gunsalus, who served on the commission, defended the broader approach, concluding: "Researchers must be willing to support the adoption of a workable federal definition of misconduct: one inclusive enough to cover the existing range of misconduct, treat all scientists involved fairly, and withstand legal challenges to investigators' conclusions" (Gunsalus 1997b:I).

In a reaction to Gunsalus's article, R. Bell, of the Office of the Inspector General at NSF, pointed out that the original, so-called narrow definition of NSF already includes "other serious deviation from accepted practices." He stressed that any research misconduct, if judged serious, falls under that definition and that the reference to "fabrication, falsification, plagiarism" is meant as indication of what is to be understood as serious. He added: "The current definition puts judgment calls front and center in that to prove misconduct, the scientists and administrators who handle allegations of misconduct in science need to develop a persuasive account of how and why an action seriously violated community standards. They need to explain and defend their judgments about seriousness" (Bell 1997:B11; see also Francis 1999; Guston 1999).

In December 2000, after four years of further debate, the Office of Science and Technology Policy released its "Federal Policy on Research Misconduct" for adoption by all Federal agencies that conduct and support research (Office of Science and Technology Policy 2000). The definition, which clearly narrows the matter to "research," defines research misconduct as "fabrication, falsification, or plagiarism in proposing, performing, or reviewing research, or in reporting research results." Its definitions for each term are:

• Fabrication is making up data or results and recording or reporting them.
• Falsification is manipulating research materials, equipment, or processes, or changing or omitting data or results such that the research is not accurately represented in the research record.
• Plagiarism is the appropriation of another person's ideas, processes, results, or words without giving appropriate credit.

It should be noted that this narrow definition is applied to research funded by the U.S. Federal agencies, and that it encompasses "all basic, applied, and demonstration research in all fields of science, engineering, and mathematics. This includes, but is not limited to, research in economics, education, linguistics, medicine, psychology, social sciences, statistics, and research involving human subjects or animals."

In other countries

Other countries are carrying on similar discussions about whether the definition of academic misconduct should encompass a broad range of suspect practices or be limited to a few specific forms of misbehavior like the American "FFP" (fabrication, falsification, plagiarism) definition, which has been used as the basis for regulations in other countries.

In the Australian "National Health & Medical Research Council Statement on Scientific Practice" (1990, cited in Lock and Wells 1996:277–284), "FFP" is mentioned as the basis of misconduct, but it also includes "other practices that seriously deviate from those that are commonly accepted." Special attention is thus paid to "misleading ascription of authorship," which means adding authors to publications without their permission or authors who did not contribute to the research, and not mentioning those who did contribute. Such emphasis on the problem of authorship seems to be directly related to a number of well-publicized cases, which Swan (1996) describes.

In 1992 Denmark became one of the first European countries to take (renewed) action on scientific dishonesty. The Danish Committee on Scientific Dishonesty bases its definition on intent to deceive. It makes an interesting distinction between *serious* wrongdoing such as the fabrication of data, the distorted representation of results, and plagiarism, and *less serious* offenses such as presenting results to the public while bypassing professional forums, and failing to credit the observations from other scientists (reported by Andersen et al. 1992; see also Andersen 2000; Brydensholt 2000).

In the wake of an "unprecedented" case of research misconduct in Germany in 1997, which shook the German academic community profoundly (Koenig 1997), the Deutsche Forschungsgemeinschaft tackled the problem. A thirteen-member international panel, "Self-Control in Science," prepared a set of vigorous and extensive *Proposals for safeguarding good scientific practice* (Deutsche Forschungsgemeinschaft 1998). Recommendation 8 asks universities and research institutes to establish procedures for dealing with allegations of academic misconduct and cites as examples "the fabrication and falsification of data, plagiarism, or breach of confidence as a reviewer or superior." The commentary on Recommendation 8 stresses the need for legal expertise in defining and implementing the procedures, since legal proceedings "raise new and difficult legal issues," including "the role of professional scientific standards within the regulations of state law, and the proof of scientific dishonesty, and with it the rules for the distribution of the burden of proof." Recommendation 14 requires universities and research institutes to have rules of good scientific practice and procedures for handling allegations of scientific misconduct as a condition for receiving any research grants. The commentary clarifies: "The definition of what constitutes scientific misconduct as such should be left to the institutions in which research is carried out, so as to ensure that they are appropriate to the specific research environment" (Deutsche Forschungsgemeinschaft 1998; for the situation in Germany, see also Christoph Schneider 2000; Stegemann-Boehl 2000).

In the wake of the same German case, the Max-Planck-Gesellschaft established a *Procedure in Cases of Suspected Scientific Misconduct* (Max-Planck-Gesellschaft 1997) in November 1997. Appendix 1 of the procedure includes a "Catalogue of conduct to be regarded as scientific misconduct." Its basic definition reads: "Scientific misconduct occurs if, in a scientifically significant context, false statements are made knowingly or as a result of gross carelessness, if the intellectual property of others is infringed, or if their research work is impaired in some other way." The details include the American "FFP" and identify as subcategories for the infringement of intellectual property:

a) the unauthorized exploitation involving usurpation of authorship (plagiarism),
b) the misappropriation, particularly in an expert opinion, of research methods and ideas (theft of ideas),
c) the usurpation of scientific authorship or co-authorship, or the unjustified acceptance thereof,
d) the falsification of the contents or
e) the unauthorized publishing and making accessible to third persons of work insight, *hypothesis, theory or research method not yet published.* (Max-Planck-Gesellschaft 1997)

The degree of "seriousness" underlying the Danish definition and as defended by R. Bell (see above), is important. However, I feel that such a label cannot be applied beforehand to specific offenses: can we say that "plagiarism" is always serious, while "omitting the recognition of other scientists" is always minor? According to the quantity of plagiarized material, plagiarism can be minor (a few paragraphs) or major (whole chapters). It may not always be misconduct, even in its mildest form, when a researcher omits mention of the work of other scientists, for it may not be feasible to mention all work done elsewhere. But if the omission occurs deliberately—for example, in a doctoral dissertation—and thus ignores or obscures major work done elsewhere on the same subject, it suggests misconduct of a rather serious degree. Carefully assessing the seriousness of a case—however the term is defined—is certainly important as a preliminary to reporting. The ORI complains that it is crushed under a workload of "trivial cases," the vast majority of which it does not pursue (reported by Friedly 1997a:I; see also Buzzelli 1999).

Further considerations

A major complicating factor is the broad gray zone between acceptable and unacceptable practice, a zone endemic to much academic research as such. Indeed, even if the end product of research is a sound and valid piece of work, a lot of stumbling and marginal scientific behavior may have preceded it. Indeed the result, the scientific article, is often, as Martin (1992:I) puts it, "a mythical reconstruction of what actually happened." This process is not abnormal in the dynamic research by which science gropes for new knowledge, involving overworked senior researchers, inexperienced juniors, insufficient supervision, breaches in continuity, faltering equipment and devices, small and more serious recording errors, and little accidents of all kinds. Moreover, divergent degrees of tolerance toward these weaknesses, according to the academic context in which they occur, create varied realms, leading to different assessments of what is acceptable and what not.

As this discussion makes clear, it is rather simple to give a general definition of "academic misconduct," but specific occurrences have divergent interpretations, as the vivid controversies between whistle-blowers and defendants demonstrate.

1.2.3 Differences between hard and soft sciences

Hard sciences, such as medicine, chemistry, or physics, rely for their research mainly on experiments, measurements, data gathering, and calculations. Research in these fields usually has these characteristics:

• The publications are short and to the point. Conclusions are based on hard figures. Research misconduct will often involve the fabrication or falsification of the experimental data.

• Research in these sciences is usually a joint venture, as is obvious from the various authors' names on one publication. Assistants are involved in the process, and their contributions, even in the form of an individual thesis or dissertation, is part of a larger whole. This characteristic has led to some famous cases where the responsibility for misconduct has had to be apportioned among several participants.

• The information published by researchers in the hard sciences is expected to add something new to scientific knowledge. This new contribution must be spelled out from the onset and clearly placed in the broader context.

• The publication is normally directed to specialized peers worldwide and bibliographical references to it appear in standard, easy-to-consult databases. Since English has become the language of scientific publication, even for non-Anglophones, the publication usually has an immediate international audience.

• Research results in the hard sciences have the potential to affect people's lives. If the information is also publicized through the media and inflated by journalistic commentaries, claims—for example, that a certain substance taken during pregnancy may cause mental retardation in the infant, or that sugar is not so bad after all—can cause large-scale changes in public behavior. As a result, the consequences of misconduct in the hard sciences are potentially severe.

• However, in general these sciences are self-correcting when misconduct appears. Publications listed in databases reach a wide audience of specialists who will take issue with the results and become part of the citations in related studies. False conclusions, it is argued, cannot stand indefinitely, for new experiments will contradict them, thus giving the hard sciences a reputation for being self-policing. At best, this is true. However, self-policing may be considerably reduced when it involves work that is less visible or has little impact.

Soft sciences, such as languages, the humanities, or philosophy, tend to present a different profile. For example:

• These disciplines rely heavily on longer, descriptive and analytical writing as the output of their research. Hence, plagiarism seems to be the most frequent form of academic misconduct in these fields.

• In many cases, the work is an individual endeavor, so that it is difficult for an author to project the responsibility for misconduct onto someone else.

• A significant number of publications in these fields do not really contribute new knowledge or insights but rather comment on other publications or summarize what others have done. Sometimes common concepts or long-standing aspects of a discipline are presented with new jargon, giving an erroneous impression of novelty. Sometimes authors unaware of preceding research reinvent the wheel or attempt to inflate the significance of a trivial discovery.

• Except for articles in major journals or books published by high-profile publishers, most of the output of soft science research is hardly noticed outside a small circle. Thousands of articles, in scores of languages, appear in specialized or local journals that are not linked to international referencing systems. Many theses and dissertations in the soft sciences are probably read by only a few persons.

• Almost none of this work has any impact on the public at large, so there is no direct public interest involved in cases of misconduct.

• Usually, no elements of self-correction function, because much of the research will never be checked and only a fortuitous discovery will bring any misconduct to light.

However, these distinctions between hard and soft sciences do not mean that the two are divided into completely separate realms with their own characteristics. It would be inaccurate to conclude that in the hard sciences fabrication and falsification are easy to ferret out and plagiarism is almost nonexistent. Such a view is based on the limited perspective of top American science but does not take into account the situation in less developed countries and in other languages. Furthermore, several notorious cases provide evidence that even high-profile U.S. research is not immune to misconduct and that establishing the facts of a situation can take years of investigation and argument. In addition, even the long-term exposure of fabrication and falsification does not eradicate them in the short run, expunge them from the databases, or eliminate the possibility of the recurrence of new cases. It seems irresponsible to neglect these grave effects by appealing to the argument that the field is intellectually healthy and will eventually correct itself. Furthermore, even with active policing, we can expect those perpetrating academic fraud to develop better techniques to cover their mischief. Plagiarism, even in the hard sciences, can be rampant, especially in translation. A researcher may republish another researcher's material in a different language for a limited audience that has no way of recognizing its origin.

When we contemplate the soft sciences, the situation is even more complex than its list of characteristics suggests. Fabrication or falsification of data can happen if the research is based on experimental work with calculation of occurrences, inquiries, tests, and the subsequent extrapolation of figures. Certain disciplines, especially in pedagogical or sociological areas, rely heavily on this kind of research, which is prone to manipulation to prove a desired hypothesis. In my own field, the "best method of learning a foreign language" is usually "proven" by comparing groups that study a language in different ways. The test results lead to the naming of a "winner," which is invariably the learning approach the researcher has invented or has been endorsing. But it is quite easy to manipulate or to forget certain variables. This lack of rigor and objectivity, combined with ignorance about previous studies, comes close to research misconduct, even if there is no real intent to deceive.

1.2.4 Differences according to the status of offenders

Casual discussion among faculty members about misconduct on campus customarily focuses on student cheating, often by undergraduates of marginal ability. This approach naturally results in the assumption that misconduct is a characteristic of individuals who do not really "belong" to academia, who are only passing through. The anecdotes are numerous and almost everyone knows them or a variation: a student who submits a paper that he or she had actually written for a previous course, another who hands in a paper downloaded from the Internet, a third who uses a sophisticated calculator that also contains all the answers to exam questions, still another who sends a look-alike co-conspirator to the Testing Center, and so on. There seems to be a growing tendency among faculty to accept these occurrences as unavoidable and to assume that people will invariably cheat when they have a chance. Faculty members who discover such improprieties may shrink from confrontation and let the matter go. On the other hand, students who are caught will seldom, if ever, be helped or backed by their peers or by members of the academic community. They just had bad luck.

The perspective changes, however, when graduate students or teaching/ research assistants are involved. They are viewed as preacademics who must prove themselves worthy of the trust of the profession. Research misconduct, in the narrow sense of fabrication, falsification, or plagiarism, is not tolerated from them. If found guilty of such behavior, they expect to receive and their professors expect to apply immediate punitive measures, including expulsion. However, at this level, relations between the protagonists have changed. Graduate students and teaching/research assistants have closer relations with the faculty, they are rendering various kinds of (personal) services, and they have not infrequently become aware of the department's or research group's internal secrets. Consequently, it is not unusual that political or other stealthy influences start playing a role in assessing alleged misconduct. If the accused is a protégé of a faculty member, if the alleged misconduct entails some responsibility on the part of the professor in charge, and/or if the misconduct occurs in a course or in a project supported by some and frowned on by others, various considerations surface that influence the accusation in different directions and create different interpretations of the conduct.

I once sat in on master's degree jury in which one professor felt that the graduate student should fail because he had clearly plagiarized a paper he turned in for this professor's course. But this faculty member was isolated in the department, and the student had the sympathy of an influential professor who could count on the collegiality of others. The vote was close but in the student's favor. The case of X2, discussed in detail below, was also strongly colored by these kinds of allegiances. As the whistle-blower, I was an outsider. X2's dissertation advisor felt that it was his immediate duty to strongly support X2, with whom he had had an intimate association for years in the same department. The doctoral committee, composed of friends and close associates of the dissertation advisor, also took an official position in X2's support, although the four members I contacted (four out of six) privately expressed serious reservations (see sections 4.3.10 and 4.4).

Once we move to alleged misconduct among faculty members, the perceptions can be heavily influenced by personal relations built up over the years, irrespective of the behavior's gravity. Friends will rally loyally to the accused's defense, while enemies will take a certain pleasure in the person's downfall. The battle over a case of misconduct clearly takes place in long-established trenches, as famous misconduct cases have repeatedly shown.

The higher the rank and the academic prestige, the less credible an accusation of misconduct. Hence the reverberation in professional journals and in the media when a highly acclaimed researcher of the stature of a Nobel Prize winner is accused of research improprieties. Whether the allegations are true or not—and it may be impossible even to hold an investigation sufficiently objective to determine the facts—an army of supporters will vouch for his or her integrity, especially if the accusations were made by lower-ranking faculty, young assistants, or foreign scientists.

The fundamental problem in such situations is that academia is expected to police itself—headed by the accused's peers and if possible within the walls of the institution. To counter the risk of cover-ups and to ensure fair treatment for both whistle-blower and accused, some recommend that only neutral outsiders should be asked to evaluate an allegation of misconduct. But in the case of alleged misconduct by a prominent researcher, even "independent" specialists are, by the very nature of their specialization, part of the worldwide network in that field. Often they will know the protagonist from professional organizations and conferences, or even from personal exchanges and close cooperation. How much objectivity can be expected in such cases?

1.3   The extent of academic misconduct

This question has been debated so extensively in many publications that my original outline did not include it. However, the extent of misconduct comes up in any conversation on the subject, showing a need to establish an informational baseline for the discussion that follows.

Some scientists have the tendency to minimize, ignore, or even deny academic misconduct. C. K. Gunsalus analyzed some reasons for such attitudes, including structural aspects of academic work—specifically that scientists are often insulated from the darker realities around them: "As a result, many of them believe that problems are rare, that the few that occur can easily be handled, and, thus, that no money need be spent to develop procedures and train people to deal with misconduct" (Gunsalus 1997b:I). Gunsalus criticizes scientists who make such minimizing generalizations without scientific proof.

Attempts in the 1980s to appraise the number of cases of academic misconduct showed significant obstacles to obtaining correct data (Phinney 1991; Sprague 1991; Woolf 1988) and triggered much controversy between the shocked scientists who had naïvely considered the problem limited to one or two "rotten apples" and the more cynical who described the scientific world as a "rotten barrel" (Broad and Wade 1982). It was some years before scientists and university administrators started to realize that they could not continue to disregard the pressing questions emerging from congressional hearings about the number of misconduct cases.

More precise figures now come from the official bodies dealing with academic misconduct, but they naturally reflect only cases that have been reported. In the United States, the Office of Inspector General (OIG) of the NSF receives reports of thirty to eighty cases per year, which are available for consultation online. The ORI reports an average of thirty-five to forty cases per year dealing only with medical and biomedical research. The number of new allegations received dropped to 166 in 1997 from about 200 in previous years, and to 129 in 1999. If the ORI comes to the conclusion that misconduct has occurred (in about one out of three allegations), it publishes the name of the accused, the related facts, and the sanction, also accessible online.

But how many cases never reach the stage of an official report? One indication is given by Swazey, Anderson, and Louis (1993), who asked 4,000 U.S. researchers (2,000 doctoral candidates and 2,000 graduate faculty) if they had ever witnessed research misconduct. Depending on the type of misconduct, 6 to 9 percent of the respondents said they had observed plagiarism or falsification by faculty. Between 13 and 33 percent, again depending on the type of misconduct, reported observing those behaviors among graduate students. When only faculty responses were studied, between 15 and 43 percent of faculty reported that other faculty had engaged in questionable research practices, as defined by the National Academy of Sciences. It is true the study by Swazey, Anderson, and Louis has been criticized, but other studies have corroborated this high prevalence of cases (Lock 1996a:15–16; Jacobsen and Hals 1996).

If these high figures of alleged misconduct are accurate, only a tiny fraction of allegations are ever reported and even fewer are published. But lists of the known cases (e.g., Lock 1996a) are still sobering in their sheer quantity. For the situation in Germany, Stegemann-Boehl lists an impressive number of known cases but continues: "German researchers and administrators in biomedical research estimate that the number of cases treated confidentially is considerably higher than the number of officially known cases of misconduct" (1996:191). Lagarde and Maisonneuve (1996:182–184), citing a "Latin mentality," also communicate a lack of confidence in how misconduct cases are disclosed in France (see also Breittmayer 2000). Van Kolfschooten (1993) published dozens of cases in the Netherlands, but also noted the reluctance, amounting to downright refusal, of universities to report cases. Similarly, the editors of three medical journals in Britain openly denounced the British General Medical Council and the Academy of Medical Sciences for failing to discuss and expose the many cases of fraud in medical research (reported by Birchard 2000).

Thus, the vast majority of cases never reach the statistics for at least four reasons. First, a probably significant amount of academic misconduct, if "well" carried out, remains undetected. Second, if discovered, many cases of alleged misconduct are never reported. Collegiality or fear of conflict or retaliation discourage potential whistle-blowers from speaking out. Third, even if people feel an obligation to report, the task itself may be impractical because of the problem of gathering sufficient evidence and the time and energy required to develop a convincing report. Whistle-blowers as a rule stand alone, not only carrying the full burden of their unwelcome chore but also the disapproval of their own colleagues. Finally, if a case is reported to the academic hierarchy, few institutions will report it further if they are able to keep it internal or if they have no legal obligation to do so. For the sake of their image, many will try to negotiate the case quietly or engage in a kind of administrative manipulation that is indistinguishable from a cover-up.

In consequence, it is difficult to determine with precision how widespread academic misconduct is, either in general or in a specific subfield. Quantitative investigations continue, however. The American Committee on Science, for example, planned to investigate the extent, if any, to which senior researchers misuse the work of investigators under their supervision (Reynolds 1998). However, the important point is not how many cases there are in the world, but that such cases do happen and that analysis shows how easily they can occur, especially in view of the items discussed in the next section.

All in all, some researchers do not hesitate to say that cheating is "reaching epidemic proportions worldwide" (Desruisseaux 1999, citing Harold J. Noah and Max A. Eckstein, and their upcoming *Fraud and Education: The Worm in the Apple*). Given the dramatic rise in cheating "over the past several decades" among American high school students (Carlson 1999; see also section 1.4.5), there is reason to believe that this permissiveness will extend to students' behavior when they are pursuing higher education or even when they themselves are part of the professoriate.

1.4 Changing circumstances and risk factors

Changing circumstances seem to exacerbate the problem. Some reinforce each other, creating ideal feeding grounds for improprieties and misbehavior.

1.4.1 The massive expansion of scientific research

The democratization of higher education and the exponential growth of scientific research since World War II have caused the numbers of students and researchers to increase dramatically (Ben-David 1991). In the United States, the NSF selects about 10,000 new research projects each year from about 30,000 proposals submitted by scientists from all over the nation. Another 10,000 awards are made to ongoing projects. From 1981 to 1998, the number of postdoctoral fellows in science and engineering rose from 18,000 tot 39,000. The budget amounts to billions of dollars. In Europe, the immense Framework Programmes of the European Union offer new opportunities to thousands of researchers in the member states.

At the same time because of this expansion, the profile of researchers has changed. Many young and inexperienced staff members and part-time graduate students are employed in various projects (see also section

1.4.4). Frequently they lack proper preparation and training because of time, money, and personnel constraints within the allotted project. Often senior researchers consider them to be a labor pool of temporary assistants rather than as future colleagues to be mentored and fostered.

In this massive and complex enterprise, where academic freedom makes tight control over an individual's performance neither easy nor desirable, the risk of improper behavior has risen proportionately. It explains the constant plea in many parts of the world for more peer review, more precise performance goals, and more output verification in scientific research.

1.4.2   The heightened pressure to be productive

The heightened pressure on researchers to produce results and publish tempt some to find easier ways to fulfill the expectations. Hiring, advancement, and tenure frequently depend on such productivity. The problem is well known in the literature on misconduct. To quote only one source:

> Conditions that favour dishonest conduct should be changed. For example, criteria that primarily measure quantity create incentives for mass production and are therefore likely to be inimical to high quality science and scholarship.... Since publications are the most important "product" of research, it may have seemed logical, when comparing achievement, to measure productivity as the number of products, i.e. publications, per length of time. But this has led to abuses like the so-called salami publications, repeated publication of the same findings, and observance of the principle of the LPU (least publishable unit). (Deutsche Forschungsgemeinschaft 1998:I)

My personal observations over my years in academia reinforce these views. Some institutions focus on good teaching as much—or even more—than strong research, especially schools that emphasize undergraduate studies. For example, departments of art, languages, philosophy, history, or religion (the latter in religiously oriented colleges) require faculty to devote much energy to the high-quality teaching of large groups of undergraduates. The same is true for basic introductory scientific courses such as in biology, chemistry, or geology. On the other hand, this emphasis does not lend itself easily to groundbreaking research or to the experimental teamwork that generates publications. As a result, many excellent teachers in higher education find themselves in a situation where they have little background, time, or means to do research. The academic evaluation system, however, requires them to obtain a doctoral degree and to publish for tenure or promotion. Fulfilling both expectations—first-rate teaching and first-rate research—can create much tension.

One way to meet the research obligation is to develop an exotic research specialty that is basically unknown to one's departmental peers, thus making it possible to dodge internal quality control. No doubt many departments have "lone-wolf" researchers, working on a subject that seems both original and marginal and that remains isolated from the rest of the group of colleagues. Such work can be valuable, of course, but it increases the risk of uncritical work and may ultimately lead to forms of unacceptable scholarship.

The pressure to look productive can make people seek other channels to pad résumés. Professional friendships, return of favors, and mutual compensations encourage some to add "honorary" authors to publications or to push for being included as a coauthor. Conversely, fierce competitiveness and mutual distrust create a premium feeding ground for unethical moves, since a feeling of enmity toward one's peers reduces a sense of professional responsibility to them. Indeed, because academic productivity is also measured in the number of projects and awards obtained and in appointments to professional journals and organizations, such "honors" are sometimes bitterly fought for.

1.4.3   Insufficient guidance and control

Academic research supervisors are overburdened with responsibilities—preparing new projects, finding new funds, administering personnel, space, and equipment, sitting on boards and committees—all apart from their core tasks of teaching, research, and writing. Many lack the time to give proper guidance to their junior researchers and to supervise their work. Even at the level of postdoctoral fellows, neglect is a major problem, as reported by Alison Schneider (2000). Since the detection of certain problems, like plagiarism, requires much effort and perseverance, there is little chance that supervisors will be the first to notice it. This lack of awareness has also been noted in connection with student plagiarism in Australia (Academics in Australia 1995).

Because the number of theses and dissertations a professor directs is also a consideration in academic appraisal, professors have strong motives for taking on more graduate students than they can competently handle. They thus have two reasons for becoming permissive on evaluation committees. First, even if their student performs poorly, they may not be aware of it if they have had no time to follow the work properly. Second, they need the student's accepted degree as an item to add to their own curriculum vitae. The case of X2, discussed in this book, seems a typical example of the combination of these factors.

More research is needed to analyze the professional activities that academic personnel carry out day by day and the impact of these time constraints on the training of junior researchers as well as on the oversight of various facets of research activities. Such findings could lead to more precise and practical recommendations—for example, on the critical minimum of training and supervision necessary in the academic research setting, and the critical maximum of work that a professor can handle adequately.

1.4.4   The impact of a new breed of academic juveniles

Having observed academic life since the mid-1960s and having been intensely involved in new developments in the humanities over the last two decades, I have witnessed a number of dramatic changes in academic personnel. Although I suspect that similar observations could be made, at least to some degree, about other academic areas and in other countries, I do not claim generalizability for the remarks that follow beyond my personal experience in my own field—the humanities in both a European and an American university.

An ever-increasing number of young and inexpensive research assistants are needed to fill positions in the numerous projects and grants available from science foundations, government initiatives, private ventures, overarching funding organizations, and so on, on local, regional, state, national, and international levels. Calls for project proposals have increased dramatically since the mid-1980s in the vast research programs launched by the European Union alone. Part-time research positions multiply the numbers of young people that can be involved. The ongoing struggle for office, staff, and laboratory space at virtually every university is material proof of this constant expansion.

At the same time, the quality of candidates is dropping. A few decades ago, only top graduates would be appointed to the few teaching and research assistantships offered. Nowadays the exponential increase in positions obliges faculty to dig deeper for staff, hiring less competent and less motivated candidates. The very best, meanwhile, often find work in the private sector where they earn higher wages and build more prestigious careers. A number of these brightest graduates have also confided to me that they have become disillusioned by observing intrigues and abuses in academic hiring and advancement; they prefer the less political environment and seemingly greater stability of a career outside of academia.

Two other institutional factors, more intense in some countries than in others, contribute to this negative development:

· The decentralization of campuses, part of the vast European educational reforms of the 1970s and 1980s, ironically has resulted in decreased quality by isolating professors from peers. All too often, each is a king or queen on a personal island, lacking competitive and critical context. To boost their visibility and prestige, many establish a research center or an institute with an impressive name and home page, but with little depth. For political reasons, the fair allocation of research funds over the various campuses allows them to obtain (major) projects and grants, even if they do not really deserve these funds. Next they must engage research assistants with the weak profile I just described, who will then also work in an academically weak environment.

· The statutory and financial conditions for research assistants funded by projects and grants are usually less attractive than the comparatively rare but more promising academic track positions. Limited benefits and low wages make the positions less appealing for the top graduate students. As a result, low-level research openings are filled by relatively inexperienced graduates who see the job as temporary, an entry-level experience, or as a chance to hang around on campus while looking for a more appealing position. However, many of these assistantships carry with them explicit expectations that the research assistant will deliver papers at professional conferences, publish, and pursue a doctoral degree.

The consequence of these conditions is, in my experience, the presence on campus of a huge population of academic juniors who are there just to have a "job." The quality of their work, the depth of their papers and publications, and/or the significance of their master's or doctoral research depends completely on the training and supervision provided by the project manager or research supervisor. If this manager lacks the motivation and/or the professional expertise to provide desirable mentoring (see section 1.4.3), we should not be surprised at the widespread erosion of what academia should stand for. I can best exemplify the problem by quoting (anonymously) this message, which appeared on a listserve for Computer-Assisted Language Learning (CALL) a few years ago:

I am a researcher at the University of (...). Since September, I am working on a research project and a Ph.D. dissertation on the subject of CALL and business communication. I am looking more precisely at the didactical implications of courseware development on the Internet. However, this is not eveolving [sic] the way I would like it to, mainly because I am working alone, quite isolated. This is why (...) suggested to contact you. Indeed, I am looking for people with experience in this research field who could give me some pieces of advice or guidance and (...) was sure that you could help me find them. Thank you very much in advance.

Such messages are not exceptional any more on academic listserves that do not filter incoming mail. In this case, we apparently have a well-meaning doctoral candidate who wishes to do proper work but is receiving deficient academic support from a department that knows nothing about CALL but landed a CALL project. If individuals in the same circumstances were less motivated or less scrupulous, they could easily exploit the ignorance and negligence of their supervisor, concluding the term with a zero return. But at that crucial point, the researchers would need to provide tangible results for the project or grant. The temptation for the assistants and/or supervisor to fill the void would indeed be overwhelming—thus setting the stage for academic misconduct.

The message I quoted above takes on special significance in considering X2's case study (see section 3.3.1). Indeed, this message was written by another graduate assistant being supervised by X2's dissertation advisor, working in the same research unit in the same period. It thus provides relevant information about the context in which X2 was working.

In an article hailing the "ancient symbol of the revered, old scholar, full of wisdom and years," J. Parini observes: "Especially in the humanities, excellence in scholarship often demands decades of preparation and immense patience. Young scholars in search of tenure and grants are too often encouraged to publish immature work—work naïvely absorbed in whatever passing approach and accompanying jargon happen to be fashionable" (Parini 2000). Of course these sweeping generalizations about immature scholars need to be softened. Despite my pessimistic observations about ill-prepared, ill-motivated, and poorly performing junior staff, I have also seen exceptionally dedicated and competent assistants in various projects and circumstances. They should in no way feel targeted by the remarks I made about others. They themselves are often painfully aware of the problems—indeed, are often compelled to witness them in close proximity—but are seldom in a position to instigate reform and improvement.

1.4.5 A cynical generation?

Articles and reports regularly indicate that cheating among college students is on the increase. Research conducted by Butterfield, McCabe, and Trevino showed that "more than three-quarters of the almost 2,000 students whom they surveyed at nine large public institutions in 1993 admitted to one or more instances of serious cheating on tests or examinations, or to having engaged in serious academic dishonesty on written assignments" (McCabe and Drinan 1999). These authors assign culpability to such factors as the erosion of traditional values, the lack of institutional support to enforce policies or to apply them equitably, and the lack of awareness, guidance, and assessment in matters of academic integrity.

Dishonesty, however, is not something that undergraduates discover. A 1998 survey by the Josephson Institute of Ethics found that 56 percent of middle-schoolers and 70 percent of high-schoolers admitted cheating on an exam—a 6 percent increase from the same survey administered only two years earlier. Concerns about this state of affairs led to such campaigns as the "Ref in your head" slogan, targeted at students aged ten to fourteen, sponsored jointly by the Educational Testing Service and the Advertising Council to reduce cheating among future high school and college students (Carlson 1999). But other reports indicate that even high school teachers and principals collude in cheating in response to the pressure for their students to reach certain levels on standardized tests (Goodnough 1999; Hartocollis 1999; Kantrowitz and McGinn 2000).

Observers express great uneasiness at how widespread the cynical view that the end justifies the means has become. Outspoken advocates of scientific integrity are particularly perturbed:

What happens to the scientific environment when people violate generally held concepts of right and wrong, and yet nothing happens to them, either because their institution chooses not to act or because it is powerless to act, as a result of inadequate rules and procedures? What happens when allegations of misconduct are poorly handled or whitewashed, or when an innocent scientist is wrongly accused by a malicious colleague and yet the investigation languishes for years, or when a whistleblower is vindicated but still suffers retaliation? Cynicism flourishes, morale erodes, and the cohesiveness of the scientific enterprise suffers, all because of a failure to honor the scientific principle of an unbiased search for the truth. The effects are particularly devastating for students, who are supposed to be learning to act according to the highest scientific and personal standards. (Gunsalus 1997b:I)

Consider this: many young scientists we and our friends have met recently view the required courses and lectures on scientific conduct as exercises in hypocrisy. The plain fact is that cheating pays—just don't get caught. And if you see the rules being broken, keep your mouth shut or you will be the target of reprisals by your colleagues and their higher-ups. Many of the papers being published these days exist only to provide entries in the bibliographies appended to C.V.'s of applicants for hiring, promotion, tenure, and awards. The actual papers are not usually read by anyone but their authors. So if there is something a little strange in a paper that has your name on it, no one will check. And if you have reached a senior position in your institution, nothing will happen if you do get caught! This is the cynical view of most of our younger colleagues, and it worries us very much, because it is largely justified. (Feder and Stewart 1994:I)

This phenomenon raises deep moral questions pertaining to the ethical education of our students and developmental direction that curricula and evaluation procedures have taken over the past decades. Has stressing the relativity of norms and values in a multicultural, global society led to a loss of the basic ethical categories of right and wrong? The strongly competitive system in which young people must succeed deserves part of the blame. Deeper roots may lie in personalities that are more prone to committing fraud. However, I will leave analysis of these moral, social, and psychological phenomena to specialists better equipped to analyze them (see, for example, Hackett 1999).

1.4.6 The international perspective

Is misconduct the same the world over? Do some cultures have different norms or traditions in assessing originality, standards of precision, data recording, and conscientiousness? If some norms and traditions are different, how are we to treat behavior that is deviant according to Western norms? The potential problem has been compounded by the fact that, especially since 1960, an ever-growing number of students now study at universities not in their home countries. What understandings do they bring about "appropriate" conduct in academic life?

Indeed, rarely mentioned in the literature but frequently discussed orally is academic misconduct among students and researchers who are studying and working in a host land. As far as I could determine, no one has yet studied international students in the context of academic misconduct on a multi-institutional scale. One study at the University of Southern California found that international students, who make up 10 percent of the student body, account for 47 percent of academic dishonesty cases ("Foreign students" 1998; see also Anderson and Louis 1994; Goodstein 1991; Heller 1997; Hudgins 1997; Walfish 2001).

No doubt the reasons for culture-specific differences are diverse. International students may genuinely and innocently hold different understandings of what constitutes misconduct. We have probably all heard anecdotes about the young foreign researcher who falsifies or fabricates data to "please the master" who is looking for evidence to prove a hypothesis. Or about the international student who copies without quoting or citing, because copying a master is a sign of respect. Or about the student who in his home country became so skilled at memorizing long passages—which was the accepted form of correct learning—that he continues to do so, unwittingly reproducing verbatim sentences from other authors in his own work.

But ignorance is a relatively easy problem to correct. Other, less acceptable reasons may also feed into the problem. The initial evaluation of candidates from abroad may have been incomplete because of difficulty in assessing the value and originality of their credentials. Dishonest techniques, such as having applications rewritten, using stand-ins for entrance exams, and obtaining inappropriate access to standardized admissions tests, are on the rise (see Walfish 2001). If deception started at an early level, it is likely to continue during advanced studies and work. A strongly felt need to preserve resident status can also be a powerful motive for cutting corners in academic integrity.

All of these reasons deserve further consideration, but I think it is important to resist the idea that attitudes toward plagiarism in an academic context vary from one culture to another—that is, that in some cultures, beliefs about intellectual property would encompass the view that plagiarism is normal (see for such viewpoints Dobrow 1993; Scollon 1995). I am aware of several cultures in which the artistic tradition views copying the master as a tribute to his talent. However, in none of these cultures is academic plagiarism considered acceptable. Chinese culture, sometimes mentioned as typical of this different cultural understanding, does not condone outright plagiarism in academia, as confirmed by various cases (Cong Cao 1996; Hertling 1995; Xiguang and Lei 1996). The high reputation of Chinese scientists could not be maintained if it did, as Chen-Lu Tsou (1998) points out.

Another aspect of the international perspective is the impact of political exigencies on personal values. Moral norms may be eroded by a system where survival or security requires dishonest practices. Bollag, citing the Czech economist Mejstrik, identifies academic misconduct as "a 'rational' response to the intellectual dishonesty enforced in academe under Communism" (Bollag 1993; see also Daniloff 1997, for plagiarism in Azerbaijani institutions). There are no doubt still countries where the whole of academia, because of its participation in a larger repressive or corrupt political system, simply requires deceitful routines if one wants to succeed or even survive. Even faculty in a democratic Western setting could rally to that need and overstep the ethical boundaries for a "good cause." A colleague of mine related the following incident:

One of my friends was trying to supervise a grossly incompetent thesis by a student from (. . .) who had also plagiarized numerous sources. If he didn't get the degree, his student visa would be revoked and he would be sent back to (. . .). Since the (. . .) government had provided a sizeable study grant for him with the understanding that he would get a degree, he would be required to pay it back. Since he couldn't pay it back, he would be, at the least, jailed, and, at the most, executed. The entire department was trapped ethically, and, after ferocious consulting up and down the line, my friend ended up writing the student's thesis so that it would be "graduate quality." The plagiarism was not cultural ambiguity but this student's desperation—he wasn't good enough not to get caught. (From a message to the author)

1.4.7 Interdisciplinarity

Interdisciplinarity has become a sought-after goal in academic circles, although it is still relatively ill-defined. (For a critical evaluation of the concept, see Wissoker 2000.) I consider interdisciplinarity to be the active mixing, in the activities of one person, of specialties from different disciplines. Thus, interdisciplinarity is different from multidisciplinary approaches, where specialists from various disciplines cooperate in a joint project, contributing their own expertise with due respect for each other's expertise. A person engaging in interdisciplinary activities is more likely to engage in academic misconduct for several reasons, which I explicate below.

Common and ill-defined border
Computer-Assisted Language Learning (CALL) forms the focus of a number of examples and commentaries in this book, not because it is more susceptible to academic misconduct than other similar subfields, but because it is my own field of expertise. Therefore, interesting cases came more readily to my attention. It could as well have been the subfields of cultural studies or human computer interaction (HCI) or any other young interdisciplinary subfield.

As an interdisciplinary field, CALL has common boundaries with language learning, culture, literature, linguistics, pedagogy, learning psychology, epistemology, computer science, and more. Each of these disciplines is further subdivided, making the interdisciplinary puzzle even more complex. From each of these subdivisions a person can throw a bridge toward a related field, even if only for an occasional excursion. In the absence of departmental colleagues knowledgeable about the subject, a researcher could easily claim bogus expertise, especially because not much "real" research is needed to write about a subject. Many publications tend to summarize what has been done by others, to compare and comment, and to conclude that more research is needed.

Moreover, it is rather easy for such a person to publish articles by using the possibilities of vague interdisciplinary boundaries. One can submit an article or a paper from a certain subfield to journals or conferences of another subfield, provided there is at least a basic link. A linguist can enter the realm of human-computer interaction, a sociologist can appear in linguistics, or a literary critic can publish in a historical journal. In the original department of the researcher, interdisciplinarity thwarts proper peer assessment. Moreover, some less-than-first-rate professional journals are rather lenient in accepting submissions that seem valuable because of the different outlook. Quite a few academic conferences need paying participants who will come only if they are allowed to present a paper. An analysis of articles and papers from a certain subfield, published in journals and conference proceedings from another subfield, but with a justifiable link, would probably reveal some empty and unoriginal contributions. But the subsequent C.V. of the participant uses these "empty" articles and papers as certification for a nonexistent expertise.

A bogus claim of expertise is not by definition academic misconduct, but it is a form of academic effrontery, sometimes to be explained because of naïveté. However, it approaches academic misconduct if it utterly "fails to respect the intellectual contributions or property of others" (see the definition of the Commission on Research Integrity, discussed in section 1.2.2). It may entail misconduct by making assertions that grossly ignore the state of the art and by disparaging experienced researchers; the "instant experts" guilty of this behavior have probably never conducted serious research and have nothing significant to offer, even if their public performance is dazzlingly convincing. One of the most famous hoaxes was Alan Sokal's success in having a nonsense article published about quantum physics and postmodern philosophy (Sokal 1996; see also the many articles and discussions devoted to it on the Internet, as well as the resulting Sokal and Bricmont book, 1997).

If interdisciplinarity remains low key, it is relatively easy for plagiarists to avoid contact with the authors they have plagiarized from and who could recognize their work in a conference paper or a publication. Indeed, a small research area from one field may develop within another domain or subdomain. An example is that learning psychology is applied to CALL, or that HCI is applied to language learning. But each of these areas often functions independently of other areas because of scientific inbreeding. Most people read only the journals of, and attend only the symposia of, their own discipline. Plagiarizing out of another discipline greatly diminishes the risk of getting caught and therefore reinforces the temptation to continue this profitable course.

Utopian projects
In certain interdisciplinary subfields it is rather easy to formulate impressive funding proposals. For example, on the topic of applying new

media to language pedagogy, it is simple to portray traditional language learning as a failure and exhibit the new media as a promising solution. With some ingenuity and the use of trendy keywords, one can formulate a visionary project, promising innovation, learning enhancement, fame for the institution, and even attractive financial returns through the commercialization of a revolutionary product. The novelty of the subject for granting agencies, the lack of a strong evaluation tradition, the mirage of an interuniversity network, and new rhetoric in talking about media and education—all these factors make it relatively easy to obtain funds given the right circumstances and gullible evaluators. But once granted, can such projects fulfill the promises? Interdisciplinary approaches, as in the case of language pedagogy with new media, are very challenging, as serious researchers and developers know. For those whose weak expertise cannot match the exigencies of the project, the deadlines virtually compel reports with fabricated results that conceal the failure of the research project.

A still limited and fluctuating base of authorities

Relatively new fields like those found in interdisciplinary endeavors are still growing toward international maturity and standards. In the case of CALL, for example, the nature of the field involves rapidly changing hardware capabilities, shifting software platforms, and constantly evolving media trends. These very characteristics hinder the establishment of a broad and stable base of international experts who are able to follow the developments over longer periods and to monitor quality. Many of the CALL researchers of the 1970s and the 1980s are no longer active in the field, either because they felt they could not keep up with the changes or because they failed to attract adequate funding and specialized staff—while inexperienced newcomers, but with a visionary rhetoric, succeed in landing new projects.

Moreover, many CALL researchers can deal with this subfield only as a side activity because their main academic commitment lies in related areas—literature, linguistics, methodology, teacher training, and so on. As a result, the field experiences a constant influx of newcomers who do not find enough helpful critical filters along the way to provide guidance, let alone sufficient academic training over several years. How many universities offer students a balanced and constantly updated program in educational technology and language learning? No doubt the same applies to comparable new subfields.

These remarks are certainly not meant to disparage the limited group of present-day CALL authorities. Some of those pioneers have been involved in the field for more than two decades, answering the challenges of change and motivating scores of new researchers. But their number remains relatively small. Some lack the courage to reprimand and censure the "instant experts," because they need them as members of their organizations, as subscribers to their journals, or as paying participants at their conferences.

In conclusion, new interdisciplinary fields are at high risk of academic misconduct. By their very nature, they easily attract new and inexperienced researchers from various backgrounds. It is clear that such new fields need thorough and high-quality research to structure and strengthen their performance and evaluation standards and to become more credible among related fields.

1.4.8   The Internet

From its inception in 1969 until the early 1990s, the Internet functioned as the scientific exchange route for a limited number of privileged researchers. Since the mid-1990s, its explosive growth—one of the major social phenomena of our time—has expanded its capabilities to virtually everyone who has access to a computer.

The advantages of the Internet for education and research are many. But ironically, it is precisely in education that one of its dark sides has become apparent. The ease by which material can be collected from the Internet has become a major threat to the integrity of scientific production. Students facing deadlines with their term papers fall prey, not only to the temptation of pasting into their work the bounteous material they can easily find, but also of surfing to a score of online term-paper providers, which have replaced the less accessible campus underground term-paper mills. The ease with which ready-made material can be retrieved has multiplied the problem of plagiarized papers, as bewildered and scandalized teachers have discovered (Atwal 1996; McCollum 1996; McLeod 1997; Rothenberg 1997). The matter has alarmed politicians like Senator Robert C. Byrd (1998). Some universities are suing the

Internet term-paper vendors (Basinger and McCollum 1997). However, because those actually misusing the material are not the providers but the students, such legal action is not likely to be successful (Guernsey 1998a).

The problems are not limited to class papers. Theses and dissertations, which usually only a small committee will ever read and even then sometimes rather superficially, can also be filled with material taken from the Internet. Fraudulent practices using computer technology also extend to established researchers, as a report of the Committee on Publication Ethics (COPE) indicates (Williams 1998). Nor is the phenomenon recent. As early as 1993, the American Association for the Advancement of Science, the National Conference of Lawyers and Scientists, and the Office of Research Integrity organized a conference titled "Plagiarism and the Theft of Ideas" in which the misuse of material taken from electronic journals and computer networks was a central item in the program (Wheeler 1993). Moreover, the problems associated with online misbehavior on campus encompass much broader copyright violations than just plagiarism (McCollum 1999).

However, the medium itself can also be used to detect plagiarism. Its capability of creating huge databases of potential source texts, combined with powerful comparison devices, makes it an ally in combating fraud (Marshall 1998a, 1998b; Wheeler 1993; see esp. discussion in section 2.3).

1.4.9 Money

Researchers are occasionally—and probably now more than before—involved in marketing the results of their research through commercial outlets. They may purposefully shape research toward its commercial potential, a direction that may even be encouraged by the university itself as it creates university-business parks and funds organizations with avowed economic purposes. There is no misconduct here as long as established rules are being followed. Many technologically oriented universities and colleges have developed guidelines, sometimes tough and sometimes lax, for the proper relations between industry and academia.

But the situation carries within it the seeds for conflicts of interests and for improprieties. Faculty entrepreneurship leads to using the research unit for personal gain, even within legal boundaries. Competition encourages researchers to assert unproven scientific statements for promotional purposes. Popular publicity for products developed in academia can easily misrepresent the research or its consequences; invariably, it uses the credibility of scientific research for its own credibility. These improprieties are only verbal. More serious is manipulating research data to prove the excellence of the product developed. This well-known problem in university-industry relationships has been treated in many publications (see, e.g., Blumenthal 1992; Campbell, Daza, and Slaughter 1999; Fassin 1991; Peters and Etzkowitz 1990; Ziman 1998). It is the focus of such organizations as the Center for Science in the Public Interest (CSPI), with their "Integrity in Science" project (Blumenstyk 2001). Though it concerns biomedical research, the following statement also has validity for other fields: "One major reason for concern is that if faculty members are profiting financially from their research either through royalties from, or as investors in, companies that market products based on their discoveries, the outcome or direction of their work may be affected. They might, for instance, be tempted (consciously or unconsciously) to design studies that are more likely than not to have an outcome favorable to the product" (Cho 1997).

But not only commercialization favoring the individual researcher and the industry may be at stake. Universities are also sensitive to the ongoing need for extra income. Financial overhead or "the contribution by projects to indirect costs" may therefore be another factor in a growing ethical laxity toward professors who generate money for the university. In an academic environment where regular public financing is diminishing or harder to obtain, university administrators welcome significant external sources of income and highly respect the researchers able to generate them, since part of the funds supplement the university budget. The past decades have seen a dramatic increase of these funds. The importance of this new form of income alters the relations between the projects' recipients and their supervisors—department chair, dean, university president. Faculty who can attract funding can often count on more privileges and less control. The quality of the research performed in such projects becomes less important than the hard cash they bring in. If questions of academic misconduct arise, a number of cases show that influential project directors are more likely to be protected and defended by the administration, especially if the institution is at risk of having to reimburse allocated funds. Harsh economical considerations overshadow moral scruples.

1.4.10   Project accounting as a fraudulent environment

"I have some project money left over to buy that" is a sentence very few professors have moral scruples with, even if the item to be purchased has nothing to do with the project. While most would balk at using the money for a personal purchase, they see nothing particularly wrong with applying it to another project or using it in the research unit in general. A vague or ingenuous description on the purchase order and the invoice is seldom questioned. However, if these administrative forms must accompany the project's final report, the professor may be put in the ethically awkward position of having to justify the purchase, even by lying about it. The reality that this involves forging official documents does not even cross the individual's mind. The practice is so frequent that it is considered standard. Thus, it has become symptomatic of much broader arrangements that are common in academia, as I have witnessed them in Europe.

For example, a project's budget includes three full-time assistants. All three are hired, but only two actually work on the specified project; the third is kept busy with other assignments. As another example, a research project has produced some side results that have not yet been published. Why not obtain funding for a new project on which those results can be used after an invented, later completion? Technically, and even legally, such practices are fraudulent, but many in the profession consider them normal, even "clever" ways of generating money, building financial reserves, and bridging employment from one project to another. It is not unusual to hear scientists talk in private in self-congratulatory tones about their unconventional accounting practices.

And indeed, why would a scientist at the lower end of the funding hierarchy feel the pinch of conscience about such arrangements? These "clever" forms of accounting exist at higher levels in university administration and have become part of the "normal" system. Large sums are quietly transferred from one project to another before a deadline would require forfeiture of the unused portion. A central administrator at the university suggests that a research assistant in the English department, where the funds are exhausted, be put on the payroll of a project in the chemistry department, a favor reciprocated at a later date. Many scientists feel perfectly justified in carrying out these schemes because otherwise, in their opinion, academic research would simply be not viable. Arguments are couched in terms of the "short-sightedness of the government," the "bureaucratic regulations of the funding agency," the "irresponsibly diminished budgeting for this project," the "strangling overhead," and so on. All these arguments basically are variations of one: the higher end, science, justifies the means.

For the purposes of my discussion, the relevant question is the extent to which this pervasive atmosphere influences the propriety of research methods and reporting per se. Are professors as lenient in their methods and data as in their accounting? Young researchers, plunged into this atmosphere, may become confused about the limits between permissive accounting and permissive research. Inquiries focusing on the researcher's ethical perceptions of both forms of permissiveness are badly needed to probe this area of academic misconduct.

1.5   Countering and curing

Against all these negative trends stands a public demand for ethical conduct in public life. During the past few years and in many countries, this demand has led to the creation of tighter guidelines to foster research integrity and of procedures for dealing with cases of suspected academic misconduct.

The decade between about 1985 and 1995 was a painful one in this regard. Several spectacular cases of alleged misconduct in various disciplines were widely publicized in almost every Western country where free speech permits, and a free press publicizes, accusations and defense. In the United States, Jeff Williams, Ned Feder, and Walter W. Stewart led the charge as whistle-blowers on several celebrated cases. The stories include attempted cover-ups, contradictory conclusions, manipulations, pressures, retaliation, dismissal, demolished careers, and broken lives.

The involvement of government officials, both elected and appointed, generated official investigations and the creation of bureaus and procedures to enforce fair treatment of both whistle-blowers and defendants.

The American Office of Scientific Integrity, created in 1989, was renamed the Office of Research Integrity in 1992 (for a history of this important institution, see Pascal 1999). That same year saw the constitution of the Danish Committee on Scientific Dishonesty. The Dutch Royal Academy instituted the Advies Commissie Wetenschap en Ethiek in 1993. The French Centre National de la Recherche Scientifique created the Comité d'éthique pour les sciences in 1994, with a broader scope than the traditional biomedical concerns. Similar agencies exist in many other countries.

These developments occur in a wider democratic context of government accountability, where citizens have ways to report alleged ill treatment and wrongdoing by officials. Nearly all respected scientific institutions and organizations have codes of ethics that define professional obligations and expectations and that condemn in more or less precise terms various forms of misconduct. Many of these codes have been updated with provisions designed to cope with troublesome recent developments. At the same time, various national scientific organizations have been organizing special committees and/or revamping their regulations.

In 1997 the Committee on Publication Ethics (COPE) was organized by the editors of nine scientific journals to control publication misconduct more systematically. It began by calling a meeting with more than 100 other editors from which clearer guidelines and a consensus for proceeding emerged (Williams 1997). COPE also called on governments to strengthen funding and evaluation procedures to deal with such misconduct. One of the problems COPE identified was that articles originally published in prominent Western journals were being plagiarized and published in less visible publications.

In April 2000, a conference sponsored by the American Association for the Advancement of Science and by the Office of Research Integrity called on scientific societies to play a stronger role in educating their members about academic integrity and in taking more extensive measures to deter misconduct. This conference issued a call to conduct more research about the causes of misconduct, to find ways to attack the problems at their root, and to provide better protection for whistle-blowers (Brainard 2000b; DuMez 2000).

The very emergence of this extensive professional and public reaction is a response to scandals that have rocked the academic community and to the growing threat posed by new circumstances that facilitate misconduct. Readers of this book who have never experienced such events in their own environment may wonder if conditions are really all that serious. The fact is that, wherever it occurs, the damage is considerable and long lasting. And it can occur suddenly, anywhere. Furthermore, the fact that "it hasn't happened here" does not actually mean that such misconduct has not happened. It may merely mean that such dishonesty has either remained undiscovered or that it has not become public knowledge.

2
Detection

2.1 Introduction

In this chapter, I delineate the problems and possibilities of various detection procedures. Important parts of this chapter and the next deal with textual plagiarism, a form of misconduct that, by its very nature, requires complex detection procedures. However, for the sake of completeness, I will also, but more briefly, mention aspects of detecting other forms of misconduct.

In the following sections, it should be understood that *possible* or *alleged* precede terms that point toward misconduct. This is an important mental addition, even if I have sometimes omitted it to cut down on repetition, because assessment of the case has not yet proven a suspicion or allegation.

2.2 The detection of fabrication and falsification

The first two forms of research misconduct, as determined in the traditional definitions (see section 1.2.2), are fabrication and falsification. What do these entail? How can they be detected? Whose responsibility is it to initiate detection?

2.2.1 Fabrication and falsification of data and statements

- "Fabrication is making up data or results and recording or reporting them."
- "Falsification is manipulating research materials, equipment, or processes, or changing or omitting data or results such that the research is not accurately represented in the research record."

These subdefinitions, as mentioned before (section 1.2.2), are those most recently adopted by the Office of Science and Technology Policy (2000) in the United States. The definitions can apply to data gathering in any discipline, including disciplines in the soft sciences, and in any form.

But fabrication and falsification can also extend beyond data and be found in the realm of statements. A common form is citing research that does not really prove what is being claimed. I take the examples below from the field of language learning, but virtually any field could produce similar examples:

• "The advantages of this strategy are supported by the findings of so-and-so (year) who reported significant effects on the reading skill."
• "The importance of this psycholinguistic approach has been demonstrated by so-and so (year)."
• "Psychologists have long since discovered that language learning happens outside conscious rule-formation."

Without checking what so-and-so *really* said, or whether that person's "discovery" is actually supported by convincing evidence, or without worrying about the identity of the "psychologists," new authors reuse such references in citations and quotations, even reinforcing the absolute character of the "discovery." It leads to the uncritical acceptance of generalizations that can be passed on for decades. Under the telling title "Future Schlock," Lawrence Baines (1997) analyzes such "mythologizing data" as they are applied to educational reform. Joel Best (2001) wrote a book on the ways statistics are being misunderstood or misused to support unwarranted claims.

Other forms of fabrication and falsification include forging names, signatures, and responses to questions on forms and surveys, concocting e-mail responses to suggest that such responses have been received, and so on. However, a survey of the ORI findings of misconduct (available on its Web site) reveals that the vast majority of the cases involve inventing or altering experimental data.

2.2.2 A paradigm of risk factors

The procedural environment in which data-gathering researchers operate is no doubt a significant indicator of potential misconduct. Laboratories with rigid professional training for their personnel, with strict written policies on recording and archiving data, as well as explicit verification procedures that are regularly applied, obviously are less vulnerable to fabrication and falsification than study sites that lack such safeguards. Between the extremes of maximum stringency and maximum laxity lies a vast array of diverse contexts. Other possible factors, which thorough research should further evaluate, include:

· The money that can be made: research that generates money, either for the research unit or for an individual, is more liable to misconduct.

· The size and coherence of the teams: within larger teams with less coherence, fabrication and falsification may be more likely to occur.

· The intensity of controlling interaction: the less interaction, the more an individual may be tempted to fabricate or falsify data.

· The personality and backgrounds of the players: foul play is seldom a first and sudden occurrence in one's life, but a trait with deeper roots; an individual accustomed to cheating may more easily slip into fabricating and falsifying data.

· The material facilities: grubbiness, disorder, outdated and/or ill-maintained equipment may be conducive to slovenliness in data gathering and hence to more serious improprieties.

· The nature of the data: research tied to complex external variables or to human factors, such as in medical or sociological investigations, is less verifiable (or may even be impossible to verify) by data audits or replications, leading to a diminished risk of being caught.

· The motives of the players: various needs may feed temptation, such as the urgent requirement to produce results confirming a hypothesis, to furnish publications for tenure or advancement, to obtain financial return for completed work, and so on.

All of these elements and their complex combinations can be factors in a paradigm of risk factors. The higher the risks, the more reason to be on guard and possibly apply detection mechanisms.

2.2.3   Institutionalized detection

Institutions can go far toward preventing and detecting fabrication and falsification by building control mechanisms into the system in both the data-gathering stage and the reporting stage. Such controls should be exercised by insiders (e.g., peers, supervisors or controllers in the laboratory, the department, and the college) and by outsiders (e.g., representatives of scientific societies, professional organizations, journals, funding agencies, and public bodies).

These mechanisms include: (1) thoroughly evaluating the methods used, (2) auditing data logs and inquiry sheets, (3) replicating experiments, (4) comparing the results with those of similar experiments, and (5) conducting other forms of investigation depending on the discipline or the kind of research. All of these monitoring mechanisms imply specific procedures and contexts, which are described in various guidelines and analyzed in the related literature. As an example, the various articles in Lock and Wells (1996) describe the procedures for verifying source data in general medical practice and in the pharmaceutical industry, as well as touching on many related issues. Johnson (1999) gives an overview of how associations and societies have elaborated their response mechanisms over the years, and Steneck (1999b) does the same for research universities. Broader perspectives pertaining to misconduct mechanisms in the hard sciences are treated in a collection of essays edited by Braxton (1999b).

Although such mechanisms have been developed for and are applied most routinely in the health sciences, they are still almost nonexistent in the soft sciences. Apart from this discrepancy between disciplines, institutionalized detection must face other challenges. First, applying such controls can be very expensive, sometimes costing as much or even more than the research that must be checked. Such a consideration makes conducting even representative sample checks virtually impossible. Second, institutional controls must still be carried out by individuals, often colleagues and others with whom one has ongoing relationships. Policing one's peers is not pleasant. Since the assignment is to search for fabrication and falsification, the monitor is automatically put in the awkward position of inspector, a function contrary to the pervasive spirit of collegiality in academia. Third, as more institutional detection is formalized and implemented, individual scientists may leave the responsibility for detecting misconduct to "the system" and will be less likely to take personal action when they suspect a serious problem. And finally, the very development of systems of institutionalized detection leads to bureaucratic overregulation and to an extravagant multiplying of paperwork for every action in academic research.

2.2.4 Private detection

Though the institutionalized approach is needed and is certainly effective in a number of contexts, undoubtedly misconduct would go unnoticed in many instances were it not for the critical and inquisitive mind of an independent individual. In previous decades, independent outsiders detected several famous cases of fabrication and falsification after the research results had been published. Sometimes the discovery is completely fortuitous. Sometimes it results from the personal drive of the whistleblower, whose suspicions are aroused by some aspect of the reported results. They may describe such intuitions by noting that "something set off an alarm bell" or "something smelled fishy."

In these cases, the attention of the reader (or of the listener at a conference) focuses on one or more irregularities: methodological protocols have not been respected; the data cannot realistically have been obtained given the lack of appropriate equipment or within the reported time frame; the description of the experiment sounds fictitious; there are discrepancies between results reported in different outlets or results of the observer's own current research; data that would tend to disprove the hypothesis have been omitted; data that tend to support it have been added, and so on. All these are first impressions. More concrete steps can be taken by requesting additional data or by trying to replicate the experiments, insofar as feasible, and then comparing the results obtained.

In many cases, outsiders start from a weak position from which to pursue their suspicion. They will need to obtain more information, which the alleged perpetrator may not be willing to give. They will need to convince institutions, such as a professional organization or the funding agency, to initiate an official investigation. They will have to face the indignation and rancor of the person they approach with their questions, even if these are not yet allegations.

Individual detection of misconduct can also happen in the intimate circle of the research unit during or immediately after the related experiments. For example, the supervisor appointed to provide direction to the junior researchers finds either the methodology or the results suspicious in some way. (Such a scenario would actually be one of the simplest forms of institutional control discussed above.) The seriousness of the offense may range from a minor but unacceptable error to intentional deceit. Within this context, the supervisor may feel free to handle it personally, or depending on the research site's protocols, the case may be passed on for institutional action. Much more difficult and challenging is the situation when a lower-ranking researcher detects apparent fabrication or falsification of data perpetrated by a senior researcher or by his or her very supervisor. A few famous misconduct cases, not least the widely publicized Baltimore case, presented exactly this quandary.

2.3   The detection of text plagiarism

Plagiarism is treated as an issue in each of the central chapters of this book. Considered the most frequent form of misconduct by some, but minimized by others, it is a complex matter in cases of misconduct. Lock (1996a:36) points out that "in established cases of misconduct [plagiarism] seems to be less frequent than either falsification or fabrication; in general allegations, on the other hand, it figures more frequently than either of the other two." This ratio, no doubt, has to do with the complexity of proving plagiarism, as this book discusses further (see sections 3.3 and 4.3).

This section deals only with the detection of possible plagiarism, suggesting methods of identifying a potential source text. In the chapter on analysis that follows, I explore the complex aspects of text comparison, in particular how authors manipulate "borrowed" texts without verbatim copying (section 3.3.3). This description will lead to assessment—that is, to a discussion of the problems associated with defining plagiarism and with determining improper use of sources (section 4.3).

*2.3.1   Finding common text clusters

Plagiarism detection relies on finding textual overlaps or a collection of common text clusters. Such detection typically consists of three steps:

* Sections 2.3.1 and 2.3.2 were written by Jozef Colpaert, project manager of Didascalia at the University of Antwerp.

Step 1:   Establish a corpus of comparison materials

Text plagiarism entails, by definition, the existence and improper use of a source text. Therefore we need a growing database of writings against which a specific document can be checked at a later stage. Four combinable approaches can be used in this respect:

• A first approach is the *locus-oriented approach*: It starts from the premise that an alleged plagiarist will have looked for a source text previously written in the same "locus," meaning for example the same institution (university or college), official organization (certifying body at county, state, or country level), or scientific organization. Because these papers, essays, dissertations, reports, books, and articles are mostly not readily available on the Web, it is important that every institution or organization establish its own database of submitted writings. Such databases, constituted locally, can eventually be put to use on a worldwide scale through the Internet.

• A second approach is the *reference-oriented approach*: It consists in establishing a corpus based on all the references used in a suspect document. Indeed, many cases of plagiarism have shown that authors sometimes copy in an inadmissible way from sources they actually cite in their text (see section 3.3.5). By tracking those sources, the investigator can assemble a corpus of materials specific to the suspect text. Each reference mentioned in a publication not only leads to these sources, but also to other references in those sources, and so on. The result is a taxonomy or tree-structured network of interrelated documents that are all potential sources of plagiarism.

• A third approach is the *subject-oriented approach*: It identifies, with the help of keywords, related documents that could have been used as sources for a specific text. These can be found with older thematic card indexes or current electronic indexes in the library and with any search engine available on the Internet. Search engines like Excite try to classify Web pages (HTML format) according to probabilities based on keywords. It is also possible to search for ideas closely related to the words in the query, or for exact phrases enclosed in quotation marks. Other symbols like the + or − signs and Boolean operators (AND, OR, NOT, and so forth) provide advanced mechanisms for information retrieval. Search engines also provide mechanisms for quickly retrieving similar documents, like the "Related texts" feature in AltaVista.

• A fourth approach is the *"track covering"-oriented approach*: Clever plagiarists will avoid using material that can be found and compared too easily by an investigator. They will avoid taking HTML material from the Web, knowing that electronic searches can quickly detect it. They will turn to little-known printed works, or to works of which only one or a few copies exist. Most of these sources are in hard-copy format (paper or microfilm), which makes it more difficult for the investigator to obtain an electronic copy in a short time. They must be retyped or scanned in order to be entered into the database, thus requiring much preparatory work, and the investigator must obtain permission to add these printed documents to the digital corpus. Downloadable documents in PDF and PS formats are also attractive to the plagiarist, because they are more difficult to trace and to convert to standard formats (such as TXT or Rich Text Format) for comparison purposes. Moreover, some organizations and journals limit free access to these documents by requiring subscriptions.

In short, an intelligent selection of writings for comparison should be based on a thorough knowledge of topic and locus (delicti), enriched by supplemental bibliographical searches. It does not proceed at random, looks at track covering strategies, and pays sufficient attention to printed and manuscript material.

Web services to detect plagiarism proceed in some of the ways described to compare a suspect text with potential source texts. The quality of their service will depend on the extensiveness of their database and the power of their search routines. The simplest service will limit itself to finding long common strings in documents available on the Internet, without a database of its own and without taking into account language alterations. This will only yield results if the plagiarist has simply copied from texts available on the Internet. Better services will constitute ever-growing databases of their own by entering masses of source material and apply refined search routines. IntegriGuard, for instance, is designed to be used by teachers. According to its promotional literature, "After the student's writing is submitted, IntegriGuard compares passages of the text against all writings that have ever been submitted to it. The submission becomes part of the database immediately following the test" (IntegriGuard 1998;

see also Falzone 1998; Meese 1998; Guernsey 1998b). The SCAM system at Stanford uses the same principle: it stores original documents in a repository on a registration server for comparison purposes, also allowing users to register their digital documents into their own databases. A signature added to each document allows the document to be traced to its origin. SCAM then checks UseNet newsgroups, mailing lists, and some Web sites daily (Shivakumar and Garcia-Molina 1995). Another example is iThenticate®, developed by researchers and alumni at the University of California at Berkeley (www.plagiarism.org). An instructor can submit student papers, which are then compared against the database to discover similar phrases (see also Carnevale 1999). EVE2 (Essay Verification Engine, at www.canexus.com) seems to work with shorter strings because it fragments the suspect text and then goes out on the Internet to find the sources. Digital Integrity does the same but works with longer strings. When one submits a suspect document, the system returns "a list of Web pages that contain any fragment of that document longer than about one line of text" (www.FindSame.com).

Step 2:   Classify potential source documents according to the probability of relatedness

The second step is to classify the documents in a corpus according to the probability of their relatedness to a particular document. I formulate this relatedness here in neutral terms, not necessarily in the immediate context of plagiarism. Indeed, texts on the same subject are by definition related and a certain degree of overlap in truisms, specific terminology, and even jargon structures is unavoidable. A response from one author to a previous publication by another author will almost certainly use a number of direct quotations and discuss matters in similar terms. In a classification of relatedness, these two publications will of course score very high without necessarily implying plagiarism. On the other hand—and this is my point—the classification should also bring to light potential source documents for a suspect document.

The computation of document similarity or relatedness, frequently used in Internet search engines, is based on linguistic patterns, collocations, frequency or occurrence lists, keywords, writing style, or more statistical features. Algorithms for pattern recognition, cluster analysis, feature selection, and lexical chaining are emerging as new research areas of information retrieval. To my knowledge these techniques are not yet commonly used to detect plagiarism, but they are valuable in determining the probability that a particular document has been used as a source for a suspect document.

Step 3: Identify, quantify, and document common text clusters between two documents

The accurate identification, quantification, and documentation of common text clusters is the core issue in plagiarism detection. It is necessary for the next phase in the procedure, assessment (see chapter 4), because plagiarism can be proven only by showing clearly the nature and quantity of unjustifiable text overlap between two documents.

Common text clusters between two presumably related documents can be studied by carefully reading and comparing the documents and noting all similarities. In cases where long passages are reused verbatim, this manual approach can yield quick results. However, in the case when the reuse is occasional, from various sources, and transformed in complex ways, a manual search becomes time consuming and frustrating, because even the slightest discrepancies between clusters hamper the comparison. Valuable items may thus be overlooked. Since the comparison is more convincing in direct proportion to the number of common text clusters, the manual approach is infeasible in complex cases.

An electronic text-comparison program provides a more objective, precise, and rapid way of comparing documents. Various systems perform string queries within a document, a folder, or an entire file system. GLIMPSE, for instance, is a powerful indexing and query system that allows the user to search through a number of files quickly (GLIMPSE 1998). SCAM (discussed above) checks for full or partial overlap and looks for similar sentences or paragraphs. It then shows contexts of detected common text clusters. The Unix DIFF utility allows for a line-by-line comparison of multiple files. Feder and Stewart (n.d.) developed a system, commonly called "the plagiarism machine," that compares thirty-character strings in different texts for matches; it leads to a measurement of plagiarism probability called the "Freeman unit."

Because no more versatile text-comparison programs seemed readily available, I built one myself. Cerberus is a simple but, I believe, high-performance tool for finding common text clusters within two or more documents. Both source code and compiled program are freely downloadable from our site www.didascalia.be (University of Antwerp, Department of Education, Didascalia).

The Appendix contains a detailed description of Cerberus, showing how easy it is to build such a text-comparison program and, at the same time, how challenging research in the field of detection and comparison routines can be.

2.3.2   Future developments

The previous sections and the Appendix provide an introduction to plagiarism-detection techniques as well as a tool, Cerberus, for checking text overlap. This tool shows how straightforward techniques can lead to accurate identification, quantification, and documentation of text overlap. Search parameters allow adjustment of text-comparison mechanisms. Naturally, the more refined the definition of the comparison operation, the slower the execution speed.

Ongoing research in DNA and chromosome decoding, music plagiarism, software plagiarism, and information retrieval will certainly require more powerful, implementable, and useful algorithms for exact or approximate string matching in the near future. In the case of text overlap detection, I believe sophisticated mathematical routines could be simplified considerably by using the knowledge already available on text-reuse mechanisms. This approach could be reinforced by research in the field of more intelligent linguistic routines—for example, detection mechanisms for sentence transformations. A second simplification could consider the redundancy of natural language on all levels (grapheme, morpheme, word, syntagm, sentence). The more knowledge that is available about the context of a particular linguistic element on a specific level, the more predictable it becomes. This predictability could reduce searching time considerably.

Finally, an automated link between browsers for information-retrieval and text-comparison programs would allow comparison of a particular document with all possible related documents available on the Internet. Even for downloadable documents in specific formats such as PS and PDF, automatic downloading and conversion could be considered.

2.3.3   The unusual-word technique

When plagiarism seems highly probable and a corpus of potential source texts within the field is available online, it is possible to search quickly for a common unusual word—that is, a word (or a structure) that would normally not appear in this context. The chance that such a word would occur "naturally" in two independent texts on the same subject is small. If it occurs, the context would immediately reveal possible plagiarism or not. If necessary, more than one unusual word could be searched for, using a compound search formula.

For example, I received a French textbook on computer-assisted learning written by a university professor, whom I call X3. When I read his section on language applications, the material sounded familiar. It seemed to be something I had written many years ago, but I could not remember the date or the place or even the language I wrote it in. In X3's text, I looked for an unusual word and decided on *chimistes* (*chemists* in French), a term unlikely to appear in a text on language learning. I applied a simple query with "search files" for *chimistes* (French), *chemists* (English), or *scheikundigen* (Dutch) to the subdirectories of all my publications, since these are the three languages I write in. One item including *chimistes* showed up within seconds, and I quickly discovered that X3 had copied several pages from a 1986 Canadian publication I had written in French. X3 did not cite this publication or list my article in either the chapter or the book bibliographies, nor did he mention my name anywhere in the plagiarized pages.

Decoo 1986	X3, 43
	(various paragraphs precede the following, also taken literally from Decoo)
… analyse automatisée de corpus en fonction d'un but spécifique, par exemple lorsque des **chimistes** anglais veulent pouvoir lire la littérature allemande dans leur domaine (projet de l'Université de Nottingham).	… analyse automatisée de corpus en fonction d'un but spécifique; par exemple on veut rédiger un cours d'Allemand pour des **chimistes** anglais qui veulent pouvoir consulter la littérature allemande dans leur domaine.

L'étude statistique de la littérature technique en question a permis d'établir une liste de fréquence lexicale et grammaticale, qui a servi de base à la préparation d'un cours de langue spécifique. On a par exemple démontré que, dans certains cas, il était inutile d'enseigner les conjugaisons puisque l'étude des corpus révèle qu'on peut se limiter à la troisième personne et à quelques temps élémentaires. Par contre, le corpus lexical ayant trait à la chimie est très riche et varié.	L'étude statistique de la littérature technique en question a permis d'établir une liste de fréquence lexicale et grammaticale qui a servi de base à la préparation d'un cours de langue spécifique. On a par exemple démontré que, dans certains cas, il était inutile d'enseigner les conjugaisons puisque l'étude des corps [sic] révèle qu'on peut se limiter à la troisième personne et à quelques temps élémentaires. Par contre, le corpus lexical ayant trait à la chimie est très riche et varié.
	etc., also taken literally from Decoo

One advantage of the unusual-word technique is that it is extremely simple and quick if the potential sources are available online: a simple search on a specific word in Windows using "find files" will suffice. Or a compound search is applied with "AND" to look for two unusual words. Moreover, the suspect text need not be available in digital form, since we only search in potential source texts. The investigator can identify an unusual word from the suspect text and type it in the search window. A third advantage is that plurilingual searches are possible, enabling the investigation to include translations by simply translating the unusual word into a number of probable languages.

The disadvantage is that, if the chosen unusual word is not common to both texts, the results are negative without even a percentage of probability, while the suspect text can still involve plagiarism. In that case, stronger detection procedures, as described in the previous sections, are necessary.

For a short description of how the X3 case was handled after the discovery of the impropriety, see in section 5.4.1, part "Memo to the accused person."

2.3.4 Some cautions

I do not wish to foster the illusion that electronic detection techniques work flawlessly and instantly. Fast and successful responses are not yet typical for most situations. Web services that provide (paid) help in detecting plagiarism have a tendency to oversimplify the matter, promising quick and definite results. Even the fastest and most effective detection devices first require the creation of a database of a vast number of potential sources in the target disciplines. The Internet corpus, gigantic as it is, does not contain everything available in traditional print. True, in rather flagrant and easy-to-determine cases, Web services can swiftly come up with a "positive" answer that will meet the inquirer's needs, but a negative answer does not mean that plagiarism did not occur. It simply means that no matching source was found. The perpetrator may have paraphrased the sentences and scrambled the paragraphs well enough to avoid identical strings. Any word processing with a thesaurus would allow a plagiarist to change key words swiftly and effectively. Or the perpetrator may have copied from an unfamiliar printed work that is not on the Internet or in a digital database. And, of course, if the material has been translated from another language, the whole principle of string matching becomes irrelevant. If dishonest people know that a detection service could be applied to their work, they will probably spend some time trying to avoid detection.

Next, even a quick and "positive" response of electronic anti-plagiarism tools requires careful manual postanalysis before any allegations can be made. The mere fact of a match does not make the material's use unacceptable. If it has been quoted and cited correctly, the author has, of course, observed proper scholarly procedures. Even quoting and/or citing in ambiguous ways opens the door to much controversy (see section 3.3).

We should also be careful that detection by Web services does not lead to games of hide and seek or, worse, to a struggle between authoritative institutions and clever hackers constantly trying to beat the system. Sympathy may go to the successful hacker, not to the plagiarized author. Such games can also lead to shady guidelines showing, in essence, "how to plagiarize from the Internet without risk." Similarly, some commercial antiplagiarism Web sites advertise themselves as big-business detective bureaus skilled in catching the thugs. Real or faked "thank you" notes to the site by anonymous teachers who successfully identified plagiarists sometimes exhibit a spirit of adventure games and revenge instead of true educational concern. Such an approach fails dramatically if the goal is to instill ethics and scholarly virtues.

A final problem is that, in the case of student work, the moment for investigating possible plagiarism often comes at a bad time, frequently at the end of each term, when papers come flooding in or when a questionable thesis or dissertation is handed in close to the defense deadline. The challenge then is finding enough time to track down the potential source. This task may take days of frustrating searching in libraries or on the Internet, while so much other work needs to be done and as the deadline for turning in the evaluation draws near.

2.4   The detection of the plagiarism of ideas

A particularly difficult kind of plagiarism involves the theft of ideas. The literature of misconduct is replete with accusations of stolen concepts on various levels of seriousness and in various settings. The plagiarism of ideas from a written source consists of the intentional misappropriation of an original concept, claiming it as one's own without proper credit to the original author. Detection of such alleged misconduct happens by identifying the obvious sameness of a unique idea and by determining the connections that allowed a person to appropriate the idea. A setting conducive to this misconduct is the review process where a reviewer, who is a specialist in a particular field, is given early access to a colleague's original findings. Such misappropriation can occur not only in the formal arena of journal or conference submissions, but also in the informal round of prepublication exchanges for collegial comments. If an idea is thus misappropriated and is later used in publications by the plagiarist, the original author will often be the first to detect it.

The paragraph above deals with the plagiarism of ideas based on a written source, which provides some material proof of the source. The matter becomes more volatile if it involves oral sources. In this case, someone discusses an original but unrefined idea with a second party, who then develops it, publishing it as his or her own. Or an interesting concept floats around within a circle of specialists, being discussed at meetings or conferences. All discussants offer contributions, some more substantive than others, but one individual finally lays claim to it. Some in academia engage in professional conversations, masking their own ignorance, and plucking any idea, however small, which they immediately begin circulating afterward as their own. Insiders quickly detect such behavior, but outsiders are often impressed by the display of knowledge.

2.5   The detection of software plagiarism

Software, like other intellectual products, can be plagiarized on at least three levels: user-interface design, content, and source coding.

2.5.1   At the level of user-interface design

Unless a software package is made with an authoring system producing the same basic user-interface for each outcome, self-designed programs have unique features developed by the author. Professional user-interface design requires working through a number of intricate phases, which require significant investment of time and resources in research coupled with personal efforts to produce quality results (see, e.g., Cooper 1999). The same characteristic, of course, applies to Web pages and the interactive engine behind them.

Such a user-interface design, including its basic concepts, can be duplicated, totally or partially, by an outsider without permission. This may constitute plagiarism or copyright infringement. A series of lawsuits during the 1990s, called the "look and feel" cases involving user-interfaces of major competitors such as Apple and Microsoft, Lotus and Borland, illustrate how much can be at stake. To the extent that much computer-related research in varied fields develops user-interfaces for programs, even if only for a prototype, the total or partial copying of an interface from another program, without proper permission, can involve misconduct issues (Donner 1994; Forester 1990; Samuelson and Glushko 1990; Samuelson 1993; Schneiderman 1990; Schultz and Windsor 1994).

I am not aware of automated devices for detecting possibly plagiarized user-interfaces. It seems that only observation and visual comparison of two identical or very similar programs would reveal potential plagiarism. As a consequence, such discoveries will be fortuitous, depending on the public availability of the programs.

2.5.2   At the level of content

Many software packages, especially for educational purposes, include printed texts, audio recordings, and videoclips as part of their program.

The production of sufficient and original content—for example, for electronic encyclopedias and electronic textbooks—is a challenging endeavor, which can be easily underestimated during the early stages of the production. Some designers of educational software, many of them from various subdisciplines, do not realize that pedagogically sound content must meet a number of complex efficiency criteria and must be composed step by step. It is tempting to avoid this time-consuming intellectual labor when "authentic material" from newspapers, magazines, brochures, movies, radio and television broadcasts, and, of course, the Internet allows the facile incorporation of a variety of sources into new programs.

The boundary between "permissible fair use" and plagiarism or copyright infringement is easily crossed, because the material taken is often extensive and used in a new application. The proper identification of the source may not be sufficient to legitimate the use.

Detecting possible misappropriated content, like the case of user-interfaces, seems to depend on personal recognition of content taken from elsewhere.

The misuse of content in software is sometimes done naïvely. In May 1999, I received a software program for language learning, produced by a person I will call X4. The program publicity, distributed by the Flemish Ministry of Education, mentioned that the content for this program came from the textbooks *Eventail-Junior 1* and *Eventail-Junior 2*, published by Van In in Belgium. When I inquired, I learned that neither Van In nor the authors of the textbooks were aware of this software's existence. Van In asked me to perform a critical comparison between the program's content and the textbooks. I found that even the software's table of contents reflected the main twenty-one units and further subdivisions of the two textbooks.

Further investigation revealed that, in fact, the textbooks' content had simply been copied into the software. This kind of detection needs to done be almost manually, case by case.

2.5.3   At the level of the source code

Detecting plagiarism in software source codes—that is, in the actual formulas and algorithms written in a programming language—is obviously important in identifying software misuses. Fortunately, such detection has already become an established subdiscipline in the field of computer science. As a research topic it is identified by keywords such as "source code authorship analysis," "software forensics," and "software similarity detection." Because a comprehensive overview of the major characteristics and accomplishments of this subdiscipline would take us too far afield, I will mention only some relevant elements and detection systems.

Plagiarism detection in source codes basically resembles the detection of common text clusters (see section 2.3)—that is, finding questionable overlap in the sequences written by two different authors. The procedures for detecting textual plagiarism also apply here. A traditional method is comparing the frequency of similar words and tokens. Because the layout of two source codes can be somewhat dissimilar, while the codes still replicate each other, another procedure is to put each source code first into a continuous stream of lexical and numeric tokens, including the personal whims of comments and variable names. Comparing the two tokenized streams results in similarity scores.

Examples of such detection devices in student research environments include Bandit at the University of Manchester (West 1999) and JPlag at the University of Karlsruhe (Malpohl and Prechelt 1999). The program MOSS (Measure Of Software Similarity) was originally conceived as a tool to detect plagiarism in programming classes at Berkeley. It is now available on the Internet as a service to instructors and staff of programming courses. It claims to be "a significant improvement over other cheating detection algorithms" but does not disclose its specific characteristics because detection devices "can be fooled if one knows how they work" (MOSS 1999). The Department of Computer Science at the University of Sidney offers YAP (Yet Another Plague), which first cleans up source codes to bring them back to their very essence. YAP3, the latest version I saw on the Web, is meant to tackle transposed subsequences (Wise 1996).

At the Software Metrics Research Laboratory of the University of Otago (New Zealand), research is pushing beyond purely quantitative measurement to detect plagiarism and so far has developed a system called Identified. They argue:

Existing numerical metrics should be supplemented with fuzzy-logic linguistic variables to capture more subjective elements of authorship, such as the degree to which comments match the actual source code's behavior. These variables avoid the need for complex and subjective rules, replacing these with an expert's judgment. Fuzzy-logic models may also help to overcome problems with small data sets for calibrating such models. Using authorship discrimination as a test case, the utility of objective and fuzzy measures, singularly and in combination, is assessed as well as the consistency of the measures between counters. (Kilgour et al. 1997; see also Gray, Sallis, and MacDonell 1997)

2.6 The detection of misused connections

The solitary researcher who makes a discovery after months or years of isolated work has become rare, though less so in the humanities and social sciences. Usually academic research is conducted in small or large teams peopled by graduate students and junior researchers who come and go according to the needs of projects or shifting personal circumstances. Overall that movement is valuable, because it provides young people with training and experience and allows project directors to select the best collaborators for further research and academic careers.

But the system also has drawbacks. People involved with a team, even in a limited and marginal way, may have little input but can easily gather valuable information that they can then use to personal advantage. The team approach allows those individuals to profit from work done by others, in part because the demarcation of the respective input of the team members is difficult to assess at a later stage. Even those who have been involved with a team only marginally can claim at least partial credit for the team's research results. On the other hand, a team leader can also take undue credit for important work done by individual researchers by stealing their ideas and by not mentioning their names or their input in reports or publications. Fierce disputes sometimes arise in such situations (see, e.g., Reynolds 1998). However, because the accuser and defendant have worked on the same team, the official bodies dealing with the evaluation of academic misconduct tend to dismiss such cases. The ORI excludes "authorship or credit disputes" from its definition of plagiarism (Office of Research Integrity 1994), as does the Office of Science and Technology Policy (2000).

Basically this situation means that official or even marginal involvement with someone else can become a source of ambiguity in determining the value and originality of their respective contributions. The matter becomes even more intricate when researchers navigate among various disciplines. It is difficult for outsiders to evaluate how much is personal work and how much is borrowed without proper credit when the research is interdisciplinary and where peers are unaware of the work done in related fields.

In summary, personal connections could be misused in various ways:

• A person is or has been officially part of a team, but uses research concepts, data, or publications of the team for personal advantage, such as lectures, publications, diplomas, or awards, without properly acknowledging either the origin of the material or the extent of the team contribution.

• Two persons come into contact with each other, either as colleagues, or in a professor-student, host-visitor, or interviewer-interviewee relationship. One profits from the sharing of information by afterward using data obtained from the other as his or her own concepts.

• A reviewer of articles submitted for publication or a conference uses this position to misappropriate concepts or data before the submitted article has been published or before the submitted paper has been given. The reviewer may even have recommended that the submission be rejected.

How can these acts be detected? The person or team that feels misused may confront the other or call attention to the misappropriation; but if the person engaging in misconduct denies the charge, the resulting controversy makes assessment by outsiders difficult. If the victims do not become aware of the misuse (for example, if the material is used for internal purposes, such as a student paper, a master's thesis, or a doctoral dissertation), only an external investigation can reveal the problem. Such an investigation might start only in the wake of other disturbing facts. In the case of X2, my inquiries into possible misused connections began only after questions were raised about the dissertation's quality (see section 3.4).

2.7   The detection of academic make-believe

By its very nature, the academic profession encourages make-believe and exaggeration. Indeed, evaluation for hiring or promotion, or the yearly assessment of productivity, are rather quantitative measurements, based on the list of publications, on the number of papers or posters presented, on the number of lectures given, on positions in academic organizations and journals, on general statements of contact and cooperation with scholars abroad, and so on. For some academics, establishing credentials becomes a matter of making readers believe that all these items are as real as the entries suggest. This make-believe also extends to other ingenious strategies, all meant to hide various degrees of emptiness and patch over the lacuna. The next two subsections discuss two common techniques:

2.7.1 Exaggerating the curriculum vitae

The Danish Committee on Scientific Dishonesty classifies as misconduct, albeit in a lesser form, the "exaggeration of the personal publication list" (Andersen et al. 1992). The padded C.V. may classify contributions to a popular daily or weekly newspaper as scientific publications in refereed periodicals, include abstracts or summaries of papers that were submitted to nonselective conferences, duplicate publications under different titles, announce as "in press" publications that are not ready yet, list as "forthcoming" publications that are barely started, and so on.

Other activities are subject to inflated description as well. A handshake and a brief hallway conversation at a conference may become "personal contact" with an academic celebrity. An informal visit to a research center is a "scientific research stay" or a "postdoctoral fellowship." Some occasional information given to a student or a colleague is worded as "academic support." A visit to a foreign country where some informal exchanges happened to take place leads to the statement that the person has become a "national advisor" to that country. Simple recognition in a remote location is presented as a "prestigious prize." A short and co-incidental connection with a project elsewhere is described as "participation in" that project. A discussion at a local meeting becomes a "seminar upon invitation." The padded C.V. may even include phoney degrees and invented honorific titles. For a discussion of the falsification of credentials, see Parrish 1996.

To detect these exaggerations, if not factual lies, we need to be critical of certain types of C.V. entries. If the C.V. contains many items that seem both vague and overstated, further inquiry is justified. Articles in a popular daily or weekly, misidentified as "peer-reviewed" publications, are comparatively easy to recognize. Other items will require a study of the professional career of the suspect to sort out the persons and places of collaboration and the validity of certain claims. In these cases, discreet inquiry of the persons referred to may produce evidence of the discrepancy. Sometimes, however, such an investigation becomes public in an open controversy about credentials (see, e.g., Basinger 1999).

2.7.2   Drawing authority from others or from oneself

It is impressive to read that researchers are being acclaimed by world authorities in the field and that reviewers of highly regarded international journals have hailed their publications. We respect such individuals for their achievements if these statements are true, corroborated by undeniable evidence. But sometimes they are made in a context that justifies distrust.

A particular technique used in publications, lectures, or even conversations is the author's reference to work in another location containing the core of the issue and necessary proofs. "As I have shown in ...," "We have conducted thorough research on this topic as reported in ..." The question is whether this claim is true. Usually, an investigator will begin digging into such claims after other facts have come to light that cast doubt on the researcher's integrity.

Does a publication contain many announcements that core issues are treated elsewhere? Does the author say *we* in a context where there is ambiguity about the real authorship? Questioning the reality behind such items will, of course, lead to a more serious analysis and to assessment. Such an analysis is not easy to conduct, for it requires carefully reading and comparing all related passages. For an example of such an approach, see the X2 investigation described in section 3.6.2.

2.8   The detection of possibly deceitful educational software

In the case of problematic software, I must stress the cardinal distinction between two different situations. On the one hand, we may be invited to discover the limited possibilities of a software prototype as the result of the honest probing of a researcher, whether novice or experienced. Such a prototype, if correctly presented, does not intend to trick the onlookers. On the other hand, there is deliberately deceitful courseware. From the analysis of a case study (see section 3.7) and from occasional experiences at conferences and fairs where software is announced or presented, I have learned to become suspicious when these characteristics of courseware are present:

- The courseware is described as an existing, working program, but an outsider cannot use it or even view it in a demonstration. Is it total fakeware?

- The courseware is described as having a number of features; however, (some of) these features cannot be viewed or studied. Is it partial fakeware?

- The courseware looks operative in a demonstration. A startup screen is followed by a number of other screens showing features of the program; however, the same screens are shown at every demonstration and outsiders are not allowed to touch the keyboard. Is it masqueradeware?

- The courseware seems to work properly as announced; however, after a very short time, the content seems exhausted. Is it emptyware?

To identify the real attributes of a courseware program requires studying it firsthand. Consulting with the author or promoter is certainly helpful, but if they restrict access or investigation, I become suspicious. Potential users must see and investigate for themselves, hands on, whether a program corresponds to its description. Only in this way can possibly deceitful courseware be detected, analyzed, and assessed.

On the other hand, we might have to take into account the following situation: at a conference or a fair, someone presents software that is not completely developed and is nervous about the possibility that a skilled user, under guise of "investigating" or checking out the program, may actually be stealing certain features. In other words, a security issue may be involved in which the user's need to explore the software collides with the originator's need to retain control. However, if this is the case, we may expect the full version of the software to be published relatively soon.

2.9 Conclusion

This chapter has dealt with the detection of misconduct, which I have separated from the next step—analysis. This separation is necessary to avoid evaluation errors and hasty conclusions.

For example, if during an inquiry on possible plagiarism, a detection system located a passage identical to the text under suspicion, the procedure simply determines that fact but cannot evaluate the significance of the overlap. During the analysis stage, the investigator must appraise the characteristics of the similarity between the two passages. If the common clusters are genuine quotations between quotation marks with a correct reference to the source, no further analysis is needed. But if the conventions of scholarly quotation have not been observed, then the presence of citation terms and of references to sources must be studied, as well as the quantity and boundaries of the common elements, the possible transformations, and so on (see section 3.3). Only then can the matter be assessed according to an established local academic code or judicial criteria (see section 4.3). Furthermore, the decision about what to do with the assessment is also a separate step. Ultimately, investigators can report their conclusions to the proper authorities or take other steps (see section 5.2). Detection is thus concerned only with the identification of alleged academic misconduct. It gathers evidence without judging. It is of some legal importance that an investigator resists the temptation to pronounce the verdict.

On the other hand, the whole procedure need not always be cumbersome. In very obvious cases, the major steps in the procedure can be taken swiftly. If a teacher immediately identifies a student's term paper as the verbatim replica, without attribution, of a scientific article published two decades earlier, not much further analysis will be needed, assessment follows forthwith, and the matter can be reported and left for judgment.

This chapter has tried to show the many facets of detection according to the kind of alleged misconduct, the varied circumstances, the possible procedures, and the range of individuals involved. All these variables may make the start of a case intricate and confused. The next chapter, Analysis, is meant to sort out and further investigate the data, in order to come to a candid picture of the facts.

3

Analysis

3.1 Introduction

The vehement reactions to allegations of academic misconduct show how vital it is to conduct a careful analysis *before* assessment and reporting. Too many times whistle-blowers are afterward accused of negligence in their account, of having overlooked essential elements, of having misunderstood core issues of the research they have denounced, or of being motivated by personal malice. Indeed, there may be alternative explanations for what at first seemed to be real misconduct. The whole matter can be turned against the whistle-blower, with very negative consequences.

Anyone who suspects a form of academic misconduct must gather the relevant data and analyze them as scrupulously as possible, taking the utmost care not to jump to conclusions. It is also advisable to conduct the investigation as discreetly as possible so as to avoid rumors. This analytical operation can be quite time consuming, especially because each case presents a range of tasks and because various factors must be weighed against each other.

A first potential problem is the extent to which someone has rightful access to the relevant data. There may be limitations as to the right of an outsider to use them. A whistle-blower can be accused afterward of having obtained incriminating material illegally or of having violated confidentiality. Next, what methods can the investigator use to identify questionable actions and data? How are they best organized and described? What criteria should be applied in preparation for the assessment phase?

The following sections do not present analyses for each form of potential misconduct but rather focus on some that seem particularly interesting because of their more complex nature or because of my personal experience. It should be clear, however, that each occurrence of alleged misconduct deserves a thorough analysis.

3.2   Analyzing alleged fabrication and falsification

Especially in the United States, the area of alleged fabrication and falsification has already received a great deal of attention, in particular in the medical, biomedical, and pharmaceutical fields. Such scrupulousness is not surprising since false data in the health sciences have the potential to affect people's lives directly, and the United States has a long tradition of sensitivity to these issues. The various fields and organizations involved have outlined the techniques and procedures for analyzing alleged fabrication and falsification in greater or lesser detail, depending on the perceived needs. As a matter of self-policing, these organizations constantly study, critically review, and improve their guidelines, responding to the challenges of new types of fabrication and falsification. I will limit myself here to a brief overview and a list of further references, since any attempt to summarize this vast area of expertise would be inadequate.

For institutional treatments, I recommend the various guidelines and reports by national and international bodies such as the American Association for the Advancement of Science, the American Medical Association and its Council on Ethical and Judicial Affairs, the Association of American Medical Colleges, the Environmental Protection Agency, the Food and Drug Administration, the National Academy of Sciences and its Committee on Science, Engineering, and Public Policy (COSEPUP), the Council for International Organizations of Medical Science, the National Institutes of Health and its Office of Research Integrity, and the National Science Foundation. All of these entities have Web sites with more information on their current guidelines.

For other disciplines and/or for some other countries, the various overarching institutional bodies and professional organizations normally provide more or less detailed guidelines to analyze and assess cases of fabrication and falsification. In many cases, considerable work apparently remains to be done to render the guidelines more practical and directly applicable. Here is a vast domain of applied research where crucial steps must still be taken, especially in some countries. As Husson et al. (1996:207) observe, even in developed nations like in the European Union, coordinated and harmonized action on the European level to better detect and analyze misconduct is greatly needed.

The review *Accountability in Research: Policies and Quality Assurance* (Gordon and Breach Publishing) is devoted to the analysis of systems for conducting research. It specializes in articles on the mechanisms of problem detection, quality evaluation, and discipline in connection with misconduct as well as in articles on problems related to conflicts of interest, research involving human subjects, audits and peer review, legal issues, codes of professional ethics governing the collection of scientific data, and more.

The statistical analysis of alleged fraudulent data can become a sophisticated endeavor. See, for example, Evans (1996), who provides many suggestions for referees and editors. Hodges (1996) discusses the English and Welsh legal framework for investigating fraud in clinical research.

3.3   Analyzing alleged plagiarism

Detection of possible plagiarism (see section 2.3) is limited to the discovery of similarities between texts. The next step is the careful examination of those similarities. Of course, if a substantial text, pages long, is the verbatim reproduction of a source that is not quoted, little further analysis will be needed and assessment can follow instantly. However, this is rare. In most cases, a long and painstaking comparison between the suspect text and potential sources awaits the investigator before any valid assessment can be made. Individuals who want to blur the origin of the sources they use—either because they really intend to deceive or because they think they are allowed to paraphrase someone else's text— will resort to a number of techniques: manipulate the language in a sentence, change the order of sentences or paragraphs, mix various sources, blur the boundaries of correct citation in order to use much more than the reader suspects, and so on. If these techniques are applied to numerous pages, and the sources pertain to various authors, the analysis will be complex, time consuming, and often discouraging. But it is a vital phase to prepare the actual assessment (see section 4.3).

3.3.1 A doctoral dissertation as case study

Background of the case

For this book I use a specific, troublesome case to show the complexity and the challenges of an explicit analysis. The elements of this case are not meant to allege misconduct, but to illustrate key issues. They are intended to provide essential groundwork and empirical data, and also to make the subject more concrete and involved.

In 1998 a European university's department of languages and literature accepted a doctoral dissertation with summa cum laude honors from a writer whom I identify as X2 for the reasons mentioned in the preface. The dissertation dealt with using the World Wide Web as information technology for language learning and was written in English. The work had been financed, first under a project of the European Union, and next under a grant from the National Science Foundation of that country. None of the members of the doctoral committee, including the dissertation advisor, was a specialist in computer-assisted language learning (CALL) or had anything to do with related professional organizations such as EuroCall or CALICO or with any CALL journal. The dissertation defense was brief and unpublicized; no CALL specialist was invited to attend.

A few months later, the dissertation advisor submitted the dissertation for an internal research award at his own university. The advisor's nomination lauded the work as a "brilliant contribution to science surpassing the traditional boundaries of research in the humanities." Indeed, X2 had, claimed the advisor, discovered "a new navigation technique in hypermedia."

As an external assessor, I was asked to be on the committee to evaluate the dissertation for the research award and received a copy of the dissertation. After a careful analysis, I submitted a report with these conclusions:

• No original research on the doctoral level had been conducted; the "new navigation technique" was a very simple, not to say naïve, idea of adapting a menu for learners.

• The dissertation was entirely based on a limited number of sources that had been extensively copied or paraphrased without, in my opinion, adequate citation.

• The references to publications, systems, and programs had been taken from these few sources but presented as if the candidate had discovered and analyzed them.

• The research X2 actually proposed, announced as the core issue of the dissertation—that is, the application of the new navigation technique to language learning—was never carried out.

• The alleged result, a courseware prototype, seemed not only very primitive to judge from its succinct description, but was also unavailable. Consequently, its very existence could not be verified.

• In view of the lack of original research and the direct use of existing sources, this small doctoral dissertation—which was financed for several years by two major funding agencies, and which granted the highest academic diploma—could very well have been written in no more than six to eight weeks.

My report to the university president prompted a hesitant and discreet investigation by the university. The president first submitted my conclusions to the author of the dissertation and his dissertation advisor, who strongly refuted my viewpoint. Both placed the focus immediately on the secondary issue of plagiarism, not on my fundamental concern—that this work was not acceptable for a doctoral degree and that, by implication, the doctoral committee had been negligent, if not manifestly guilty, in its oversight. The university president next submitted my report as "a complaint regarding plagiarism"—which again avoided the fundamental question—to the very same doctoral committee that had granted the degree and of which the dissertation advisor was the central figure. The doctoral committee responded that they upheld their original assessment, although the committee members (four of the six) whom I contacted personally as part of my evaluation assignment privately admitted to me that there was a problem.

To also go outside the group that had actually granted the degree, the university president next asked an ad hoc, informal group of three faculty members, but from his own institution, to evaluate possible plagiarism—

once again, not the fundamental question of unacceptability of this work for a doctoral degree. One of the three members was a coauthor with a member of the doctoral committee; two of the three were close colleagues to four members of the doctoral committee, belonging to the same departments. After studying the matter secretly for several months, the ad hoc committee submitted a two-page report in which they first stated they did not evaluate the quality of the dissertation, thus explicitly avoiding the fundamental question. They next confirmed serious "short-comings in the citation" and "misleading reuse of sources," but concluded that the word *plagiarism* did not really apply. They did not define how they were using the term. Their short report was next submitted to the university's research council, which, after a discussion, decided only to "take note" of the report, not to endorse it. This report essentially closed the case as far as the institution was concerned. During the whole investigation, the chief concern, explicitly articulated on several occasions and at various levels, had been "how to safeguard the reputation of the university." I respected the decision made and did not attempt to continue the process.

Irrespective of any formal judgment, the analysis of this dissertation encapsulates the challenges and risks of research as an interdisciplinary endeavor. The matter raised questions about the assessment of research originality without proper specialists, about the appropriate way to identify and praise "exceptional work," about the functioning of a doctoral committee, about the definition of plagiarism, about assertions in connection with courseware, and about reporting and handling alleged academic misconduct. In short, I felt the matter provided a case study from which the profession could learn.

My analysis of this dissertation is basically an extensive critical review. Such reviews are de rigueur and indispensable in the academic tradition. Normally, one would identify the author. I considered that option, along with inviting him to respond. But since the dissertation is not available through any traditional channel, is not being publicized in any way, and cannot be borrowed from the university library without consent (a standard procedure for all theses and dissertations), there is little chance that it will ever be read widely. Furthermore, it is obviously in the interests of X2 and his dissertation committee to keep the dissertation away from critical eyes. A colleague of mine who tried to borrow it from the library was refused permission. Still, a copy of the dissertation can be consulted in that university's library and can, within the customary scholarly conventions, be quoted.

I have also included in my analysis (and, later, in the chapter on assessment) the essence of the responses to my report by X2 and by the dissertation advisor. I do so not only to be fair to them, but also to show how divergent interpretations can become in a defense. I would like to stress again that X2 was exonerated from the charges implied in my report. To the assessors of that university the techniques used by X2 for his dissertation are considered acceptable academic conduct.

Readers who find the following description and detailed analysis of examples tedious may proceed directly to section 3.4. For others, however, perhaps because of their involvement in assessing research conduct, these details will constitute important data for proper evaluation and are necessary for a full understanding of the problems underlying alleged academic misconduct, in particular plagiarism. The detailed analysis shows how much effort it takes to provide a fair and serious appraisal of a case. The matter also serves as concrete background for several related issues that will be discussed.

Brief description of the dissertation

The dissertation is 157 pages long, followed by a bibliography of 22 pages. It is written in British English. After a five-page introductory chapter (chapter 1), the dissertation consists of two main parts. The first part is the most elaborate (88 pages) and has three chapters:

• Chapter 2 presents concepts and aspects of adaptive hypermedia systems (AHS). Its information is completely available in other sources. I will analyze the contents of chapter 2 in sections 3.3.3 to 3.3.9.

• Chapter 3 introduces what its author calls a "new" idea for more effective learning in a hypertext environment: visual links on the screen are adapted according to what the learner knows; links for which the learner is not yet ready are hidden, disabled, or removed. X2 explains this "proficiency-adapted model" in a few sentences without referring to related studies or programs that have used similar approaches for many years, and without elaborating on the educational implications. The chapter itself is filled with already-known information about mental processing in hypertext, all taken from other sources. I will also analyze this chapter in sections 3.3.3 to 3.3.9.

· Chapter 4 describes an already-existing application of such a "proficiency-based" learning model in an Internet course on hypertext. X2 draws some of his description from material published previously by the dissertation's coadvisor, who also created the course. I will analyze this personal and scholarly connection in section 3.4.

The second part of the dissertation is thirty-nine pages long and provides some discussion of implications for language learning on the Web. It contains two chapters:

· Chapter 5 gives in seventeen pages a sketch of language-learning methods and forms of computer-assisted language learning. All of this information is taken directly from a few sources published in the 1980s. I discuss this chapter from time to time in sections 3.3.3 to 3.3.9).

· Chapter 6 presents in twenty-one pages the core of the dissertation—a description of designing a language-learning site on the Web using this learner-adapted method. I will analyze this part in section 3.7.

An appendix of seven pages concludes the dissertation. My discussion of the appendix appears in section 3.6.2.

From detection to analysis

Leafing through X2's dissertation would give the casual reader a positive impression. Here is a carefully structured text, with numbered chapters and sections, a neat layout, tables and figures, and much descriptive material, with many references to sources and a bibliography of 225 items. Such a reader would naturally conclude that the author has read large amounts of specialized literature, done original research, and produced a fine end product.

However, close reading produced other impressions:

· The *peripheral* and *preparatory* material from the research field on hypertext and human-computer interaction is quite rich and varied compared to the vagueness and sterility of the discussion of the dissertation's *core* subject, namely, implications for language learning.

· X2 often refers to other sections of the dissertation that purportedly describe his own work in more detail. Checking these cross-references quickly showed that these places did not, in fact, provide the descriptions that he said they would.

• The relative paucity of actual quotations (i.e., sentences between quotation marks), even when the text sounded as if taken from quality sources, is noteworthy.

These clues, which emerged from a close but quick reading, raised the suspicion in my mind that X2 might have plagiarized material as a cover for his own deficient research. To carry out a serious program of detection (see section 2.3), I assembled from Internet sources a corpus of material written in English that I thought might have been the basis for the alleged plagiarism. I then applied search routines with parts of sentences X2 had written. The detection program grew in tree-branched linkages. A dozen authors had been extensively used, without, in my opinion, proper citation. I compared the material and identified various patterns of reuse. I counted the average number of words tied to one reference, calculated the average number of subreferences taken from a source, and identified the percentage of cited material versus the author's alleged own material.

Due to the space limitations of this book, the following sections summarize only some of the findings. I recognize that I am quoting from X2's dissertation without identifying him. But these quotations are obviously taken in turn from others, whom I do identify. Moreover, in the chapter on assessment (see section 4.3.10), I will provide reactions from some of the main authors X2 used. They confirm their intellectual property and assert their view that X2's claims to having done original work are unacceptable.

When quoting from X2, I have preserved the style he uses as well as the British spelling. Elements between parentheses and numbers between square brackets are part of X2's text. However, except for the sources from whom X2 took material, I did not include in my bibliography the internal references included in his text or his sources.

3.3.2   Blurring the boundaries of citations

For bibliographical references, X2 uses a citation form that identifies sources by a number between square brackets—for example (boldface added):

X2, 24
Sometimes such a set of goals can even be very small [**111**], [**125**]. In this case the current user goal is included into a user model. In more advanced representations, the current user goal may be included in a hierarchy of goals [**210**] or in a set of "goal-value" pairs, where the "value" identifies the probability that the given goal is the actual goal of the present user [**153**].

The numbers refer to the alphabetized list of bibliographical entries at the end of the dissertation. Such a citation form is standard in a number of disciplines, including computer science.

In the hands of a careful, honest author, this system is certainly admissible. Its advantage is to present a text less cluttered than the usual author-date citation style used in many of the social sciences. Of course, an honest author will make sure that the material pertaining to the reference is well identified by adding quotation marks or by marking the boundaries of the citation with elements from indirect speech (for the difference between quotation and citation, see section 4.3.2). From time to time X2 quotes or cites with sufficient clarity, but such instances are rare. For example (boldface added):

Example of quotations (X2, 8)	In order to show how difficult it may be to agree on a univocal definition of hypertext, here is a list of informative quotations given by prominent researchers in the field: • *"A network representation of information is one of the defining characteristics of hypermedia."* [5] • *"The essential feature of hypertext systems is machine-supported links."* [55]
Example of distinct citation (X2, 48)	**Bly and Rosenberg [11], for example, have shown** the impact of different window layouts on users. **They have proven that** there is an intrinsic difference between tiled windows and overlapping windows and that the former ones are easier in use and can bring to higher accuracy of performance.

However, X2's more usual method—which is to omit quotations or distinct citations—results in false impressions in at least two ways:

• The lowered visibility of the names of the source authors gives a false impression that the work is X2's own.

• The failure to specify the boundaries of the citation means that an unlimited amount of material may have been borrowed.

The consequences of this method will become apparent from the analysis in subsequent sections (see sections 3.3.4 to 3.3.9). Moreover, even in the examples of quotation and distinct citation given above, those very quotations and citations were taken directly from elsewhere, because X2 copies series of references from a certain source without clear attribution (see section 3.3.7).

3.3.3 The linguistic manipulation of source material

A common way to reuse material without verbatim copying is to alter the language of the sources. In the following overview of linguistic manipulation techniques, I compare examples from X2's dissertation with source material. (See also further comparisons in sections 3.3.4 to 3.3.6, where the broader context of the use of these techniques will become apparent.) Again, at this stage I am not alleging plagiarism; I am analyzing the text. It is true that, viewed separately, these examples can be perceived as single occurrences of limited importance. It is their *sequential quantity* in long unattributed passages that makes them questionable. The total pattern is more important than individual items.

From this point, I juxtapose X2's text with his sources in columns, arranged in various rows for easier comparison. When X2 uses a reference figure between brackets, I add the equal sign and the name of the author to show its correspondence with an identical reference also named in the source.

Replacing words with synonyms

The technique of replacing words with synonyms or equivalent expressions is an obvious way to alter sentences. It is a technique that X2 uses extremely frequently. I will limit myself here to a few sample sentences from one source. (I identify synonyms by the use of boldface.) Other examples in later sections, dealing with different problems, will continue to illustrate the phenomenon.

Thüring, Haake, and Hannemann 1995:I	X2, 46, 48
Empirical studies have **shown** that a **reader's ability** to understand and remember a **text** depends on its degree of coherence.	**Empirically**, it has been **proven** that the **user's capacity** to understand and to remember a **document** depends on the document's degree of coherence.
Even for smaller **hyperdocuments** this can **result in** a considerable memory load **if** no external **orientation cues** are given. In order to provide cues that appropriately **capture** the net-like structure of most hyperdocuments, authors may employ graphical presentation formats that **give** a visual **impression** of the "information space."	Even in small **documents** all this can **give rise to** a considerable memory load **insofar as** no external **help** is provided in the form of navigational cues. And such cues have to allow users to **grasp** the hyperdocument net-like structure by **providing** a visual **snapshot** of its information space.
One interpretation of this result is that memory for content and memory for spatial information **are different aspects of the same** mental representation, i.e., the **reader's** mental model.	**It seems indeed** that memory for content and memory for spatial information **belong to the same** mental representation, i.e., the **user's** mental model.

Syntactic permutations

Syntactic permutations produce sentences with more or less significant changes in word order. Such alterations, especially if combined with a few synonym replacements, diminish the length of identical strings, thus making reuse of material more difficult to detect (see section 2.3). Within the permutations, it is possible to discern various patterns. Each of the following examples is part of a much longer sequence of sentences used from the indicated source. I will move from simple to more complex ones, but the list is far from exhaustive.

	Brusilovsky 1996:I	X2, 25
Coordinate permutation	For example, MetaDoc uses two **dimensions** of classification **and two sets of stereotypes** (novice—beginner—intermediate—expert one).	MetaDoc [15], for instance, uses more **sets of stereotypes** (novice; beginner; intermediate; expert) **and** two classification **dimensions**.

	Brusilovsky 1996:I	X2, 25
Pronoun/ noun permutation	**This** can be just a binary value (known—not known), a qualitative measure (good— average—poor), or a quantitative measure, such as a probability that the user knows the concept.	**Such an estimation** may be either a binary value, i.e., known/not-known, a qualitative measure, i.e., good— average—poor, or a quantitative measure, i.e., a probability of the user knowing that concept.

	Kendall 1996:I	X2, 37
Verb/noun permutation	A highly nonlinear **presentation** of these fragments of thought is meant to parallel the random-access nature of human memory.	**They are presented** in a highly non-linear way in order to simulate the characteristic random access of human memory.

	Chapelle 1989:60	X2, 118
Participial phrase/independent clause permutation	**Focusing on** the syntax of language, intelligent grammar checkers (IGCs) perform an analysis of students' written work to point out errors.	Intelligent grammar checkers (IGC): **they focus** on the syntax of the language in order to analyse students' written production, to detect grammatical mistakes.

	Bloomfield 1994:I	X2, 9
Subordinate clause/gerund phrase permutation	**As the node size decreases,** connectivity increases, and with this, Begoray suggests, user disorientation increases.	**By decreasing node size,** connectivity increases and, consequently, user's disorientation with it.

	Wyatt 1987:88	X2, 114
Subject/ complement permutation with linking verbs	Tutorial, drill and practice, holistic practice, and many types of game software **are examples** of instructional programs.	**Examples** of instructional CALL programs **are** tutorials, drill and practice, holistic practice, and several kinds of game software.

	Brusilovsky 1996:I	X2, 25
Relative clause/parti- cipial phrase per- mutation	For each domain model con- cept, an individual overlay model stores some value **which is an estimation** of the user knowledge level of this concept.	So, for each knowledge ele- ment, the overlay model stores a value **corresponding to the estimation** of the user's knowledge relative to that particular concept.

	Thüring, Haake, and Hannemann 1995:I	X2, 48
Active/pas- sive permu- tation	A number of **empirical stud- ies demonstrate the effects** of such features on various kinds of user performance.	**The effects** of such features on users' performance **have been revealed by** several em- pirical studies.

	Wyatt 1987:88	X2, 114
Active/pas- sive permu- tation with subject ex- clusion	[...] the computer **presents language learning materials** in a highly structured, pre- determined manner.	[...] **the language learning material is presented** in a highly structured and pre- determined way.

	Eklund 1996:I	X2, 50
Independent/subordinate clauses permutation	**The nodes are** declarative elements of knowledge **while the links represent** procedural and structural understanding.	**Whereas the nodes** are declarative elements of knowledge [...], **links represent** their procedural and structural understanding.

	Dieberger and Bolter 1995:I	X2, 53
Compound sentence/adverb clause permutation	Navigation in such systems becomes a matter of moving through the imagined environments **and spatial proximity indicates** context and geographic relatedness.	And in spatial hypertexts navigation actually becomes a mere matter of moving through several environments **where spatial proximity indicates** both the context and the relatedness between nodes.

	Dieberger and Bolter 1995:I	X2, 53
Chiasmic permutation	A **geographical** metaphor **needs** to be stable; an **abstract** map, in contrast, can be changed according to the user's needs.	[...] since an **abstract** map **need not** be graphically stable as a **geographical** metaphor does, the spatial hypertext can be shaped according to users' needs.

	Brusilovsky 1996:I	X2, 25
Prepositional structure/adverb clause permutation	[...] the majority of AH systems use a rather advanced domain model **with several types of concepts which represent different** kinds of knowledge elements or objects **and several kinds of links which represent different** kinds of relationships between concepts.	[...] the primitive concepts defining that particular domain, **where several kinds of concepts identify different** types of knowledge elements **and several kinds of links identify the different** possible relationships between them.

More complex treatment of a source, such as compound sentence permutation where more than two sentences are combined, split, or reordered, even over various paragraphs, goes beyond the syntactic level and will be discussed below.

Shortening sentences

The simple technique of shortening sentences allows a person to borrow the essence of the source material.

Brusilovsky 1996:I	X2, 25
Sometimes a simpler stereotype user model is used to represent the user's knowledge (Beaumont, 1994; Boyle & Encarnacion, 1994; Hohl, Böcker & Gunzenhäuser, 1996).	Alternatively, a simpler stereotype classification can be introduced [4 = Beaumont], [15 = Boyle & Encarnacion].
For example, MetaDoc uses two dimensions of classification and two sets of stereotypes (novice—beginner—intermediate—expert: one) to represent user's knowledge of general computer concepts, another to represent user's knowledge of UNIX (which is the domain of the system). A particular user is usually modelled by assigning this user to one of stereotypes for each dimension of classification (for intermediate for general computer concepts, novice for UNIX).	MetaDoc [15], for instance, uses more sets of stereotypes (novice; beginner; intermediate; expert) and two classification dimensions, i.e., the user's knowledge of general computer science concepts and the user's knowledge of UNIX. Any user is modelled by assigning one stereotype for each classification dimension (e.g., novice for UNIX concepts).
A stereotype user model can also be represented as a set of pairs or "stereotype-value", where the value can be not only "true" or "false" (what means that the user belongs or does not belong to the stereotype) but also some probabilistic value (what represents the probability that the user belongs to the stereotype).	A more sophisticated version of the stereotype model is obtained by associating probalistic values to every stereotype.

Combining sentences

Independent clauses can easily be combined into compound clauses or into an independent clause with an adverbial clause.

Bloomfield 1994:I	X2, 8–9
The first four definitions are limited in that they all define hypertext in terms of its components without addressing what concept might underlie hypertext. The fifth defines it in terms of what it is possible to do in a hypertext [...].	We can see that, whereas the first four definitions only address hypertext in terms of its components, from a mere technological point of view, the fifth one explicitly focuses on the user and on what she may possibly do in a hypertext environment.

Splitting sentences

Conversely, a sentence composed of an independent and an adverbial clause can easily be split into two independent sentences.

Thüring, Haake, and Hannemann 1995:I	X2, 46
If we want to increase the readability of a hyperdocument we must assist readers in the construction of their mental models by strengthening factors that support this process and by weakening those that impede it.	Therefore, the readability of a hyperdocument can be enhanced by assisting users when constructing their mental models. This ultimately means that all factors fostering this process have to be increased, whereas those biasing it minimised.

Depersonalizing the original

Original authors will use a personal identifier *(I, we, my, our)* or a term such as *paper* or *article* to refer to one of their own specific publications. When using such sentences, X2 replaces these identifiers or terms by words that depersonalize the original or adapt it to the needs of the dissertation.

Kendall 1996:1	X2, 37
I wanted to give the reader maximum flexibility in changing the ordering of material	[...] **they** [floating links] **allow** the reader maximum flexibility in changing the sequence of the material
I wanted to exert a high degree of control over the reader's progress	**they still allow** the author a high degree of control over the reader's progress

De Bra 1996:1	X2, 70
In order to give the students some hands-on experience with hypertext while studying this course **we decided** to offer the course text in hypertext form, using World Wide Web technology. **We also decided** to offer the text as a real hyperdocument, not having a linear or strictly hierarchical structure.	In order to give students some practical experience with hypertext while studying this course, **it was decided** to offer the course text in hypertext form, using World Wide Web technology. **It was as well decided** to offer the text as real hyperdocument, without having a linear or strictly hierarchical structure.
In this paper we focus on the use of World Wide Web technology to make such a course possible, and on **the tools we developed** and/or used to help both the teacher and the student throughout the course.	**In this chapter** we focus on the use of World Wide Web technology to make one such course possible and on **the functionalities offered** by the courseware in the light of the theoretical proficiency-adapted framework discussed in Chapter 3.

Changing the order of sentences and paragraphs

The reuse of material can be identified easily if longer passages have been used from a source, in a similar sequence of sentences. Changing the order of sentences and even of paragraphs will impede recognition. Combined with all the preceding techniques, the result will look quite different and will be more difficult to detect. To make the similarities more obvious in the following complex example, I have boldfaced words that indicate the beginning of some of the similar sequences and added arrows.

Brusilovsky 1996:I	X2, 29
Annotation can be naturally used with all four possible forms of links. This technique **supports** stable order of links and avoids problems with incorrect mental maps. Annotation is **generally** a more powerful technology than hiding: **hiding** can distinguish only two states for the nodes—relevant and non relevant—while annotation, as mentioned above, up to six states, in particular, several levels of relevancy as implemented in Hypadapter (**Hohl**, Böcker & Gunzenhäuser, 1996). Annotations do not restrict cognitive overload as much as hiding does, but the **hiding** technology can be quite well simulated by the annotation technology using a kind of "dimming" instead of hiding for "not relevant" links. **Dimming** can decrease cognitive overload in some extent (the user can learn to ignore dimmed links), but **dimmed** links are still visible (and traversable, if required) which protects the user from forming wrong mental maps.	In itself annotation is therefore not very dissimilar from hiding, although it is **generally** a more powerful technology than this latter one, since annotation **supports** a stable ordering of links and avoids incorrect mental maps formation [...], though annotation can not reduce cognitive overload as much as hiding [62]. **Hiding** can nevertheless be simulated rather well by adaptive annotation by means of "dimming" (instead of just hiding) non-relevant links. To a certain extent, i.e., as long as the user can learn to ignore dimmed links, **dimming** can indeed limit cognitive overload, but can not eliminate it completely, since **dimmed** links are still visible, therefore also recognisable as such (links) and traversable. Still, the fact that they are visible prevents users from forming wrong mental maps [191]. Finally, while **hiding** can only distinguish between just two node states, i.e., relevant or non-relevant nodes, annotation can recognise more levels in each node's relative relevance (see Section 2.3.4) [108 = **Hohl**, Böcker & Gunzenhäuser, 1996].

The visual comparison of such passages is arduous, even with the help of the juxtaposed columns and arrows. However, when one applies the detection device Cerberus (see Appendix), the number of identical or highly similar parts becomes obvious. In the following comparison for the same passage, I have included *all* elements from the above left and right columns. The elements from the right column (X2's text) remain in original order, but I have repositioned those from the left column so that they are next to the elements X2 used. This rearrangement makes it clear that the match is almost perfect.

Brusilovsky 1996:I	X2, 29
	In itself annotation is therefore not very dissimilar from hiding,
Annotation is generally a more powerful technology than hiding:	although it is generally a more powerful technology than this latter one,
This technique supports stable order of links	since annotation supports a stable ordering of links
and avoids problems with incorrect mental maps.	and avoids incorrect mental maps formation [...],
Annotations do not restrict cognitive overload as much as hiding does,	though annotation can not reduce cognitive overload as much as hiding [62].
but the hiding technology can be quite well simulated	Hiding can nevertheless be simulated rather well
by the annotation technology using a kind of "dimming" instead of hiding for "not relevant" links.	by adaptive annotation by means of "dimming" (instead of just hiding) non-relevant links.
in some extent	To a certain extent,
(the user can learn to ignore dimmed links),	i.e., as long as the user can learn to ignore dimmed links,
Dimming can decrease cognitive overload	dimming can indeed limit cognitive overload,
but dimmed links are still visible	but can not eliminate it completely, since dimmed links are still visible,
(and traversable, if required)	therefore also recognisable as such (links) and traversable.
which protects the user from forming wrong mental maps.	Still, the fact that they are visible prevents users from forming wrong mental maps [191].
hiding can distinguish only two states for the nodes	Finally, while hiding can only distinguish between just two node states,

—relevant and non relevant—	i.e., relevant or non-relevant nodes,
while annotation, as mentioned above, up to six states, in particular, several levels of relevancy as implemented in Hypadapter (Hohl, Böcker & Gunzenhäuser, 1996).	annotation can recognise more levels in each node's relative relevance (see Section 2.3.4) [108 = Hohl, Böcker & Gunzenhäuser, 1996].
Annotation can be naturally used with all four possible forms of links.	

The element [...] reads: "(for an analysis of the cognitive impact of hiding on users see Appendix A)." The value of this insertion is studied in section 3.6.2 in the part on the appendix of the dissertation.

3.3.4   Extended use without acknowledgement

Analysts pinpoint extended use without acknowledgement as the most blatant form of plagiarism. Thorough investigation requires, by the very nature of the material, lengthy examples; but because of space limitations, I will shorten them and indicate continuations of the comparison with *etc.*

For example, in subsection 2.4.2. of the dissertation, X2 describes an alternative hypertext approach that provides information adapted to users so that they can experience literature in a different way. The introductory sentence to the subsection includes a reference to the hypertext poem used as example but provides no reference to the source on which X2 based his description of the procedure. It is a paper by Robert Kendall available on the Internet (Kendall 1996).

Kendall 1996:I	X2, 37
A Life is a lyric poem in which the speaker reflects on his past. It opens with an essentially linear prologue, followed by a hypertext in which each node constitutes a memory or rumination [...].	'*A Life Set for Two*' is a lyric poem where the author reflects on his past. It starts with a linear prologue, followed by a series of nodes representing the author's memories.

A highly nonlinear presentation of these fragments of thought is meant to parallel the random-access nature of human memory. The work is organized by a system of *floating links* [...].	They are presented in a highly non-linear way in order to simulate the characteristic random access of human memory. Such a randomised navigation is realised by means of floating links.
Floating links. Dynamic links, or what [89 = DeRose] calls "intensional links," [...] As with links in static hypertext, the end point of a floating link is fixed, always leading to one predetermined node.	Floating links, or "intensional", i.e., implicit links [70 = DeRose] (see Chapter 1), are given a fixed end point, i.e., they lead to one pre-determined node, just like any other static links.
The source points, however, are not anchored to specific nodes. [...] The availability of a particular link at any given time depends less on the particular node currently on screen than on other parameters in the reading environment.	But, as they are stored separately from nodes, their source points are not anchored to any specific node. Therefore, the availability of a particular link does not depend much on the node currently accessed, rather on some other criteria in the reading environment.
etc.	etc.

In his reaction to my report, X2 explained for the example above that a reference to Kendall's paper appears two pages earlier in his dissertation, on page 35, and that he chose not to repeat that reference on page 37, since he had already referred on page 37 to the hypertext poem as such. He does not comment on the misleading impression—that he himself is the author of the comments—which Kendall confirmed to me as unacceptable scholarly practice.

The following example shows that X2 took this material, including citations, from an unpublished dissertation available on the Internet, to fill section 1.2 of the dissertation.

Bloomfield 1994:I	X2, 8–9
A few definitions from researchers in the field will give some different visions of what hypertext is before looking at it in more detail: • A network representation of information is one of the defining characteristics of hypermedia (Begoray, 1990). • The essential feature of hypertext systems is machine-supported links (Conklin, 1987).	In order to show how difficult it may be to agree on a univocal definition of hypertext, here is a list of informative quotations given by prominent researchers in the field: • "A network representation of information is one of the defining characteristics of hypermedia." [5 = Begoray] • "The essential feature of hypertext systems is machine-supported links." [55 = Conklin]
	[The third definition is different.]
• [They are] methods of online information management and/or presentation in which textual documents are parsed into nodes. Usually each node contains a single concept, data element, idea or chunk of information. The nodes are connected to one another using links (Mohageg, 1992). • True hypertext should also make users feel that they can move freely through the information according to their own needs (Nielsen, 1989).	• "[They are] methods of online information management and/or presentation in which textual documents are parsed into nodes. Usually each node contains a single concept, data element, idea or chunk of information. The nodes are connected to one another using links" [156 = Mohageg]. • "True hypertext should also make users feel that they can move freely through the information according to their own needs." [161 = Nielsen].
	[A sixth definition is also different but is taken from another source used.]
The first four definitions are limited in that they all define hypertext in terms of its components without addressing what concept might underlie hypertext. The fifth defines it in terms of what it is possible to do in a hypertext, but there are systems (for example, those that use "guided tours", such as NoteCards (**Trigg**, 1988) which explicitly prevent the user from navigating in this undirected way through hypertext systems.	We can see that, whereas the first four definitions only address hypertext in terms of its components, from a mere technological point of view, the fifth one explicitly focuses on the user and on what she may possibly do in a hypertext environment, although systems based on the notion of 'guided tours', such as the more traditional NoteCards [202 = **Trigg**], for example, prevent users from navigating in such a loose way.

In his response to this comparison, X2 stressed that the whole series of definitions is not identical because definitions 4 and 6 are different. Therefore, he argued, he used several sources. In the case of the last paragraph, which includes Bloomfield's identical subreference to Trigg and which clearly shows the unattributed source from which X2 took the preceding material, X2 argues that such use is not plagiarism because he does not share Bloomfield's ideas. The rest of his section, he pointed out in his answer, "defends a different concept of hypertext." In other words, X2 argues that it is permissible to use unattributed material as long as one does not agree with the material copied. Moreover, further analysis of the dissertation revealed that X2 took the sixth definition, by Holland, from Burbules and Callister (1996), again without correct attribution, after including still more unattributed material from Bloomfield.

All this shows that extended use without clear acknowledgment can become a complex matter of intertwined sentences and paragraphs from various sources, opening the way for much controversy.

3.3.5   Extended preuse or postuse with a citation

A frequent form of plagiarism is referring correctly to a publication but using its material extensively, before and/or after the citation, without indicating the boundaries of the use. I call this phenomenon *extended preuse* (extensive material already used before the reference appears) and *extended postuse* (extensive material used after the reference appears). In X2's dissertation, many pages seem to fall under one or both of these two categories. Again, because of the nature of this phenomenon, complete examples would require many pages. I therefore indicate by *etc.* that the borrowed material continues. I also mention the total number of words in the comparison passage.

Example of preuse

Reference [73], identifying Dieberger and Bolter, comes at the end of a passage of ninety-five words using this publication as a direct source. X2 provides no indication of where the citation begins.

Dieberger and Bolter 1995:I	X2, 53
Navigation in such systems becomes a matter of moving through the imagined environments and spatial proximity indicates context and geographic relatedness.	And in spatial hypertexts navigation actually becomes a mere matter of moving through several environments where spatial proximity indicates both the context and the relatedness between nodes.
A geographical metaphor needs to be stable; an abstract map, in contrast, can be changed according to the user's needs.	In addition, since an abstract map need not be graphically stable as a geographical metaphor does, the spatial hypertext can be shaped according to users' needs
The user may even use and navigate several views of the same hypertext to look at diverse relations among the same nodes.	and, eventually, users can navigate within different views of the same (spatial) hypertext whenever focusing on diverse relations of the same nodes
In one view nodes having the same author may be placed close together; in another view textually similar nodes may be close. This environment may be visualized graphically in two or even three dimensions.	(e.g., one view can focus on nodes which are textually similar, while another view on nodes with identical graphics [sic]) [73].

Examples of postuse

Section 1.3 of the dissertation includes a definition of nodes. The initial reference to [10]—that is, to Bloomfield—is meant to identify the verbatim quoting of a few words from this source. These words are put between quotation marks, reinforcing the impression of careful quotation; however, X2 has taken the rest of the passage from the same source without attribution.

Bloomfield 1994:I	X2, 9
A node is a discrete block of editable media.	Nodes are the fundamental units of a hypertext. They are "*discrete* blocks *of editable media*" [10], typically containing different grained and sized pieces of information about a well-defined topic.

Granularity: As the node size decreases, connectivity increases, and with this, Begoray suggests, user disorientation increases.	Granularity ultimately affects connectivity: by decreasing node size, connectivity increases and, consequently, user's disorientation with it (see Chapter 3).
A hypertext will exist at some point on a fine-grained/coarse-grained dimension, and will generally lie between having a large number of small nodes or a small number of large nodes (Begoray, 1990).	Depending on its fine-grained/coarse-grained dimension, the resulting hypertext system will indeed range from a large number of small nodes to a small number of large nodes.
Typed nodes can ease the modularisation process by taking advantage of structure that may be in what is to be represented.	Typed nodes can therefore ease the modularisation process by taking advantage of the structure that may be in what is to be represented.

In the following example, X2's first sentence includes a reference to [218]—that is, a publication by Wyatt. The next few paragraphs could possibly be understood as an extension of the announcement made in that first sentence. But the commentaries that follow continue to use material from Wyatt, without attribution, for a total of 420 words borrowed from Wyatt. X2's text includes a reference to a table, "adapted from" Wyatt's publication (see also section 3.3.9). He actually copied it verbatim. If that table were included in the example below, the total number of words X2 has lifted from Wyatt here would amount to 634.

Wyatt 1987:88–90	X2, 114–115
More insight into CALL approaches can be provided by examining the interactional relationship between student and computer. On this basis, three fundamental categories of language-learning programs can be distinguished: instructional, collaborative, and facilitative (Wyatt, 16). [Wyatt is referring here to his own earlier work, published in 1984.]	Examining the interactional relationship between the user and the computer, three fundamental approaches to CALL may be distinguished: instructional, collaborative, and facilitative [218 = Wyatt].

A. INSTRUCTIONAL Students are responders, not initiators, despite their high level of activity. [...] Predetermined learning path(s). The computer instructs the student; students learn *from* the computer.	*INSTRUCTIONAL* Students are responders, not initiators, despite their high level of activity. Predetermined learning path(s). The computer instructs the student; students learn from the computer.
B. COLLABORATIVE Students are initiators, take more responsibility for their learning [...]. No predetermined learning paths. Elements of discovery learning; students learn *with* the computer.	*COLLABORATIVE* Students are initiators, take more responsibility for their learning. No predetermined learning paths. Elements of discovery learning: students learn with the computer.
etc.	etc.

Examples of preuse and postuse

On pages 45 through 48 of his dissertation, X2 writes a subsection of 1,060 words, 860 directly based on a publication by Thüring, Haake, and Hannemann and also utilizing part of that article's structure. The passage includes five references to [200]—that is, the publication by Thüring, Haake, and Hannemann. Thus, X2 averages one reference per 172 words, without delineation of the boundaries.

X2 also includes thirteen references to other authors, taken from the same source, as if he had discovered and studied these himself (see section 3.3.7).

Thüring, Haake, and Hannemann 1995:I	X2, 45–48
In cognitive science, comprehension is often characterized as the construction of a mental model that represents the objects and semantic relations described in a text [24 = Van Dyck & Kintsch].	In the cognitive science tradition, comprehension indicates the user's ability to build up a mental model representing the objects and the semantic relations implicit in the document the user is analysing [206 = Van Dyck & Kintsch].

If we want to increase the readability of a hyperdocument we must assist readers in the construction of their mental models by strengthening factors that support this process and by weakening those that impede it.	Therefore, the readability of a hyperdocument can be enhanced by assisting users when constructing their mental models. This ultimately means that all factors fostering this process have to be increased, whereas those biasing it minimised.
Two factors in particular are crucial in this respect: *coherence* as positive influence [23 = Thüring, Haake & Hannemann] and *cognitive overhead* [3 = Conklin] as negative influence on comprehension.	Two factors in particular seem to affect this construction process: coherence [199 = Thüring, Haake & Hannemann] and cognitive overhead [55 = Conklin].
Coherence Empirical studies have shown that a reader's ability to understand and remember a text depends on its degree of coherence [...]. A document is coherent if a reader can construct a mental model from it that corresponds to facts and relations in a possible world [12 = Johnson-Laird]	**3.4.1 Coherence** Empirically, it has been proven that the user's capacity to understand and to remember a document depends on the document's degree of coherence, which is related to the user's ability to construct a mental model corresponding to facts and relations in the subject domain of the document [119 = Johnson-Laird].
Empirical studies of linear text indicate that establishing coherence at a local and global level is facilitated when a document is set out in a well-defined structure and provides rhetorical cues reflecting its structural properties [24 = Van Dyck & Kintsch].	In a linear (book-modelled) document, both local and global coherence can be achieved if the document is structured properly and provides rhetorical cues which mirror one such structure [206 = Van Dyck & Kintsch].
Applying this result to hyperdocuments implies that authors should provide cues for both types of coherence at two levels, i.e., at the node level (within nodes) and the net level (between nodes). [...] In order to *increase local coherence* at net level, authors should limit "the fragmentation characteristic of hypertext" [16, p. 22 = Marshall & Irish]	In a hyperdocument it is not as simple. If we take the local coherence to be at the node level, i.e., within the hyperdocument pages, and the global coherence as the one between nodes, or at the network level, i.e., between hyperdocument pages, then system designers have to *"limit the fragmentation characteristic of hypertext"* [147 = Marshall & Irish].
etc.	etc.

3.3.6 Extended use, but only referring to a table

X2's reference [54], identifying C. Chapelle, comes after a passage of 227 words that uses this publication as a direct source, including Chapelle's references to other authors. Reference [54], however, refers only to a table "adapted from" this source. Moreover, the table itself is copied verbatim, not "adapted." It is clear that X2 has lifted not only the table but the entire passage.

Chapelle 1989:60	X2, 117–118
The resulting intelligent language courseware can be divided into three kinds of systems....	The main kinds of intelligent CALL systems are:
Intelligent tutoring systems (ITSs) attempt to "combine the problem-solving experience and motivation of 'discovery' learning (typified by microworlds and intelligent grammar checkers) with the effective guidance of tutorial interactions" (Sleeman and Brown, 1982, p. 1).	Intelligent tutoring systems (ITS): they attempt to combine the problem solving approach and motivation of discovery learning (which is instead typified by both microworlds and intelligent grammar checkers—see further) with the effective guidance of tutorial interactions [187 = Sleeman and Brown].
etc.	etc.
[Identical table in Chapelle 1989:59; see also 3.3.9.]	The following table (adapted from [54]) gives an overview of how the above mentioned systems might improve language instruction.

3.3.7 Including references of the original's sources

A striking feature of X2's use of a source is his frequent inclusion of the same references, citations, and quotations as in the source. I identify these embedded sources and materials as *subreferences*. They prove beyond doubt the origin of the source since the quantity and the same sequence of the references, tied to similar sentences, cannot be explained as coincidental. I have already given examples of this phenomenon in previous sections. I add one more here to show how these subreferences can also pertain to examples of systems and programs.

Brusilovsky 1996:I	X2, 24
As a rule, each system supports a set of possible user goals or tasks which it can recognize (**HyPLAN, ORI-MUHS, PUSH, HYPERCASE, Hyne-cosum, HYPERFLEX**).	Normally, every system recognises a set of possible goals which it can support (as, e.g., in **HyPLAN, PUSH, HYPERCASE, Hynecosum**).
In some cases, the set of goals is very small and the goals are not related to each other (**Höök et al.**, 1996; **Kaplan, Fenwick & Chen**, 1993). To model the current user goal, the system includes one of these goals into the user model. [...]	Sometimes such a set of goals can even be very small [111 = **Höök et al.**, 1996], [125 = **Kaplan, Fenwick & Chen**, 1993]. In this case the current user goal is included into a user model.
The most advanced representation of possible user goals is a hierarchy (a tree) of tasks (**Vassileva**, 1996). The most advanced representation of user current goals is a set of pairs "goal-value" where the value is usually the probability that the corresponding goal is the current goal of the user (Encarnacio, 1995; Grunst, 1993; **Micarelli & Sciarrone**, 1996).	In more advanced representations, the current user goal may be included in a hierarchy of goals [210 = **Vassileva**] or in a set of "goal-value" pairs, where the "value" identifies the probability that the given goal is the actual goal of the present user [153 = **Micarelli & Sciarrone**].
User's knowledge of the subject is most often represented by an overlay model (**Hypadapter, EPIAIM, KN-AHS, ITEM/PG, ISIS-Tutor, ELM-ART, SHIVA, HyperTutor**) [...].	The most common way to represent the user's knowledge is by an overlay model (as, e.g., in **Hyadapter** [sic], **KN-AHS, ITEM/PG, ISIS-Tutor, ELM-ART, SHIVA, HyperTutor**).
Sometimes a simpler stereotype user model is used to represent the user's knowledge (**Beaumont**, 1994; **Boyle & Encarnacion**, 1994; Hohl, Böcker & Gunzenhäuser, 1996).	Alternatively, a simpler stereotype classification can be introduced [4 = **Beaumont**], [15 = **Boyle & Encarnacion**].
etc.	etc.

According to my calculations, at the present stage of the analysis, X2 took from twelve authors a total of sixty-two subreferences pertaining to publications and to examples of systems and programs as if he had discovered and studied those himself.

3.3.8 Use of loose elements without attribution

This phenomenon is more difficult to detect because it involves only single sentences, a few sentences, or a small paragraph, appearing between others that may be original or taken from completely different sources. I give examples of two such occurrences from X2's dissertation.

Kendall 1996:I	X2, 64
This can make the hypertext reading experience smoother and more satisfying in many ways—for example, by better enabling the text to avoid presenting the reader with illogical sequences or unwanted recurrences of nodes.	Generally speaking, the hypertext reading experience is made smoother and more satisfying, for instance by avoiding to present the user with illogical sequences or unwanted recurrences of nodes.

The following example shows that X2 took a few sentences from Wilkinson, Crerar, and Falchikov 1997 without any reference to that source. Also note that, within the text, the reference to Spiro and Jehng (boldface) becomes part of the material taken from Wilkinson, Crerar, and Falchikov:

Wilkinson, Crerar, and Falchikov 1997:I	X2, 65
[Title of the article] "Book versus hypertext: exploring the association between usability and cognitive style"	[Title of the section] Book versus Hypertext: What is the relationship between Usability and Cognition?
Paper-based books as a 'technology' are very mature. [...] Nevertheless, there have been those who have pointed out that books are not perfect as tools to support all types of learning. **Spiro and Jehng** (1990, p. 163) argue,	Paper-based books are very mature as educational technology. Nonetheless, they do not seem to be perfect as tools able to support all kinds of learning. **Spiro and Jehng**, for instance, claim that,

"Linearity of media is not a problem when the subject matter being taught is well structured and fairly simple. However, as content increases in complexity and ill-structuredness, increasingly greater amounts of important information are lost with linear approaches and the unidimensionality of organization that typically accompanies them."	"Linearity of media is not a problem when the subject matter being taught is well structured and fairly simple. However, as content increases in complexity and ill-structuredness, increasingly greater amounts of important information are lost with linear approaches and the unidimensionality of organization that typically accompanies them." [192 = Spiro and Jehng]
One potential solution to the problem of linearity is to use a technology like hypertext or its media rich variant hypermedia.	One possible solution to overcome the problems associated with linearity is therefore to use a technology that allows multiplicity and contingency in reading.

X2 responded to the report identifying this instance by saying that the first lines of the above text are "a truism in the research field" and that, after the similar passages in the comparison, he develops an argument different from the one defended by Wilkinson and colleagues. In short, X2 uses the same "defense" as for his extensive use of Bloomfield (see section 3.3.4): "Because I handled the problem in more general terms, I did not see the need to refer in my text to the article by Wilkinson et al."

3.3.9   Use of tables and figures
X2's dissertation contains eight tables and four figures. All are taken directly from eight different sources, without any significant modification; however, two small figures (figures 4.1 and 4.2, p. 97) first appeared in a publication coauthored by X2 and his coadvisor. The other ten tables and figures come from other sources.

Two characteristics of this copying are disturbing:

• X2 never once includes the reference to the source together with the table or figure; rather he puts it in another location in the text, often on a different page from the table or figure itself. Readers browsing through the dissertation will normally think that the tables and figures are the genuine output of X2's own research.

• The textual reference to these tables and figures always says "adapted from"—for example,

• "There exist a number of techniques which are exploited in combination with the above mentioned methods—as depicted in Table 2.2, adapted from [19]" (X2, 31).

• "Thus, learning can be viewed as the accumulation and subsequent organisation of knowledge structures, which are represented in terms of links and nodes (see Figure 3.1, adapted from [51])" (X2, 50).

However, the verbatim copying of these ten tables and figures shows that they are not "adapted from." One could argue that in certain languages some less-educated persons may understand "adapt" as "taken from," but in X2's native language and cultural tradition the term "adapt" unmistakably points to altered or reworked material. Moreover, in his own dissertation, X2 always uses the term in that sense as a central notion ("learner-adapted," "adapted to the user," "adapt a system to user's needs"). I limit myself to two examples of this verbatim copying presented with a reference on a different page, and as "adapted from."

Table 2.1 in X2, 19	
Educational Hypermedia Systems	Anatom-Tutor, C-Book, ELM-ART, ISIS-Tutor, ITEM/PG, HyperTutor, Land Use Tutor, Manuel Excel, SHIVA, SYPROS, ELM-PE, 2L670, Hypadapter, HYPERCASE
On-line Information Systems	Hypadapter, HYPERCASE, KN-AI IS, MetaDoc, PUSH, HYPERFLEX, CID, Adaptive HyperMan
On-line Help Systems	EPIAIM, HyPLAN, Lisp-Critic, ORIMUHS, WING-MIT, SYPROS
Information Retrieval Hypermedia	CID, DHS, Adaptive HyperMan, HYPERFLEX, WebWatcher
Institutional Hypermedia	Hynecosum
Personalized Views	Basar, Information Islands
Table 2.1. AH systems classified according their application areas.	

Compare with Table I in Brusilovsky 1996:I

Educational Hypermedia Systems	Anatom-Tutor, C-Book, ⟨Clibbon⟩, ELM-ART, ISIS-Tutor, ITEM/PG, HyperTutor, Land Use Tutor, Manuel Excel, SHIVA, SYPROS, ELM-PE, 2L670, *Hypadapter, HYPERCASE*
On-line Information Systems	Hypadapter, HYPERCASE, KN-AHS, MetaDoc, PUSH, *HYPERFLEX, CID, Adaptive HyperMan*
On-line Help Systems	EPIAIM, HyPLAN, Lisp-Critic, ORIMUHS, WING-MIT, *SYPROS*
Information Retrieval Hypermedia	CID, DHS, Adaptive HyperMan, HYPERFLEX, WebWatcher
Institutional Hypermedia	Hynecosum
Personalized Views	Basar, Information Islands

Table I. Existing adaptive hypermedia systems classified according their application areas. Second entries for the systems that fit two categories are shown in italics. Bibliographic references are provided in Appendix 1.

The only differences between the two tables are the addition in X2's table of the Internet course "2L670," which X2 describes in his dissertation, the use of selective italics in Brusilovsky's original table, and X2's omission of the program "Clibbon."

A second example, also showing the extent of verbatim copying, is X2's table 5.2, lifted from Wyatt:

Wyatt 1987:87–88 Figure 1: Some Types of Programs Used in CALL		X2, 116 Table 5.2: Relational Classification of CALL Approaches.	
Program Type	**Examples of Functions and Contents**	**Program Type**	**Examples of Functions and Contents**
Tutorial	introducing new material—e.g., the Cyrillic alphabet in beginning Russian	*Tutorial*	Introducing new material—e.g., the Cyrillic alphabet in beginning Russian.

Drill and practice	allowing mastery of material already presented—e.g.,grammatical forms, culturally appropriate behavior	*Drill and practice*	Allowing mastery of material already presented—e.g.,grammatical forms, culturally appropriate behaviour.
Game	adding elements of peer competition, scoring, and timing to a wide variety of practice activities.	*Game*	Adding elements of peer competition, scoring, and timing to a wide variety of practice activities.
Holistic practice	providing higher level, contextualized practice activities—e.g., cloze passages	*Holistic practice*	Providing higher level, contextualised practice activities—e.g., cloze passages.
Modelling	demonstrating how to perform a language task—e.g., how a good reader handles difficult sections of a reading passage	*Modelling*	Demonstrating how to perform a language task—e.g., how a good reader handles difficult sections of a reading passage.
Discovery	providing situations in which linguistic generalizations can be made —e.g., inferring rules for generating comparative forms	*Discovery*	Providing situations in which linguistic generalisations can be made —e.g., inferring rules for generating comparative forms.
Simulation	allowing students to experiment with language use—e.g., levels of formality in a conversational simulator	*Simulation*	Allowing students to experiment with language use—e.g., levels of formality in a conversational simulator.
Adventure reading (interactive fiction)	offering "participatory" reading materials—e.g., student as detective explores murder location, gathers clues	*Adventure reading*	Offering "participatory" reading materials—e.g., student as detective explores murder location, gathers clues.

Annotation	providing a wide range of language "notes" (vocabulary, syntax, plot, etc.) available on demand during reading or listening activities	*Annotation*	Providing a wide range of language "notes" (vocabulary, syntax, plot, etc.) available on demand during reading or listening activities.
Idea processor	planning and editing outlines—e.g., before writing activities, after listening to lectures	*Idea processor*	Planning and editing outlines—e.g., before writing activities, after listening to lectures.
Word processor	creating and editing written assignments	*Word processor*	Creating and editing written assignments.
On-line thesaurus	expanding vocabulary, improving writing style	*On-line thesaurus*	Expanding vocabulary, improving writing style.
Spelling checker	guarding against errors during or after writing activities	*Spelling checker*	Guarding against errors during or after writing activities.
Textual analysis	revealing structural and stylistic aspects of written work—e.g., complexity and variety of sentence types, subject/verb agreement errors	*Textual analysis*	Revealing structural and stylistic aspects of written work—e.g., complexity and variety of sentence types, subject/verb agreement errors.

The only differences in X2's text are:

· Capital letters at the beginning of each example entry and a period at the end

· British spelling *(behaviour, generalisations, contextualised)*

Otherwise the two tables are identical.

3.3.10   Copying from oneself

A peculiar system to help fill pages and thus expand the text is to copy one's own paragraphs (or paragraphs already taken from another author) and repeat them elsewhere in the same work. X2 does this sometimes as part of an introduction and a conclusion, which could justify some repetition, but the extent and the perfect match of the paragraphs make the technique questionable:

X2, 4	X2, 148–149
Within such a framework language learning is viewed as a situated, mainly communicative process where learners are exposed to authentic meaningful material in a learner-driven and tailored (for what concerns her proficiency level) exploration of a teacher-controlled instruction presentation.	Within such a framework language learning is viewed as a situated, mainly communicative process where learners are exposed to authentic meaningful material in a learner-driven and tailored (for what concerns her proficiency level) exploration of a teacher-controlled instruction presentation.
Eventually, the identification of a (pedagogically) sound learning theory and the recognition of well-defined and grounded learning objectives to attain, combined with an understanding of the technology that will be used to achieve those goals, will help in exploiting that technology adequately and successfully.	Eventually, the identification of a (pedagogically) sound learning theory and the recognition of well-defined and grounded learning objectives to attain, combined with an understanding of the technology that will be used to achieve those goals, will help in exploiting that technology adequately and successfully.

In the following examples significant parts of sentences are reused, more than would be possible by chance (boldface added):

X2, 3	X2, 149
For example, does the mainly quantitative advancement fostered by the technology, i.e., **the increase in the amount of information students can access, correspond** as well to an improvement in **the quality of its understanding and of the knowledge that results from it?**	[...] the extent to which the technology has ultimately enhanced learning, i.e., they can not determine whether **the increased amount of information learners can access** by means of the present technology **correspond as well to an improvement in** its understanding and in the knowledge resulting from it.

X2, 4	X2, 99
This **can be achieved by updating both the hyperdocument link structure and the content presentation** [...], i.e., by enabling only the link structure and the content presentation mode that match the user's present needs, which are assumed *a priori* as confirming to some predefined knowledge stereotypes and to some recognised learning procedure. **This would nevertheless be impossible without considering the user's cognitive skills as well as her learning styles in processing information.**	We have seen how this **can be achieved by updating both the hyperdocument link structure and the textual context of links. This would nevertheless be impossible without considering the user's cognitive skills as well as learning advancement in processing information.** As such, an adaptive link structure is used to unify two complementary (hyper)-books which are intimately very different: a course text for learning and a reference text for later use.

From the same paragraph, shown above, the nonbold text actually appears in another place in the dissertation. Thus, X2 seemed to have copied a previously composed paragraph, then fragmented it to use the different parts in other sections of the dissertation.

X2, 4	X2, 62
This can be achieved by updating both the hyperdocument link structure and the content presentation, i.e., **by enabling only the link structure and the content presentation mode that match the user's present needs, which are assumed *a priori* as conforming to some pre-defined knowledge stereotypes and to some recognised learning procedure.** This would nevertheless be impossible without considering the user's cognitive skills as well as her learning styles in processing information.	But the same user adaptivity can be guaranteed more easily **by enabling only the link structure and the content presentation mode that correspond to the user's learning requirements** (i.e., by putting introductory information or summaries in separate nodes that provide links to nodes with detailed information), **which are assumed *a priori* as conforming to some pre-defined knowledge stereotypes and to some recognised learning procedure.**

3.4   Analyzing the misuse of professional connections

In section 2.6 I discussed the issue of possibly misused professional associations. The case of X2 illustrates this problem in general. It also shows how researchers in an interdisciplinary field are in an anomalous situation that they can exploit to their advantage.

3.4.1   Establishing professional connections

X2 is neither a linguist nor a computer scientist, but comes from a general field outside languages. In the course of his graduate studies he showed an interest in aspects of artificial intelligence and human-computer interaction. A job opening on a multimedia project about language and culture brought him into a department of languages at another university. Neither X2 nor his dissertation advisor had ever done research on computer-assisted language learning or on second-language acquisition. Within the framework the project provided and because his presence in a language department required a connection with language, X2 decided (or was encouraged by the project promoter) to obtain a doctorate on using the Internet for learning languages.

X2 does not seem to have sought out the work of experienced CALL researchers, either because he was unaware of their existence or because he thought it was not necessary, given his assumption that CALL did not contain leading-edge research. The analysis of his dissertation shows only insignificant references to CALL research. In the seventeen pages of chapter 5, in which he introduces both language methodologies and CALL, he copies the data of three older and cursory overviews of CALL, which happened to be available in his university's library (Cook 1985; Wyatt 1987; Chapelle 1989), including their references to even older works. X2 does not cite any relevant research in the field of CALL and adaptivity, even though this issue is the core of his dissertation. Moreover, he also leaves unexplored the even larger field of computers in education, with its major studies on adaptivity.

In contrast, X2 draws heavily on the research realm of hypertext and human-computer interaction (HCI). From these two fields come the vast majority of the 225 references in his bibliography. However, it should be noted that most of these bibliographical references are actually sub-references taken from a limited number of sources (see section 3.3.7). Of course a limited angle of approach, such as hypertext and HCI, can be perfectly justified if the methodology and the results of the research concur with the objectives. But the objectives of X2's dissertation were to show the methodological implications of an HCI framework for language learning (X2, 3).

3.4.2   Profiting from professional connections

X2 came into contact with a professor of computer science, a specialist in hypertext. This professor had put one of his computer courses on the Internet in an interactive mode and had published a journal article about this endeavor. X2 met this professor at a conference and subsequently became involved in the professor's activities.

In the dissertation's chapter 4 and appendix, which both discuss this Internet course, X2 uses ample and nearly verbatim material from an early publication by this professor as sole author, but without reference to the source. I limit the comparison to only two paragraphs, but the re-use is extensive.

Article by professor	X2, 70ff.
The course places a focus on principles and practice, not on fancy features and multimedia applications. The aim of the hypermedia course is to teach students how to create hyperdocuments that are easy to use, how to develop hyperdocuments from information items and semantic relationships, and how to build hypermedia systems that offer a rich set of useful navigation aids.	The course focuses on hypertext principles and practice, not on fancy features and multimedia application. Its aim is to teach students how to create hyperdocuments that are easy to use, how to develop hyperdocuments from information items and semantic relationships, and how to build hypermedia systems that offer a rich set of useful navigation aids.

Tracking Students' Progress	Tracking Students' Progress
The non-linear, non-hierarchical structure of the course text makes it difficult for students to keep track of their progress, i.e. to decide how many, and which pages they still have to read.	The non-linear, non-hierarchical structure of the course text makes it difficult for students to keep track of their progress, i.e., to decide how many and which pages they have already read and how many and which ones they still have to read.
The anonymous nature of World Wide Web access implies that this information is not present in the server log files either.	The anonymous nature of World Wide Web access implies that this information is not present in the server log files either.
etc.	etc.

I do not identify the professor whose work was borrowed because he became X2's dissertation coadvisor, thus suggesting considerable responsibility for X2's use of sources. As part of my assignment to evaluate the dissertation, I asked this professor if he could clarify the relation between his work and X2's. He answered in writing that he had met X2 at a conference, then explained: "The course [name of the course] has been developed by me, both as to what concerns the content and as to what concerns the related adaptive software. The input of [X2] was limited to ideas and discussions about the methods of adaptivity which can/could be applied."

In a subsequent e-mail, probably realizing the implications of the preceding, he wrote that "I do not want to reduce the input of [X2] to less than what it was. We had very productive discussions about the various forms of adaptive linking.... The various subsequent versions of the adaptive course [name of the course] have completely been created by myself, but do contain ideas which we developed together."

However, in his written answer to my report, X2 responded in these terms: "The concerned Internet course about hypermedia, which existed at the University of (...), was thoroughly optimized by Prof. [name of the coadvisor] and myself, starting from an existing experimental Internet course."

Whatever the truth about the course's development, it is clear that X2 was involved to a certain extent in some further versions of this Internet course, once it had it been launched in its first versions by the professor alone. In view of publication dates, there is no doubt that the original and fundamental work had been done by the professor before X2's involvement and that he had published on it alone. But does the later involvement of X2 justify the extensive use of the professor's earlier publication by X2 in his dissertation without giving proper credit?

At a later stage, X2 and the professor became coauthors of a few abstracts and papers on this Internet course, which were published through the usual channels. From at least one of those joint publications, X2 uses extensive material in his dissertation in various chapters (pp. 43–51, 61–62, 66, 73–77, 80–84, 87–102, 154–55). But he provides only two references to this joint publication (pp. 69, 70), each referring to a single preceding sentence, without clarifying the far-reaching extent of the use, covering forty pages of the dissertation.

All in all, it seems that X2 profited from a rather large amount of work done by the professor. At no place in his dissertation does he describe when and how he got involved with the organization of the Internet course, nor does he quantify the respective contributions of each participant. In a joint publication such a lack of delineation is customary, though even in such cases the input of each should be mentioned. In the context of a doctoral dissertation, which bears the name of a single author and which by definition is supposed to reflect independent research, one would definitely expect such a description.

The matter raises questions about a professor's responsibility in such a situation and the reasons that could have prompted such leniency with the use of his material. It is true that his responses to my inquiries showed that he was annoyed by the situation and was willing to explain as much as possible without incriminating X2. He wrote to me: "It was then [after describing the existing courseware] the intent that [X2] would investigate if the concept of adaptivity, and in which form, could usefully be implemented in CALL. That was necessary for the European project for which [X2] works. I would have liked to see [X2] work this out first and evaluate it and then only complete the doctoral work and defend it. For reasons that are not very clear to me it had to go faster."

Indeed, chapter 4 of X2's dissertation describes the professor's Internet course on hypermedia as an already-existing application of a "proficiency-based" approach, outside the language-learning realm. It was meant as an introductory step: "In Chapter 4, we will describe an actual courseware where this proficiency adapted formalism has been successfully applied, i.e., the course [name of the course], whereas in Chapter 6 we will attempt to extend it to a CALL application" (X2, chapter 3, 45).

As we will see in section 3.7, chapter 6 of the dissertation does not fulfill that objective, which should have been the core element of X2's personal research. As we just read, even the coadvisor of the dissertation confirmed that fundamental problem, though he did not question the "not very clear" reasons why the dissertation was not completed as planned. On the contrary, he joined the committee in granting a summa cum laude doctorate. See also section 4.4 for an assessment of possible misconduct by a whole doctoral committee.

3.5   Analyzing the self-promotion of one's own work

Authors refer occasionally in print to their own work, either as a matter of necessity or to enhance their own credibility and prestige. But the technique becomes questionable when a reference to one's own work appears at the end of a paragraph that uses material taken directly from another author.

Even if authors refer to their own work, containing similar material (but perhaps also taken from the work of others?), the lack of attribution to the obvious source could be viewed as a kind of "double plagiarism," first by using the material without proper attribution, and second, by claiming that it originated in their own publications.

In the following examples from X2's dissertation, each passage is clearly taken from Thüring, Haake, and Hannemann, including a reference to Dillon, McKnight, and Richardson, taken from that source. Still, at the end of each passage X2 refers to a four-page publication that he coauthored with his dissertation advisor, not to Thüring, Haake, and Hannemann.

Thüring, Haake, and Hannemann 1995:I	X2, 48
Even for smaller hyperdocuments this can result in a considerable memory load if no external orientation cues are given. In order to provide cues that appropriately capture the net-like structure of most hyperdocuments, authors may employ graphical presentation formats that give a visual impression of the "information space."	Even in small documents all this can give rise to a considerable memory load insofar as no external help is provided in the form of navigational cues. And such cues have to allow users to grasp the hyperdocument net-like structure by providing a visual snapshot of its information space [**42 = ref. to a 4-page paper from 1995 by X2 and his advisor**].
A visual presentation fulfilling these requirements also should provide an overview of the document structure to increase global coherence. Besides simplicity of the user interface, an important argument supporting this claim is the close relation between comprehension and orientation. Empirical studies summarized in [5 = Dillon, McKnight, and Richardson] revealed a correlation between comprehension and memory for location.	Such a visual device would not only improve easiness in understanding the user interface, but it would as well suggest the existence of a positive correlation between comprehension and orientation [75 = Dillon, McKnight, and Richardson], more specifically, between comprehension and memory for location [**33 = ref. to a 3-page contribution from 1996 by X2**].
In addition to supporting orientation and navigation, an adequate interface for hyperdocuments also has to cope with the third potential source of cognitive overhead: user-interface adjustment.	By the expression user-interface adjustments cognitive scientists normally refer to the mental effort required by users to cope with the several changes undertaken at interface level and to their consequent necessity to cope with them [**32 = ref. to a 6-page paper from 1996 by X2**].

It is an equally questionable practice to use material from an author and replace an element in that material so as to be able to refer to one's own work. In the following paragraph, X2 clearly uses material from V. J. Cook (it is part of a sequence of 610 words), replaces the words "communication in the classroom" with "target language culture," and adds a reference to his own publication on culture.

Cook 1985:15	X2, 112
3. The communicative model	5.3.3 The Communicative Model
Perhaps the model most favoured at present among language teachers is the communicative, which not only takes communication as the goal of teaching but also tries to attain this **through the use of communication in the classroom**; people learn to communicate by communicating.	But probably the most dominant model to-date is the communicative approach (see also Section 5.7), which not only takes communicative competence as the primary goal of language teaching, but also tries to attain it **in the context of the target language culture** (see Section 5.1 and, e.g., [43] for an overview of recent research in this field). [43 = reference to an edited work from 1997 by X2 and his advisor about culture]

3.6   Analyzing academic make-believe

In section 2.7, I discussed forms of academic make-believe. The case of X2 gave us a chance to detect some of these elements as potential problems. In the following sections, I use them as examples of possible analysis.

3.6.1   Drawing authority from others

After I submitted my report on X2's dissertation, he reacted by stating that he had been recognized for his outstanding work by "world authorities" and "top reviewers." X2's dissertation advisor produced equally strong comments on his behalf. A particular "world authority in hypertext," working at a prestigious American university, reportedly vouched for the quality of X2's research. X2 and his advisor also referred to "dozens of reviewers from highly respected scientific journals," and "international referees" for important academic conferences, whose acceptance of X2's contributions showed their approval.

However, a quick investigation revealed that the "world authority in hypertext," though known and active in his field, was actually a job-seeking, visiting researcher from a foreign country only temporarily at this American university. He became a member of X2's doctoral committee, an honor few job-seeking scholars would refuse. This appointment naturally put him in a difficult position for critiquing the dissertation. Indeed, at the very time X2's dissertation was being submitted, this researcher sent an e-mail to the coadvisor of the doctoral committee, and probably also to other members, in which he mentioned that he would be applying for an academic position at several American universities and solicited letters of reference to include with his application. However, he sent his e-mail to a public mailing list of the coadvisor's students, a list that can be viewed worldwide. At the time I wrote this chapter, the letter was still there for public scrutiny. I do not want to disparage this person's request for letters of reference or his mailing error, but the facts definitely reveal his awkward position and the relations between committee members that can seriously erode scholarly objectivity. I should also add that I had friendly and collegial e-mail exchanges with this researcher, who conceded some of the problems in the dissertation (see section 4.3.10).

As to the "dozens of reviewers" and "international referees" who reportedly thought highly of X2's publications, the analysis of his articles and papers led to a different assessment (see section 4.5). Moreover, I know of at least one reviewer who had his international professional organization reprimand X2 for his inadequate citation habits. X2 had submitted a paper that, by chance, this reviewer evaluated. Since X2 had ambiguously presented this very researcher's work as if it were his own, the paper was refused with that criticism. This is a far cry from "outstanding work recognized by world authorities and top reviewers," as X2 and his advisor would have us believe.

3.6.2   Internal references to the author's own work

X2's dissertation provides ample evidence of his practice of citing his own work (see section 2.7.2), even when much of the material in those earlier publications had also been borrowed from other scholars. However, within the dissertation he also refers lavishly to other sections of his own dissertation. A detailed analysis will illustrate this point.

X2's dissertation is liberally sprinkled with references to other chapters and sections, pointing both backward and forward—for example, "We have already stressed before that ..." (p. 18); "... as we have already clarified in Section 3.7.1 ...” (p. 55); “As we will discuss extensively in Chapter 3 ...” (p. 22); “As we will illustrate in Chapter 4 ...” (p. 33); “In the subsequent sections we will describe ...” (p. 72).

On superficial reading, these internal references give constant reassurance that the dissertation is well structured and tightly organized. But these internal references do not, in fact, point the reader to discussions that cover the points X2 says they do. As examples I will take the internal references that appear in chapter 6 and the appendix, because X2’s references lead the reader to expect that the innovative results of the actual research are found there. Despite their length, I believe that extensive quotation is necessary to show both the scope of the problem and the need for a thorough analysis to place these references in the context of the whole dissertation.

Make-believe for Chapter 6

X2 repeatedly refers to chapter 6 (the last chapter) as the core of the dissertation, for there the “implications for language learning on the WWW” (subtitle of the dissertation) will be discussed and the developed “CALL system” or “CALLware” will be presented as “the litmus paper” of his “ambitious proposal” (X2, 100). I cataloged the passages referring readers to that chapter (boldface):

• In the CALLware, however (see **Chapter 6**), we will be experimenting with link disabling as a sub-category of link hiding, with the link text still looking like a link, but not leading to its destination since it is disabled. On that occasion we will also discuss the implications of one such choice from a cognitive and ergonomical point of view. (X2, chapter 2, 28)

• The course [name of the existing course on hypermedia] exploits content adaptation to provide both additional and prerequisite explanations in combination with some form of explanation variants (see Chapter 4). Analogously does the CALL system described in **Chapter 6**. (X2, chapter 2, 31)

• As we will illustrate in Chapter 4 and in **Chapter 6**, both the course [name of the existing course on hypermedia] and the CALLware do employ the fragment variants technique to represent concepts to users. (X2, chapter 2, 33)

• In Chapter 4, we will describe an actual courseware where this proficiency adapted formalism has been successfully applied, i.e., the course [name of the existing course on hypermedia], whereas in **Chapter 6** we will attempt to extend it to a CALL application. (X2, chapter 3, 45)

• ... in Chapter 4, we will show how this formalism has been successfully applied to an intelligent tutoring system in the field of hypertext didactics, whereas in

Chapter 5 and in **Chapter 6,** how, both methodologically and functionally, this can as well be extended to CALLware. (X2, chapter 3, 56)

• In **Chapter 6,** we will, as a matter of fact, show how the design model discussed in Chapter 3 and the authoring environment that originates from it (see further) may be extended to a CALL application. (X2, chapter 4, 69)

• ... since we aim to provide an authoring environment which is also suited for the development of non-computer science courses (a first attempt in this direction is the CALLware described in **Chapter 6**), authoring needs to be kept simple and intuitive. (X2, chapter 4, 92–93)

• In an absolute sense, this chapter's [chapter 4's] contribution therefore consists in the elaboration of some design principles for the actual implementation of the above mentioned proficiency-adapted model. Ideally, such design principles might be later generalised and reused to other content/context-specific applications. In primis, the litmus paper for such an ambitious proposal will be, as already anticipated, the CALLware described in **Chapter 6.** (X2, chapter 4, 100)

• But its [chapter 4's] main contribution lies nevertheless in the elaboration of a new authoring environment, by fully exploiting the WWW technology ... And, once again, **Chapter 6** will demonstrate the extent to which an attempt at exploiting such an authoring environment for an AH system in language learning has succeeded. (X2, chapter 4, 100–101)

At the beginning of Part II of the dissertation, "Methodological Implications for Language Learning on the WWW," X2 announces the two respective chapters, 5 and 6.

• In Chapter 5 we will situate CALL research to-date, outlining briefly its theoretical referents, its methodological development, and focusing on its still open problems. In **Chapter 6** we will present an illustrative CALL application, where the principles focused on so far have been applied to language learning. (X2, 105)

In chapter 5, the following internal reference appears:

• Nevertheless, because of the uncertainties and ambiguities of natural language, CALL programs have almost never been developed within the communicative methodology (we refer to **Chapter 6** for a detailed analysis of the present issue). (X2, chapter 5, 113)

And in the conclusion of chapter 5:

• ... we refer to the discussion in Chapter 3 as well as to the CALLware described in **Chapter 6** for details. (X2, chapter 5, 121)

The introduction of chapter 6 again confirms:

• The present chapter examines the design of a pilot CALLware on the Web [36] which is based on the proficiency-adapted framework discussed in Chapter 3 and which applies the authoring environment illustrated in Chapter 4, thus circumventing the limitations both drill-and-practice-based applications and intelligent tutoring systems present when complying with L2 learners' needs (see Chapter 5), as well as the difficulties intrinsic in more traditional CALL design to take advantage of the potential expressed by the Web. (X2, 126)

In X2's bibliography, reference [36] in the preceding paragraph denotes the announced pilot CALLware (see section 3.7.1).

All these announcements have made it clear what readers can expect in chapter 6, where "the litmus paper for such an ambitious proposal" is allegedly found. But the twenty-one pages of this final chapter do not even begin to fulfill these promises. All X2 does there is to briefly repeat a few simple and long-known principles. As to his intended courseware program, he only copies the table of contents of an existing book as the "course structure" of this program. The courseware itself is nonexistent (see section 3.7). Even the coadvisor of the dissertation had come to the same conclusion, but did not act on it (see section 3.4.2).

Make-believe for Appendix A

Similar announcements in the course of the dissertation point at the highly interesting and supposedly convincing data found in Appendix A:

• ... for an analysis of the cognitive impact of hiding on users see **Appendix A.** (X2, 29)

• ... see **Appendix A** for a definition of the possible searching behaviors in a Web-based environment. (X2, 45)

• ... see **Appendix A** for the details concerning the evaluation procedure. (X2, 72)

• Empirical findings [19] seem to support our claim to prevent, by disabling them, the usage of those links for which students are not yet ready, because this ultimately does enhance learning, while simply discouraging their usage by de-emphasising them gives students more navigational freedom and, eventually, worse learning results (see **Appendix A**). (X2, 88)

• ... the experience that has been gained so far (and that will be briefly anticipated in **Appendix A**) will clearly foster further advancements in this same direction. (X2, 100)

• Finally, link disabling means that the link text looks like a link, so it is visible, but it does not lead to its destination since it is disabled. It may therefore be disturbing for users because it shows them which possible directions they might follow, but it does not let them select any of them (since they are disabled)—see however detailed discussion in **Appendix A.** (X2, 101)

• The reason behind such a shift ... has to be sought in the results of a preliminary evaluation (see **Appendix A**). (X2, 136)

• A preliminary evaluation of the results collected by experimenting with the application described in Chapter 4 closes this work (**Appendix A**). (X2, 149)

However, none of these promises are realized in the seven pages of Appendix A. In this appendix, X2 first mentions that it is difficult to do such evaluations, then explains the simple and limited multiple-choice testing of the previously existing Internet course on hypermedia, the results of which are kept in student log files. But, the reader learns:

... this is but a preliminary evaluation awaiting for [sic] all the log files from each student's learning process to be compared exhaustively. The results collected so far show that, in general, students feel uncomfortable about links being removed because they perceive there is still information out there they could eventually access, but they do not know how to access it, actually. (X2, 154)

The preceding sentence is the only indication of a result. X2 provides no quantitative data on how many student reactions were solicited, collected, or analyzed. No figures on the evaluations, no empirical data, and no statistics are provided. Moreover, this sketchy evaluation pertains only to the non-CALL Internet course developed by the coadvisor of the dissertation, which is supposed to be the model for the proposed CALL-ware. At the end of the appendix, X2 brushes off the need for a more thorough evaluation of his own CALLware:

For what concerns the pilot CALLware discussed in Chapter 6, trial sites still have to be set up. But the same more general paradigm specified above will be followed. And, because of our main underlying assumption, i.e., learning a language does not change significantly from learning any other material (see Chapter 5), coupled with the adoption of an equal design model as the one discussed in Chapter 3 and applied in Chapter 4, the same (preliminary) empirical evidence collected now is very likely to be expected also in that situation. (X2, 156)

3.6.3 Improper use of *we*

X2 writes his dissertation using the first-person plural pronoun, *we,* an acceptable practice. However, at numerous points in the dissertation, X2 also utilizes *we* in sentences involving internal reference—for example, "we have illustrated ...," "we have been identifying ...," and "we have introduced...." Careful checking shows that many of these references do not pertain to work done by X2 but by others. I will limit myself to a few examples. The salient elements appear in boldface.

Example 1

The technologies we have just illustrated are not mutually exclusive. Some of them are, e.g., used in combination in the ISIS-Tutor [21 = Brusilovsky & Pepsin 1994] and in Hypadapter [108 = Hohl, Böcker & Gunzenhäuser 1996]. (X2, 29)

This paragraph concludes a description of systems several pages long (pp. 24–29) taken directly from Brusilovsky (1996). Even the paragraph itself is taken from that same source, including the same examples and references to ISIS-Tutor and Hypadapter.

Example 2

There exist yet other kinds of adaptive hypermedia systems, even if they are not recognised as such by the "official" literature in question—and this explains why they do not appear in the above tables; still, they do apply some of **the principles we have been identifying in Section 2.2.** (X2, 35)

The principles described in section 2.2. were directly taken from Brusilovsky 1996.

Example 3

In the previous section [3.7.1.], **we have introduced the idea** that through the activities provided by the hypertext users discover structure. In the present section, we will therefore discuss the structure of such activities from the user's point of view to give a more theoretical foundation to the approach for information filtering **we have been developing.** (X2, 57)

The idea that users discover structure through hypertext activities can be found in basic works about hypertext. The one-page "section 3.7.1" in the dissertation does not present any new ideas but uses material from a couple of authors. The sentence "we have introduced the idea" is therefore misleading. As to the "approach for information filtering" that X2 claims to have developed, namely that learners would have access only to information they are ready for, we can leave the assessment of its originality to readers conversant with the history of computer-assisted language learning since the 1960s.

Example 4

But surprisingly, most previous studies on adaptive systems have only focused on dynamically assembling information and presenting it according to the user's class and/or knowledge state without including the user's learning procedure in identifying which information to present to students. They lack the notion of a model of human cognition that describes both problem solving and the acquisition of procedural skills. **We have introduced such notions (see Section 3.4.1),** describing the learning paradigm encompassed by such an adaptive model of structuring information. (X2, 66)

Notice the contrast between "previous studies," which are criticized for their lacuna, and the **we**-introduction of new notions. Analysis shows that the concepts mentioned in section 3.4.1 of the dissertation were all taken directly from Thüring, Haake, and Hannemann 1995. Moreover, no adequate citation was provided for this source. When I contacted the authors involved, they confirmed the unacceptability of the presentation by X2 (see section 4.3.10).

3.7   Analyzing possibly deceitful courseware

Again the work of X2 provides a basis for analyzing alleged academic misconduct in the presentation of courseware.

3.7.1   The invisible courseware
At the introduction of X2's chapter 6, he declares: "The present chapter examines the design of a pilot CALLware on the Web [36]" (X2, 126).

Reference 36 in the preceding sentence refers in X2's bibliography to a program entitled *Capire l'economia italiana*, with its author X2 himself. There is no other identification, only a URL address, which points to the homepage of the coadvisor of the dissertation. I tried the address for several months after the publication of the dissertation, but the URL was constantly "not found." I sent three inquiries, at intervals of a month or so, to the webmaster of the site, to ask for clarification, but I never received an answer. Search tasks on the Web to locate *Capire l'economia italiana* as CALLware also failed to yield results. In his reaction to the critical report of his dissertation, X2 did not clarify this point.

In the dissertation, however, X2 makes it clear that the announced CALLware is not a theoretical projection, but that it does exist:

In a previous chapter (Chapter 4), we have presented a new authoring environment which we have claimed to be intuitive and relatively simple and, because of this, better suited for the development of any instructional system beyond the more traditional Computer Science applications. The present CALLware exemplifies the extent to which an attempt at exploiting such an authoring environment for an AH system in language learning has succeeded. (X2, 127)

3.7.2   The purportedly existing courseware

If we give X2 the benefit of the doubt and presume that the courseware exists but was not to be shown for some reason, it is still possible to analyze its characteristics based on the description X2 provides.

On the level of content

For the design of his courseware, X2 argues that what is valid for the existing Internet course on hypermedia (described in chapter 4 of the dissertation) is also valid for language learning:

> What ultimately allows us to apply exactly the same principles used for the course [name of the course] to a CALL application is the certainty that, from the point of view of a (constructivist) theory of learning, learning a language is a process analogous to learning any other material. (X2, 127)

X2 next asserts that "designing any courseware" includes three steps:

> 1. conceiving the course structure, keeping in mind the functional dependencies among concepts;
> 2. writing the Web pages;
> 3. putting the Web pages to work using the given software in order to make the courseware adaptive according to the features described thus far. (X2, 128)

X2 continues:

> In the following presentation we will only limit ourselves to the first point in the above mentioned taxonomy, i.e., to an illustration of the design decisions behind the actual course development. We refer to Chapter 4 for all the technicalities, with their intrinsic advantages/disadvantages and their decision options, regarding the actual implementation of one such courseware. (X2, 128–129)

In other words, for the actual writing of the Web pages and for the implementation of the software, X2 refers only to the description of an existing Internet course on hypermedia.

X2's work for his courseware application is thus limited to the first step—that is, "conceiving the course structure." However, the next paragraph states that "the courseware is based on the (linear) overview on the Italian economy published by the most authoritative Italian financial editorial group" (X2, 129). Indeed, the courseware content, which is described in the dissertation as a short list of chapter titles, reflects the same sequence as the chapters of *Come si legge il Sole 24 ore*, a best-selling discussion of the Italian economy.

In other words, "conceiving the course structure" equals copying the table of contents of an existing book. X2 performed only that activity as "the litmus paper" of his "ambitious proposal" (X2, 100). Moreover, it is fair to ask why X2 has identified himself as the author of the bibliographical entry *Capire l'economia italiana*, while the content of this presumed software is fully taken from another source.

On the level of interactivity

From X2's description, it appears that his language courseware allows reading text passages in a normal hypertext environment, with links toward flat lexical, grammatical, and cultural explanations, without any further interactivity. X2 mentions that users can obtain more lexical, grammatical, and cultural information by following the suggested links, visible in the text, to the appropriate nodes with extra explanation. These simple and well-established principles are presented as though they were innovations.

The "proficiency-adaptive model," however, should be the kernel of the innovation. X2's formula is that the system would record how the student processes information and then the system would adapt its presentation accordingly by making certain knowledge "forbidden." To have the system do this, X2 proceeds from the following assumption:

We assume that once, e.g., the rules for gender and article agreement have been introduced, or a definition of the concept "aliquota" has been seen, these nodes are no longer pointed to and therefore conditional links leading to them are disabled. Being preliminary notions, the student is indeed expected to master them soon after her first visit to their corresponding nodes, otherwise she could not advance in her learning. (X2, 132)

And a little further: "We assume each student's proficiency in the factual knowledge corresponds to the set of concepts she has read about" (X2, 133).

In other words, the whole system is based on the supposition that seeing a page once is equivalent to having mastered the content of that page; consequently, the student must not be allowed to access it later.

The student's comprehension of the text passages is evaluated in this courseware through a multiple-choice test. Anyone with even a limited experience in computer-assisted learning will wonder why this program is presented as either original or as adding value, compared to even the most elementary courseware.

3.7.3   The utopian courseware

The description of the courseware by X2 continues as follows:

This CALLware, among the wide range of learning activities CALL systems might ultimately concentrate upon, like [sic], for instance, error correction, text analysis, machine translation, vocabulary instruction, pronunciation, listening or reading comprehension, text manipulation, only deals with text comprehension in Italian for specific purposes. Such a reading comprehension ability may eventually be further extended to writing, i.e., to support advanced learners of Italian in the active production of text by determining whether they use the proper factual vocabulary and correct grammatical and syntactical structures, together with more general text production issues in Italian, possibly by means of natural language generation (NLG) techniques. (X2, 126)

X2 is correct in saying that the courseware he described (though invisible and not controllable) "only deals with text comprehension." His projections to the next, extremely complex and challenging stages, like creative language evaluation and production "by means of natural language generation" by the computer, are laid out as if they merely involve a further extension of his work.

3.8   Analyzing the plagiarism of ideas

In section 2.4 we distinguished between written and oral sources in the case of plagiarism of ideas. Whatever the form of "the theft of a concept," one senses the complexities of the ensuing analysis: How original was the idea? How much was already shared or common knowledge? What is the relationship between the concept and the way it was presented in writing?

Recognizing the plagiarism of ideas that exist in oral form is even more challenging because of their casual and fleeting nature. If an idea emerged from discussions, how can we determine what came from one participant or another? One needs witnesses to state what was said at which moment in what context, and even then, witnesses memories—especially if months have elapsed—are apt to be unreliable.

3.9   Conclusion

This chapter has concentrated on a case in which I was personally involved as whistle-blower. Some of the material I used in this chapter was part of the report that I submitted to the chair of the committee responsible for granting research awards. This chair had requested my evaluation.

In this chapter I have done my best to preserve impartiality and objectivity. This is a challenge whistle-blowers must be aware of. Indeed, if they are driven by the feeling that they have a point to prove, they may easily generalize beyond the facts or use legal language without realizing the implications. How can they remain impartial if they are yielding to the temptation to be rash or judgmental? How can they remain objective if they are spurred on by indignation? Any whistle-blower should be aware of these dangers.

My solution to this quandary was to take sufficient time for the analysis and to frequently reread and amend what I had written. Moreover, I had my analysis checked and rechecked by colleagues I could fully trust, before submitting it to a higher authority. They helped me eliminate remnants of emotional language and marginal arguments that weaken analysis. Still, even the best analysis will have weak spots, which the accused will mercilessly identify, amplify, and use against the whistle-blower.

4

Assessment

4.1 Introduction

In the introduction to the chapter on analysis (see section 3.1), I emphasized the importance of scrupulously gathering and examining relevant data. The next step is the assessment of the data: to what extent do they demonstrate misconduct, defined as deliberate deception to gain undeserved profits? Part of this assessment process was covered in the previous chapter, where a number of analytical considerations automatically led to some form of evaluation.

This chapter elaborates on some of these evaluative elements, without pretending to be exhaustive. I deal with this subject before the chapter on reporting (chapter 5), because the potential whistle-blower should try to evaluate, after analysis and before reporting, how strong the evidence is and what chances of success any whistle-blowing efforts may have. Indeed, even in the face of an apparently strong case, accused individuals can deny or minimize the charges if they can present arguments that whistle-blowers have not anticipated. Whistle-blowers should try to imagine how the accused will interpret and possibly counter the allegations. That exercise should help them decide whether to report and, if the answer is yes, how to report (see sections 5.2 and 5.4).

By their very nature, the elements pertaining to assessment also belong to a later phase in the procedure, namely, the appraisal of the case by the persons to whom it is reported, the arguments of the defense, and, finally, the conclusion by the appointed evaluators. It is only in that very final phase that assessment becomes a verdict. It will be clear from the discussion that some elements described in this chapter apply equally or more to the whistle-blower's assessment prior to his or her report, while others apply equally or more to a supervisor or an investigative committee after the initial reporting. Therefore this chapter pertains to the evaluative activities of a whistle-blower as well as to further checkpoints along the road.

The purpose of this chapter is also to show how problematic some of the facets can be, how much interpretations can diverge, and therefore how ambiguous and frustrating the assessment of academic misconduct can become. The issue at stake is how to distinguish between shoddy research, serious errors, and questionable practices on the one hand and "real" misconduct on the other.

4.2   Fabrication or not? Falsification or not?

Sometimes assessment of fabrication or falsification can occur quickly and unambiguously because the material evidence of the misconduct is undeniable. The literature on misconduct often refers to the "felt-tip mouse" of William Summerlin as a prototype of falsification in the present era (see, e.g., Hixson 1976; Lock 1996a:19). Here the researcher had simply blackened a portion of the skin of a white mouse to fake a successful skin transplant from a black mouse. More recent examples of easy-to-identify fraud include the manipulation of slides to show certain effects or the fabrication of e-mail responses to surveys. Analyzing such falsifications—for example, by use of electronic control devices—uncovers the truth unequivocally.

Matters become more difficult when evidence must be found outside the primary elements or circumstances of the case. Has this anonymous survey form been filled out by real respondents or by the researchers themselves? Have these data been recorded on the exact date mentioned in the report or at some other time? Have data that tended to disprove the hypothesis deliberately been overlooked? Investigative committees face complex and time-consuming tasks as they try to unearth the truth. There are many borderline cases, as the "Summaries of Closed Investigations Not Resulting in Findings of Misconduct" on the Office of Research Integrity's Internet site reveals. Much of the assessment task must focus on determining unintentionality, inadvertent error, divided responsibilities, and misunderstandings. Indeed, much can go wrong in recording data—mixing cards and labels, miscounting totals, applying wrong variables, or simply pressing the wrong key at the wrong moment. The most widely publicized assessment quandary pertains to the so-called Baltimore case, where the determination of whether "real fraud" or "minor error" had occurred took more than a decade, passing through alternate conclusions and finally involving a congressional committee and the U.S. Secret Service. Daniel J. Kevles (1998) devoted a whole book to the matter, and the case continues to stir emotions and to have ramifications (see e.g. , Guterman and Heller 2000).

Assessment becomes much easier when the accused, if guilty, is willing to confess as soon as the charges are made or the investigation is started. Indeed, the perpetrator may (and should) realize that denial creates a need to construct even more lies, which, once uncovered, bring even greater harm (see also section 5.6.1). Much time, energy, and expense can be saved by a candid acknowledgment of the problem. In its reports of proven cases, the ORI includes a record of a defendant's willingness to cooperate fully with the investigation. Such notations represent a bright spot on an otherwise dark record.

Finally, one should also warn for derailments when oversensitiveness to misconduct becomes the norm. For example, research in the arts, humanities, history, and social sciences may include persons being interviewed. Valid concern for the well-being of "human subjects" oblige researchers to request permission for their work from institutional review boards, similar to those in the hard sciences. However, bureaucratic shortsightedness may lead to aberrant situations, for example when an innocent chat with a subject, but not formally approved by a board, can plunge a sincere researcher into the torment of a misconduct case. Examples of such "regulatory mania" are given by Shea 2000.

4.3   Plagiarism or not?

Probably no other question has stirred up so much debate in cases of alleged academic misconduct. My analysis of X2's text (see section 3.3) showed the many areas that lend themselves to controversy, because the similarities with source texts are complicated by numerous nuances, the boundaries of citation can be explained differently, the limits between truisms and original thoughts are disputable, and so on. Still, it should be our duty to try to determine criteria that would enable valid assessment.

4.3.1 Defining plagiarism

It seems deceptively easy to define plagiarism. Dictionaries give us such traditional phrases as "the action of using or copying someone's else's idea or work and pretending that you thought of it or created it" (Collins), or "to take (words, ideas, etc.) from (someone else's work) and use them in one's own work without admitting one has done so" (Longman), or "to steal and pass off as one's own (the ideas or words of another)" (Webster). We do not need to give the precise references to these sources, for they are common knowledge in the public domain. Of course, we are considering plagiarism here only in its fundamentally negative sense and are not dealing with constructive uses of the word in marginal cultural trends, as for example in Home 1995.

There are clear-cut cases of undeniable plagiarism. For example, it is unequivocally plagiarism when a student hands in a paper that has been copied, completely and verbatim, from a published source, without any reference to that source. It is also blatant plagiarism when a faculty member publishes someone else's work under his or her own name. However, such cases are rare. Often plagiarism is not so easily defined, as numerous cases show. Allegations of plagiarism are countered by excuses such as:

- The wording is quite different from that of the alleged source.
- The overlap is minimal and accidental.
- The sources used were properly cited, but in a different place.
- Every competent reader would know what the obvious source was.
- The sentence is a truism that many people would write the same way.
- The copying of that part was inadvertent.

Sometimes the blame is placed on material factors: word processing hid the citation, footnotes accidentally disappeared during electronic transfer, the quotation marks were unintentionally dropped in typesetting, and so on.

One senses the predicament in the subjectivity of the adjectives: *different, minimal, accidental, proper, competent, obvious, inadvertent, unintentional.* These adjectives are all subject to interpretation—hence the need for rule books and style guides on how to cite and quote correctly, which are recommended to students and regularly reedited (e.g., Crews and VanSant 1984; Fowler and Aaron 1989; Hacker 1991, 1993; Trimmer 1989). Moreover, as a quick survey of the Internet shows, many institutions and even departments have developed their own written guidelines to help students avoid plagiarism. All these guidelines are well meant, sometimes containing detailed instructions and clear examples. But it seems difficult to make the guidelines unequivocal once we leave the clear case of extended verbatim copying without reference. For example, one such guideline states:

The best way to avoid accidental copying (it is a still a violation whether you meant to or not), is to read the passage and then express it in your own words. Afterwards, compare your text to the original and make sure that they are sufficiently different. Take care to avoid paraphrasing.... Yes, sometimes there is no good way to make the sentence substantially different and still convey the information with the same effectiveness. It is perhaps OK to do this once or twice in an assignment, but certainly no more than that. Remember, the wording must be your own! Express information in your own words. Remember: Paraphrasing is plagiarism!!! (University of Kentucky, Department of Chemistry, n.d.)

The rules of this department also provide convincing examples of what is *not allowed.* But at what point does a rephrased sentence become "sufficiently different" to be *allowed*? One can easily understand why students can get confused. On the one hand, the message says "read the passage and then express it in your own words;" on the other hand, "paraphrasing is plagiarism." Specialized linguists can explain the matter by pointing at the difference between integrated concepts in mental representation versus expression in "surface structures," but few individuals would be able to master those distinctions consciously when asked to reexpress something. Even if all the significant words are replaced by synonyms, even if the syntactic structure is drastically altered, the specificity of the content still rides on the input of a source. Much will depend on the degree of specificity to determine how unique that input is. And how does one define "your own words"?

John Rodgers (n.d.) mentions: "The ethical paradox that we must acknowledge is that the more serious forms of plagiary are those that are most difficult to detect and for which the intent to plagiarize would be hardest to prove." There is thus a broad gray zone in which it is impossible for the whistle-blower and the accused to agree on a definition of what is acceptable and what is not.

Even unacceptable copying and paraphrasing of numerous passages can still be denied as plagiarism. Lawyers have their ways of refuting accusations of plagiarism. They could claim that what is at stake is "a failure to cite sources properly" or "a lack of respect for authors' rights," while arguing that "authentic" plagiarism can only pertain to intentional fraud. If the accused did not make money from the plagiarism (as in student papers, dissertations, or journal articles) or did not hurt anyone substantially, those lawyers may have a case. In a famous plagiarism case in the Netherlands, the defense even argued that, in an academic milieu, plagiarism can apply only to the fraudulent usurpation of original research results. Since Professor D., the defendant, "only" paraphrased known material for popular scientific publications, his lawyer argued that the term *plagiarism* could not apply and won the case. In view of the public notoriety given to the case, the man was forced to resign anyway. Taubes (1995) reports another case of a successful plagiarism suit.

In the context of research misconduct, the ORI provides as its working definition of textual plagiarism:

Substantial unattributed textual copying of another's work means the unattributed verbatim or nearly verbatim copying of sentences and paragraphs which materially mislead the ordinary reader regarding the contributions of the author. ORI generally does not pursue the limited use of identical or nearly-identical phrases which describe a commonly-used methodology or previous research because ORI does not consider such use as substantially misleading to the reader or of great significance. (Office of Research Integrity 1994)

This definition includes some important but subjective elements, such as "substantial" versus "limited," "nearly verbatim," and "mislead the ordinary reader."

• The difference between "substantial" and "limited" is clearly necessary to rule out trivial cases. This important issue is pursued in section 4.3.4. Let us not forget, however, that the ORI adds that the "limited use" must pertain to descriptions of a commonly used methodology or previous research. Such use is permissible, but it must remain within narrow bounds. It is a technique found in the introductions to articles or reports that define the methodology used or that situate their research in the framework of previous research. Filling whole pages or most of a thesis or dissertation with such content would be plagiarism.

• "Nearly verbatim": plagiarists cannot hide behind the excuse that their text is not exactly the same as the original. However, as we have seen (see section 3.3.3), language is malleable, allowing for many degrees of divergence. At which point does a sentence become "not nearly verbatim" to make it acceptable? But even if it is really divergent, detailed comparisons of longer paraphrased passages may show that the "copied" text is derived so directly from the original content that it would generally be viewed as unacceptable, especially if that content is rich in valuable information that was obviously "stolen."

• "Mislead the ordinary reader": plagiarists cannot claim that the origin of the source would be clear to experts and specialists. If an ordinary reader is misled about the real authorship, plagiarism has occurred. I will return to this useful criterion in section 4.3.5.

It is helpful to apply the ORI's working definition to the X2 case and also to see how the three-member ad hoc committee, appointed to evaluate the allegation of plagiarism, assessed the matter. It seems difficult to deny that X2's dissertation presents "substantial unattributed textual copying," making use of "nearly verbatim copying of sentences and paragraphs." The substantial character is evident from the hundreds of sentences under suspicion of insufficient attribution. The ad hoc evaluation committee itself found the use of that material "misleading to the ordinary reader." The three committee members confirmed that all the problems I reported were true—that the dissertation contained misleading reuse of sources without indicating the boundaries of citation, misleading reuse of subreferences as if they were the result of X2's research, and misleading literal reuse of tables and figures under the rubric "adapted from." All these techniques would fall under the ORI's definition, especially in view of the fact that most of the dissertation is made up of such misleading material.

But the ad hoc committee concluded that these "shortcomings" did not qualify as plagiarism, "taking into account the special circumstances proper to this case," namely "the citation tradition in the discipline" and "the nature and origin of some of the cited texts." The ad hoc committee did not provide the definition of plagiarism they were using, nor did they elaborate on what they meant by the "citation tradition in the discipline" or the extent to which X2 complied with this tradition (see section 4.3.3 for a discussion of this aspect). They did not clarify "the nature and origin of some of the cited texts" nor why those characteristics made the exploitation of such texts acceptable in the formats X2 had used. In contrast to the committee's reactions, the authors from whom X2 borrowed extensively and who are major scholars at the heart of the discipline, found that use unacceptable (see section 4.3.10).

The hesitation of an investigative committee to resort to the word *plagiarism* is not uncommon, for it allows the committee to attempt a compromise between the factions. The art is to indict and not to indict at the same time, so that everyone can read what he or she wishes into the verdict, even though no one is totally pleased. In a complex and widely publicized case at Texas A&M, a three-member committee defined the infraction as "intentionally failing to credit sources in a work product in an attempt to pass off the work as one's own," but not as plagiarism (Leatherman 1999a). A committee at the Dutch University of Nijmegen reached a similar conclusion when evaluating a 1994 doctoral dissertation containing pages that were almost identical to pages in several books published in the 1980s: the matter was judged to be "uncareful processing of sources," but not plagiarism (Jansen 1996). If a report thus avoids the explicit denunciation of "plagiarism," which is a convicting term in an academic context, it allows the accused to claim that he or she has been exonerated, even if the report's description of the behavior matches the formal definition of plagiarism. It shows that a whistle-blower should be careful with the word *plagiarism*, for the term opens the avenue for an evaluation committee to reject this allegation, thus exonerating the offender and putting the whistle-blower in the wrong, whereas the committee in fact concedes serious problems of source citation (see also section 5.4.2).

4.3.2   From quotation to citation to ambiguity

Assessment requires a cautious use of terms. Though *citation* and *quotation*, or *to cite* and *to quote*, are often used as synonyms, some differentiate shades of meaning between the terms, especially in view of their etymology. A quotation requires quotation marks and is a direct rendering of another's words. A quotation would be properly introduced by an element such as (example invented):

Peter Johnson (1999) wrote in his essay on postmodernism: "I believe that the essence of civilization consists of …"

Or the reference could come after the quotation marks:

"I believe that the essence of civilization consist of …" (Peter Johnson 1999).

Citation, on the other hand, makes use of indirect speech:

Peter Johnson wrote in his essay on postmodernism that he believes the essence of civilization consists of …

In the preceding example, one can see where Johnson's words start, though they are in indirect speech. One assumes that they stop at the end of the sentence. But this linguistic structure opens the way, not only for slight alterations in the wording, but also for unclear endings and therefore for ambiguity. Indeed, the next sentence could also be part of Johnson's input. Just as ambiguous are citations in which the reference appears at the end of a passage, because it becomes difficult to know where the citation actually started. Still using the same example, an unidentified number of sentences preceding this sentence could be from Johnson:

… There is indeed a belief that the essence of civilization consists of … (Peter Johnson 1999).

The next question is the extent to which indirect speech reflects someone else's exact words. Shouldn't exact wording take the form of a quotation? But if we change the wording in indirect speech, how precise are we in rendering the content of the author we cite?

Further, a citation does not always refer to the words of a single author but may allude to a general concept or a specific subject that various people have dealt with. In such a case, a sentence ends with references to various sources. But there is no way of knowing exactly how much each referenced author has contributed to the preceding words.

Quotation therefore is a much clearer and safer way to avoid misunderstandings, not only to precisely render a person's words, but also to avoid ambiguity about where the quotation starts and ends and who the author is. However, this safe way of including someone else's input is sometimes too verbose to be a practical solution. Especially in introductions or summaries, where the author presents the status of the topic under discussion, it is customary to cite previous work in a compact form with references to the various authors after virtually every sentence. This convention for short introductions and summaries is unambiguous and therefore perfectly acceptable.

But overall, the shift from quotation to citation opens a Pandora's box of potential plagiarism. An analysis of questionable citation practices must make careful comparisons between the sources and the suspect text. Next comes the assessment of whether plagiarism has occurred. Clearly, both accuser and defendant will interpret the case differently. If the matter pertains to a small number of occasional sentences, it could be easy for the defendant to refute plagiarism, especially if he or she has referred to the source in other parts of the publication. On the other hand, if the quantity of obviously reused elements makes up the core of the publication, without clear references indicating the boundaries of citations, the case will probably involve lengthy pro and con disputes. Assessors can count on receiving document after document, either to add to the allegations or to refute them. The matter will become very cumbersome. Outsiders who need to evaluate such a discussion must therefore cope with a high level of detail and carefully study the sources and the various arguments before reaching a decision. This explains why many complex plagiarism cases are never definitively resolved.

4.3.3 Disciplinary differences in citation/quotation norms

In my report on X2's dissertation, I quoted the following statement from the American Historical Association as a supporting definition of plagiarism, particularly because it also referred to the phenomenon of extended postuse, which is so prevalent in X2's work:

Both plagiarism and the misuse of the findings and interpretations of other scholars take many forms. The clearest abuse is the use of another's language without quotation marks and citation. More subtle abuses include the appropriation of concepts, data, or notes all disguised in newly crafted sentences, or reference to a borrowed work in an early note and then extensive further use without attribution. All such tactics reflect an unworthy disregard for the contribution of others. (American Historical Association 1986, amended 1995)

My use of this citation from the American Historical Association turned out to be a strategic error. In their written response to the allegation of plagiarism and in subsequent letters and oral justifications, both X2 and his dissertation advisor argued that I had applied citation norms from the field of history to the field of computers, implying that in computer science the citation techniques of X2 were perfectly justified. Their explanation seemed to satisfy some of the dissertation advisor's close colleagues, allowing them to escape the controversy and avoid collegial conflict. I heard comments of this kind: "The whole affair was only a matter of different citation norms. Prof. Decoo had applied criteria from American history writing to citation in computer science." It was interesting to note the relief in these comments, illustrating the need faculty members have to escape internal controversies and safeguard academic cohesion. The experience also taught me how careful one has to be with arguments, because the accused will seize the slightest opportunity to undermine the whistle-blower's line of reasoning.

But the point is important. Do different disciplines have different quotation and citation norms? Generally speaking, in the soft sciences longer quotations and citations are more frequent than in the hard sciences because of the conventions of paper preparation and thesis development. In the soft sciences many publications thrive on commenting about what others have said, on analyzing and nuancing their texts—hence the need to quote or cite extensively. Moreover, quite a few publications in the soft sciences are lengthy, because journals tend to provide the space needed. In the hard sciences, the IMRAD structure (Introduction, Methods, Results, and Discussion) used by publications in reporting experiments imposes conciseness, and journals generally offer limited space for every article. This convention imposes a tradition of compact referencing, with short sentences that summarize previous research. A common space-saving citation style is in-text numbers in brackets that refer to a numbered alphabetic reference list.

Most fields have their own citation guidelines, such as those of the Modern Language Association (MLA), widely used in the humanities, or the American Psychological Association (APA), widely used in the social sciences. Such guidelines usually apply only to norms of bibliographical entries and do not provide training in exact ways that source material should be cited or quoted.

My intention here, however, is not to point to variations in the length of correct citations or quotations, but rather to emphasize the ethical norms of clearly acknowledging sources used extensively, whatever the discipline. It is unthinkable that computer science, or any discipline, would reject the general criteria of the American Historical Association and find acceptable "the appropriation of concepts, data, or notes all disguised in newly crafted sentences, or reference to a borrowed work in an early note and then extensive further use without attribution." But this position is, in essence, the core of X2's and his thesis advisor's argument that the AHA definition could not be applied to computer science.

Moreover, this defense by X2 and his advisor was not persuasive to the misused authors themselves, who are key figures in the subject of the dissertation and who found X2's approach unacceptable by the norms of their profession (see section 4.3.10).

It is also interesting to note that X2's approach shows an internal contradiction when it comes to the citation traditions he is using as justification. On the one hand he uses numbers in brackets to refer to a numbered reference list, which is indeed part of the compacting approach of some hard sciences; on the other hand, he employs extensive borrowings from other authors, to the point of filling almost the entire dissertation with it. I asked one of the dissertation committee members, the foreign researcher in the field of human-computer interaction, how he felt about the extensive use X2 had made of one of his publications in the dissertation. He answered in writing that such extensive use is rare in computer science. But he thought such a procedure was usual in languages and literature, so he was "not surprised" by X2's "doing that too." In other words, to counter the allegation of plagiarism, X2 claimed that he was following a computer science tradition, while the computer specialist on his own dissertation committee thought that the extensive copying was part of X2's humanities background.

It should be clear that alleged differences between traditions cannot be used to deny plagiarism.

4.3.4   How much use constitutes plagiarism?

An important criterion seems to be the quantity of questionable material. How many words or sentences must have been identified as having been used without proper attribution before plagiarism has occurred? No mathematical criterion exist (yet), but we can at least suggest a few points that should be taken into account.

Some vivid plagiarism cases in the literature on misconduct involve only a few unattributed sentences, or one or two short paragraphs. Even if juxtaposed to the original sentences and thus showing undeniable copying, is this amount sufficient to warrant a conclusion of plagiarism? The context should be taken into account. If the accusations are made against a background of preceding professional antagonism between the whistle-blower and the accused, if the rest of the (voluminous) work of the accused shows no sign of similar occurrences and respects the conventions of scholarly use, the grounds seem too fragile to support an argument of plagiarism. One should accept the defendant's traditional defense that the passage in question is the result of an "error of transcription," of a "missed reference," or of the "negligence" of a secretary or other assistant. The defendant is unlikely to make the same mistake again. However, the same small amount of clearly copied and unattributed sentences in a student's paper, submitted at an early stage in his or her education, should certainly prompt the professor to at least inform the student that this practice constitutes plagiarism and must be avoided. Thus, depending on the context, the same small amount of copied material can be assessed differently.

The next quantitative stage to be considered occurs when the passages challenged amount to more than just a few sentences—say an average of one sentence per page, to establish a minimal measurable criterion. If such sentences appear throughout an author's work, it points to a pattern of loose usage of sources and constant low respect for citation rules. Normally, any scrupulous assessment should then conclude that plagiarism has occurred. From that point on, any greater amount of material used without proper attribution should leave no doubt about the nature of the offense and the label that should be applied.

Complicating the quantitative criterion, however, are a number of variables that mitigate the weight of the unattributed usage of original material:

· *The degree of paraphrasing.* Should one assign lesser weight to changed sentences, even taking into account scales of deviation? Although the sources of these sentences are indisputable, such alterations open up a large area of controversy about the extent to which they can be considered fully plagiarized. On the other hand, the very changing of sentences may indicate intent to deceive, making the offense not less but more serious. But such a judgment requires determining the author's motivation, a controversial area in itself.

· *The importance of the sentence in terms of scientific originality.* There does seem to be a difference between using, without attribution, key sentences containing original information, and, for example, a paragraph briefly describing the invention of the first computer. The first topic is unique; the second now belongs to the realm of common knowledge. But in many cases there is a continuum from the one extreme (i.e., high originality) to the other (i.e., universal knowledge). Moreover, the degree of familiarity one has with the subject greatly influences the perception of originality versus general awareness. It is not uncommon to hear someone accused of plagiarism claim that, for specialists in that field, the origin of some statements is so obvious that citation is unnecessary.

· *The distance of the sentences from the reference in the case of extended preuse and postuse* (see section 3.3.5). At what point and to what extent should sentences from a correctly cited source but that appear at a considerable distance from the citation count as plagiarized? Here again, an intent to deceive may have played a role in shaping the way the accused has worked out his material, purposely keeping citation borders ambiguous and keeping, as an escape route, the justification that "there is a reference." See also section 4.3.7.

My analysis of X2's work shows how those variables impact assessment. In his written defense against the allegations, X2 used exactly these margins of interpretation. Passages I identified as problematic became, in X2's words, "summarizing, paraphrasing passages, which give the state of affairs of current research without claiming original input." These passages are "only rendering what the discipline considers as accepted data, as common knowledge." Or: "The hypertext researcher, whom I had in mind when composing my text, knows that e.g. Brusilovsky or De

Bra own the intellectual property of the material I cite." If the citation occurs after the copied material, the reader is, according to X2, "unambiguously led to the source text."

But here also, the sheer volume of the suspect material should be considered an indicator. If there are only a few controversial sentences in a larger work, a reprimand should suffice. But dozens, if not hundreds, of slightly paraphrased sentences without proper attribution, or extensive passages at an unconventional distance from a reference, as in X2's dissertation, would normally lead to a conclusion of flagrant plagiarism.

Moreover, another important quantitative criterion can be added here, namely the proportion between used sentences from proven sources, and original ones by the author within the same publication, provided the sentences can all be correctly categorized as one or the other. In the case of X2, the analysis allowed me to calculate that nearly all sentences in the dissertation had simply been drawn from other sources without, in my opinion, sufficient attribution. Since X2 conducted no original research as such, this lack of a convincing proportion of original sentences is not surprising.

Finally, in the interest of completeness, I should note that the intense attention paid to plagiarism in the past few decades, especially in training students, has also been counterproductive at times. Heightened sensitivity about even the smallest incorrect attribution has had unexpected consequences. John J. Schulz, head of Boston's University's mass communications department, resigned from that post because he had failed to attribute one sentence at the end of a lecture that he was quickly wrapping up because of time constraints (Leatherman 1999b). It was clearly a minor, unintended oversight in an oral presentation. But the lapse was pointed out in an on-line discussion between students and led to a debate about whether the university had a double standard for students and professors. In that context, the problem escalated in such a way that Schulz decided to set what he felt was the proper example of consequences to be faced in the case of "plagiarism." He resigned as department chair. He refused to draw on the usual excuse of "unintended" or "inadvertent" error, which would have been credible in this case. No doubt he made a commendable and intelligent decision in view of the unfolding controversy. But the incident also illustrates the danger of overreaction by immature critics. It seems that Schulz's resignation sent as strong a signal about the folly of fanaticism as about the obligation to cite correctly. We can only hope his decision did not feed the vanity of arrogant juveniles who rush to judgment.

4.3.5   Will the ordinary reader be misled about the authorship?

In plagiarism cases controversy arises over whether citation boundaries are clearly marked. For accusers it is clear that certain passages are unattributed, but defenders insist that the public, for whom their work is intended, will not be confused about the original authorship. X2 used this argument is his defense.

The ORI's working definition of plagiarism mentions that the offense pertains to "sentences and paragraphs which materially mislead the ordinary reader regarding the contributions of the author" (Office of Research Integrity 1994). This definition suggests a simple test: Ask a few "ordinary readers," independent of each other, to go through a number of disputed pages, which normally also include citations and quotations, and indicate in two colors what, in their perception, is clearly cited or quoted and what is evidently the author's own input. To avoid disagreement over the test, I believe that the "ordinary readers" should be persons for whom the work is intended—that is, academics interested in and familiar with the subject. Both the whistle-blower and the accused could agree beforehand on the identities of these referees, but it is important that these "ordinary readers" receive no hints about the origin of the text to be evaluated. Next the result is compared to the allegedly plagiarized passages. If the number of "culpable" passages is large—say, several hundred words at various spots in the work—the test provides convincing proof that the text has misled the reader.

4.3.6   What if no source can be found?

Alison Schneider (1998) reports on the case of an adjunct professor who had a major conflict with his university over an alleged plagiarism case. A certain Professor C., who taught a composition class, had accused a student of plagiarism. The essays the student handed in over a period of several months contained numerous typical errors and were graded accordingly. Then suddenly the student handed in a couple of perfect essays. Professor C. claimed that there was no way the student could have written the essays herself. The student took the case to the department head. Another professor reviewed the work and found no evidence of plagiarism. Professor C. took the case to various higher levels at his institution, but each of them found no evidence of cheating. The dispute escalated. According to the adjunct professor, he finally lost his job because of the case.

Even if Professor C. were right, his story shows flawed assessment on his part. Lacking concrete proof, there is no case, even if educational experience and common sense tell us that there must have been cheating. In the case of Professor C.'s student, perhaps other ways could have been found to assess the student, such as having her write essays under supervision or having her perform a cloze test on her own work, that is, leave out a number of words and have her fill in the blanks.

In assessing the probability of plagiarism, a system like Glatt does not try to find a source against which to compare the original but uses a cloze test. The Glatt Plagiarism Screening Program replaces every fifth word of the suspect student paper with a blank. The student is requested to supply the missing words. To calculate the Plagiarism Probability Score (PPS) a number of factors are taken into account, such as the number of correct responses and the time interval between when the individual hands in the paper and takes the test. The technique is useful in cases where a student has copied material without much personal effort to understand the content and to reword the source. However, when plagiarists are conversant with the subject and skilled in rewording, or if they prepare themselves for the screening, such a cloze test is not convincing.

4.3.7   When does extended preuse or postuse constitute plagiarism?

The analysis of X2's dissertation revealed as the most frequent problem the extensive preuse and postuse of material around a correct reference (see section 3.3.5). The phenomenon is well known in the literature on plagiarism:

Some forms of plagiarism incorporate source attribution but still manage to steal. A plagiarist might paraphrase from a source for three paragraphs before or after a direct quotation properly attributed, giving the impression that all but the quotation itself is original material. Or she might quote directly from the source, crediting it in a footnote but without indicating by blocking or quotation marks that it is a direct quote, thereby implying that the wording is her own. (Watkins 1994:26)

The accused might respond that there is a reference to the source, that there was no intention to deceive, and that anyone familiar with the subject would immediately know to what extent the source was used.

Disentangling such a case requires thorough assessment and policy agreement to determine the answers to the following questions:

• When can we speak of "extended use," meaning clearly crossing the border of appropriateness? Do we limit the appropriate use to one sentence, or several, or to a whole paragraph—or even more? What kind of indications and how many should there be in those sentences or paragraphs to clarify that an identified source is being used?

• What about the criterion of familiarity with the subject to explain a difference in assessment? Are we to accept the argument that a person thoroughly acquainted with the subject is able to recognize the boundaries of extended use, whereas an outsider feels deceived when discovering the true authorship?

• How many occurrences can there be of extended preuse or postuse in a publication? A rare and ambiguous occurrence is quite different from a regular pattern, covering many paragraphs or even many pages of extended use.

4.3.8   Between plagiarism and copyright infringement

Plagiarism may, but does not always, include copyright infringement. Copyright infringement may, but need not, include plagiarism. This ambiguity creates confusion that enables lawyers to deny that plagiarism has occurred.

Under what conditions is the reuse of someone's text legitimate? The answer is to be found in citation rights that fall under copyright laws. Though varying according to the country, these laws usually allow a "fair use" of up to 300 words that may be cited without authorization of the copyright owner. The origin of the text and the name of the copyright holder must be mentioned. But the application of this simple rule becomes difficult when the uses differ. What about a lengthy paraphrase of more than 300 words? What about the lack of generally accepted criteria for evaluating the degree of paraphrasing (from "closely" to "loosely" reworded)? What about the reuse of ideas or concepts, where the wording does not matter, but the origin is undeniable? There may be plagiarism, but no copyright infringement.

Copyright laws are not meant to judge the subtle distinctions of plagiarism but rather to regulate the relations between authors and publishers, the commercial rights to reproduction, the effect of the reproduction on the potential market of the original work, and so forth. The verbatim copying of a copyrighted text, without identifying the source, falls under copyright law, but cannot be successfully prosecuted under civil law if no monetary damage can be claimed (as in student papers or in academic articles and reports). Nonverbatim plagiarism, which seems more common than verbatim plagiarism, is more a concept of "unacceptable behavior" determined by ethical and professional traditions and as such eludes legal definition.

Complicating the matter further is the fact that some works, especially on the Internet, are not (yet) clearly protected by copyright law. The digital environment poses complex legal issues—a scientific subfield in itself (see Davis 1999; Hugenholtz 1996; Leibowitz 1999; Samuelson 1994; Strowel and Triaille 1997). To reuse digital, noncopyrighted materials, even without citation, may not constitute copyright infringement but may be plagiarism.

Another strange twist, particularly in the academic environment, is that it is not uncommon to commit autoplagiarism and/or copyright infringement, without its becoming a matter of concern. Suppose that for a publication or a course syllabus, a researcher reuses parts of his or her own article, previously published in a journal that owns the copyright (though who is actually the owner in such cases is another complex question). If the author does not mention the source and did not obtain proper copyright permission, this is autoplagiarism and violation of copyright. Nowadays such cases happen more frequently because of the ease of copy-and-paste in word processing, combined with the pressure to produce new publications.

Whether plagiarism or copyright infringement is involved, or both, requires careful assessment. Answers are not always evident. Much depends on the nature of both the original publication and the one con-

taining the alleged plagiarism, the commercial value of both, the extent
of the alleged plagiarism, the measure of academic merit or other profits
derived from it, and so on. For an annotated bibliography on the subject,
see Anderson 1998. For further study, see Buranen and Roy 1999.

4.3.9   Where is the line between "inadvertent" and intentional plagiarism?

Those accused of plagiarism sometimes blame inadvertence: a few notes
taken years before were mistakenly reused as personal writings, electronic editing made one or two footnotes disappear, or a couple of sentences from various sources became garbled in text processing. All these
explanations can be perfectly valid, and each of us should be aware that
these things can happen to us. A measure of comprehension and tolerance should not be absent from our assessment, especially when dealing
with a prolific author whose work is generally characterized by quality
and care.

However, if more occurrences of such "inadvertent" lapses are identified, the sheer quantity becomes a criterion (see also section 4.3.4). But
at what point does the number of plagiarized sentences tip the balance
toward a decision that such occurrences are not inadvertent? The opinions of the whistle-blower and the accused will naturally differ greatly.
A range of opinions may also be expected even from fairly objective
observers. In the published case of X1, fifty-nine passages in his writings
were identified as copied or inadequately cited from eleven authors whose
work had appeared in eight separate books or articles published between
1987 and 1994. The executive committee of the professional journal that
evaluated the case came to the conclusion that plagiarism had occurred.
X1 courageously confessed to plagiarism and apologized to the authors
and the professional community but still claimed it was inadvertent.
While this may be true, the conclusion is inescapable that his working
habits were sloppy beyond the point of acceptability for a professional.
The question finally remains the same: At what point does sloppiness
become misconduct for a trained academic professional?

"Plagiarism requires intentional misconduct. All the errors were inadvertent," said the lawyer defending a professor in a famous 1995 academic
plagiarism case (Magner 1995:I). This defense seemed to be successful and

the matter would no doubt have ended there, were it not that some time later other irregularities were found in another of the same professor's publications. Those who use the defense of "inadvertence" should be aware that, once suspicions are aroused, a person's colleagues and competitors have every reason to begin carefully checking other publications. If a repetitive pattern is discovered, it becomes difficult for the defendant to continue to claim inadvertence. (See also Brown and Murphy 1989.)

4.3.10   The perceptions of misused authors

Plagiarism means the misuse of someone else's words and ideas. An author whose work is misused is the wronged party. How does such a person assess the plagiarism? Reactions vary according to the status of the plagiarist (e.g., a student versus an established researcher), the amount of text plagiarized, the distinctness of the source, and the profits obtained from the mischief. The plagiarized author will generally feel outrage at being robbed of fundamental rights.

If a plagiarized author declares indifference, this does not render the plagiarism harmless. On the contrary, it undermines the ethical standards needed to protect integrity and professionalism. One cannot morally agree with being burglarized; rather, such a reaction raises questions about covert pressures and hidden motives.

In the case of X2, we were faced with an interesting phenomenon. Of the dozen authors that X2 used extensive material from, two were members of his doctoral committee. These two, assuming they read the dissertation, were almost certainly aware of the way X2 had made use of their material. The first was a foreign visiting researcher in the field of human-computer interaction at an American university. As part of my evaluation assignment, I asked him, via e-mail, how he felt about the extensive use X2 had made of one of his publications. He answered that in computer science such extensive use is rare. But because such a practice was, in his view, usual in languages and literature, he was "not surprised" by X2's "doing that too" (see also section 4.3.3). He was, of course, mistaken about the acceptability of such a practice in languages and literature. Still, he admitted in a later e-mail after the conclusion of the case that X2's thesis had been "written possibly in a kind of rush." He added: "I wish all Ph.D. students could have opponents like you—it will lead to the increasing of quality. I think that [X2] as well as people around got a very good lesson."

The second author was the coadvisor of the dissertation. He told me in writing that he was bothered by the whole situation and not happy about the fact that the dissertation had to be completed very quickly "for reasons that are not very clear to me" (see section 3.4.2).

The other misused authors, who had no personal connection to X2, were more outspoken about the appropriation of their material. X2 and his advisor had claimed that the dissertation used an accepted citation tradition in this scientific field. I gave five authors whose work had been used extensively in the dissertation the pages drawing on their publications but identifying X2 only as "a graduate student who did an important research work." I asked if they found their work "adequately attributed." Their answers were as follows (they afterward gave written permission to quote them in this form here):

1. I have just read the complete chapters you provided last week. I am sorry to say that I can find very little in those pages that the student can claim as work of his/her own. I therefore propose that he/she clearly declares that those chapters summarize some of the ideas we described in our ACM article. (Manfred Thüring)

2. It's clear that the student is quoting from my work without adequately making it clear which are his/her ideas and which are mine.... This is not acceptable scholarly practice. Clearly there's a problem here that needs to be fixed. (Name withheld upon request)

3. In my opinion, my work was not cited adequately in the paper you sent. The author needed to cite mine as he introduced the three types of CALL. His/her use of the exact references and the same or paraphrased words used in my paper indicates to me that he/she took them from mine.... I would call what you sent "dishonest citation" (not just "uncareful"), and that is essentially what "plagiarism" is—presenting the work or ideas of another person as your own. (Carol A. Chapelle)

4. Thank you very much for sending me the respective chapter via fax. The student really just copied most parts out of our article and mainly changed some of the wording. There are very few places where he/she added something minor. However, since the student never clearly acknowledged the source and the way it was used in this chapter I would

regard it as a kind of plagiarism. Clearly, this is not acceptable in any decent scientific work. Thank you very much for taking your job as a reviewer that serious. Unfortunately, not many people are doing it that well. Only if the risk of getting caught really exists (due to serious reviews, like yours) the bad behavior may be limited. (Joerg M. Haake)

5. I found reading the text a slightly eerie experience. It was as if I were reading another draft of something I had written, adapted slightly for a more formal context. It was paraphrased and reshuffled but it was all there. I know that there is a quick reference at the beginning but it is not stated clearly enough that the whole of this section is taken from my article. If we crossed out everything in the work that is not the student's and marked only what was left, I guess very little would survive here. (Vivian J. Cook)

The most striking reaction came from the author who requested that his name be withheld here: he immediately identified X2 as the same person who had submitted a paper to an international conference some time earlier. Asked to review the paper, he discovered that it contained much of his own work without adequate citation. Some of the same material was also in the pages of the dissertation I had sent him. The author preferred not to be named here because of the anonymity of the conference review process.

I submitted these authors' statements and information to the president of the university where the case occurred with the request that their testimony be considered in the assessment. At that time, however, the university had just submitted the exonerating report of the small ad hoc committee to the Research Council to obtain its approval and quickly close the case (see section 5.5.1, tactic 6). The misused authors' statements were not added to the dossier intended for the members of the Research Council. The vicepresident of this university, who chaired the meeting's Research Council in which the case was presented, refused to consider my extra information so he could close the case.

4.4   Can a thesis or doctoral committee be guilty of misconduct?

The final granting of a master's or doctor's degree depends primarily on the committee that evaluates the quality of the thesis or dissertation. If they do their work seriously, if every member takes up his or her academic responsibility and judges according to the standards of the profession, it is unlikely that serious misjudgment or errors will occur. Of course, we can expect committee members to contest particular aspects of the candidate's argument, point out overlooked or underused sources, require parts to be reworked or expanded, and even disagree among themselves, but such a healthy process of evaluation—as long as there are no elements of personal malice—will result in improvement. The final outcome would be a justified decision supported by all, which the candidate genuinely deserves, and which will maintain the status and prestige of a degree granted by the institution in question.

But what if committee members close their eyes to obvious infractions? What if some, or even all, do not read the candidate's work but rather rely on a general impression of "work well done"? What if a member, because of lack of time or interest, simply asks another committee member for his or her assessment and echoes that opinion? What if a member follows the judgment of another out of collegiality or to return a favor? What if several know that the thesis or dissertation is far from finished, or grossly copied from existing sources, yet still accept it as outstanding work? What if political machinations succeed in removing from the committee a member who is not that indulgent?

In X2's case, the immediate and extensive discussion around possible plagiarism instantly diverted attention away from what, to me, was the most fundamental question: Is this work as such, with or without formally recognized plagiarism, acceptable for a doctoral degree? If it is proven that this dissertation is unacceptable because of a basic lack of original research, because of extensive and misleading reuse of sources, and because the announced research was never carried out, shouldn't the responsibility be borne by the members of the doctoral committee who awarded the degree—especially since they judged it "summa cum laude"? Moreover, they reconfirmed their verdict after they were given a chance to review it in the light of my report.

Such behavior on the part of the doctoral committee makes the possible culpability of X2 seem less egregious and that of the committee itself quite large. This student finished his dissertation at a rate that made committee members themselves uneasy by their own admission, composed the dissertation itself with material from others, and never performed the research for which the degree was awarded. Under such circumstances, standard academic procedure dictated that the dissertation advisor, supported by the committee members, reject the work, denounce the process being used, set stringent conditions under which the work must be redone, and then supervise both the process and the result closely. They failed to do these things. The coadvisor, in an e-mail to me, admitted that he was aware of the fundamental problem: The intended investigation of the concept of adaptivity in CALL did not take place and "for reasons that are not very clear to me it had to go faster." Other members of the doctoral committee also confirmed to me—but only in private messages—their awareness of a deep structural problem caused by poor quality and the "rush" to finish the dissertation. But in the committee meetings—insofar as they were held—and in their personal reviews of the written chapters as submitted to them—insofar as this happened—none of them seemed to have displayed the ethical courage or the academic integrity to resist the dissertation advisor's insistence that they play the roles he expected from them. But why?

Equally disturbing is the fact that one of the original members of X2's doctoral committee was quietly removed. This professor, an external expert eminently qualified to evaluate the topic, was included in the original committee, formed in 1995 by a departmental decision. He never received any information about the progress of the dissertation, contrary to the rules that oblige doctoral candidates to report regularly to their committee. He told me afterward he thought the candidate had withdrawn from the program. Three months before the deadline for submitting the dissertation, the dissertation advisor arranged for the replacement of this professor by the person who became the coadvisor. The professor was not informed of this change. He was still unaware of the fact that X2 had defended his dissertation when I told him about it.

The assessment of the work of a thesis or doctoral committee poses peculiar legal problems. In the case of X2, the university president submitted the evaluation of possible plagiarism in the dissertation to the same doctoral committee that had awarded the degree, because, according to him, the country's legal framework has no mechanism for appealing the decision of such a committee as to the quality of the work done.

On the other hand, he also allowed "plagiarism or not" to be evaluated by an external ad hoc committee, as if plagiarism had nothing to do with the quality of the dissertation (see also section 5.3.4). Comparative research on local and national control of degree-granting processes and appeals systems would be welcome with an eye to recommending more homogeneous and legal handling of such assessments. Proper provisions should enable thesis or doctoral committees to be scrutinized and, if need be, their decision overturned and undeserved degrees revoked.

4.5   Can publications become misconduct?

As a reviewer and advisor for several journals (*CALICO Journal, Computer Assisted Language Learning, ReCALL*), I sometimes have to evaluate submissions that show no trace of original research. These articles, mostly written by people who have recently entered the field or dabble in it, often have impressive titles and make use of fashionable jargon. But the articles themselves seldom do more than summarize and reiterate what others have said about a certain subject (though normally with proper citations, quotations, and scores of references). Typically, their contribution is limited to an occasional comment, the posing of a question, the rephrasing of an argument, and a conclusion that further research is desirable.

It should be obvious that I do not include in this criticism high-quality articles summarizing the state of the art of an aspect of a related subdiscipline. All serious researchers in my field of language learning are eager to receive regularly updated information on current international research dealing with such subjects such as voice recognition, intelligent parsing, or human-computer interaction. Balanced and up-to-the-minute overviews answering such questions, written by experts in the field, are treasures in multidisciplinary scholarship.

But the poor-quality articles I refer to are of a different type. They stem from a tradition of student papers in which gathering, summarizing, and commenting on sources constitute the core activity. For students who must first become acquainted with the field itself, this activity can be defended as a justified and valuable learning experience. Yet some researchers seem unable to move beyond that tradition and think they have done scientific research if the article is well structured, filled with technical terms, and replete with references. Such an article, however shallow and trivial, cannot be called misconduct.

However, questions can be raised about the scholars themselves when their curriculum vitae lists only these kinds of contributions, some of which, minimally reworked, are published in a series of unrelated journals and conference proceedings over a period of years. X2's case study provides material for this kind of assessment. In the bibliography of his dissertation, X2 lists his own publications—twelve items published over a period of three years, three of them in journals, eight in conference proceedings, and one in a reader. Most of them are only a few pages long. It was difficult to locate some of them, because they could not be found through normal interlibrary loan requests and were not available through the Internet. Still, I persevered until I found most of them. Comparing them with each other, I discovered that several of these small publications were variants on the same theme, though the impressive titles differed. Moreover, the basis for these related publications was an article by someone else.

In light of these findings, it was not persuasive to read the claim of X2 and his dissertation advisor that my critique of the dissertation was unfounded because of X2's "many publications in outstanding journals and proceedings." They argued that, since these "international publications" had successfully passed "severe peer-reviewing" by "dozens of reviewers," the quality of X2's work was beyond criticism.

I reemphasize that publications as such, even weak ones, do not constitute research misconduct (leaving aside the possible plagiarism in these publications). But isn't the use of such weak publications to prove a nonexistent international prestige, on its face, deception? Isn't it misconduct when the authority of anonymous and distant reviewers is evoked to block the investigation of pressing and obviously apparent local problems?

With all due respect for reviewers (and I am one of them), is it possible that some articles and papers too easily pass the control posts of journals that need to fill their pages and of conferences that need paying participant/attendees? One senses the predicament. Only objective evaluators, thoroughly familiar with the state of the art and with all the publications of the accused, and with a proper mandate, can assess the extent to which the subsequent use of references to these publications becomes deliberate deception, perpetrated to conceal inadequate work and to gain the prestige and monetary rewards associated with academic positions. Even if such an assessment is feasible, it will seldom be requested.

4.6   When do research projects become deceptive?

We may, of course, assume that many, if not most, projects are well intentioned, well prepared, well carried out, and, in the case of student work, well supervised. My focus in this section is on the others.

Some fields and subjects lend themselves easily to the creation of proposals that are attractive to funding agencies at the university, national, or international level. Language technology, for example, combines salient ingredients that speak to the imagination and are understandable to nonspecialists who must assess applications. Among these clearly desirable goals are the significant improvement of foreign-language learning, use of multimedia technology, individualization and intensification of education, and automated translation, in written and even oral form, when communicating in different languages. An American having a telephone conversation with a Chinese person, with immediate oral transposition of the spoken word—who could resist such a promising venture? Moreover, it is easy to formulate such a project convincingly within the limited space on application forms by using the right jargon and promising impressive results.

However, once the project is funded, numerous pitfalls appear. First, the project director, who is usually knowledgeable about only one aspect, must supervise and coordinate the complex facets of interdisciplinary research. Interdepartmental and interuniversity projects are particularly vulnerable in providing adequate coordination because each piece of an intricate project may develop separately and at a different pace. Second, it is difficult to find personnel with expertise and experience in the various subfields. In the case of language technology, such personnel problems span advanced technology, language engineering, language processing, and language learning-methodology. The young graduates applying for such research positions are seldom adequately trained to meet these needs because the programs in many departments seldom offer training aimed at building interdisciplinary expertise, nor is the project director equipped to steer them properly in many cases. If specialized researchers can be found, it may be difficult to keep them long enough to guarantee continuity, because they may be in high demand elsewhere and can easily leave a project where they have no career opportunities. Next, especially in research involving computer applications, hardware and software are evolving at a rapid pace, making some achievements obsolete even before they are finished. Finally, in the case of educational applications, it is easy to grossly underestimate the difficulty of developing sufficient content: the framework is only one aspect, while the development of subject matter is time-consuming. Meanwhile, there is the pressure of deadlines to contend with.

If these challenges are tackled courageously and reported honestly, there is no misconduct. Even an unsuccessful academic project can constitute a valuable learning experience. But critical questions should be raised at each phase of projects that are doomed to fail. It is possible to argue that faculty members who apply for project funding are being irresponsible and deceitful when they ask for money to finance projects that they are incapable of bringing to fruition. Even if the faculty researchers are genuinely overoptimistic during the application process, the same generosity in evaluating their motives cannot be applied when, during the course of a project, it becomes clear that the objectives cannot be reached and they resort to such cover-up techniques as manipulating objectives and data, and grossly embellishing progress reports. And unquestionably, it is misconduct at the completion of the project to produce a final report composed of a clever introduction and conclusion summarizing irrelevant data, in which the authors cite their own impressively titled publications. Equally unacceptable are efforts to convince readers that the project led to valuable results waiting for further implementation, or, worse, that funding a new project will advance knowledge significantly in the same area.

4.7   When do educational media become deceptive?

Many educational projects since the 1980s have included the production of new media to enhance learning—videodiscs, courseware, distance-learning packages, and so on. If I limit myself to courseware for language learning, criteria for evaluating the quality of such products have been with us for quite some time (see, among others, Bonekemp 1994; Chapelle 1997; Cohen 1983; Decoo 1984; England 1984; Fetter 1984; Hubbard 1987, 1988; Kenning 1991; Knowles 1992; Levy and Farrugia 1988; L'Huillier 1990; Murray and Barnes 1998; Poulsen 1990). This is not the place to discuss such norms, but we ought to stress their value in connection with our subject. Many producers and users of courseware have learned to profit from these criteria, which are meant to refine our analytical perceptiveness and to improve quality. We also recognize that these criteria evolve over time as the capabilities of hardware and software evolve, and with new insights into learning and into human-computer interaction.

However, the application of these criteria should also help us differentiate between courseware of dubious quality and courseware that is deliberately deceitful. Low quality is regrettable but not reprehensible. The assessment of deceit, on the other hand, could be centered around the following criterion: What is the degree of discrepancy between what an author or promoter says or writes about an educational product and the actual capabilities of this product? In applying this criterion, we need to differentiate between commercially made and presented products (with the promotional language and advertising hyperbole that are endemic in such presentations) and products presented in an academic environment as a result of research. The latter could more easily be implicated in misconduct when there is discrepancy between representation and reality.

Subquestions of the following nature could be asked:

- What terms are used to describe the state of the educational medium ("almost finished," "ready to be launched," "ready as prototype," "used with pilot groups") and to what extent are these descriptions true? (See section 3.7 for a discussion of invisible, or purportedly existing, or utopian courseware.)
- Does the quantity and scope of the content in the medium really exist as announced to reach the objectives for the intended target group? Or is it "emptyware," cobbled together just for demonstration purposes?
- To what extent are affective statements such as "the students are really excited about it" or "the users love to work with it" based on scientifically valid evaluation?

• To what extent are efficacy statements such as "the results have really improved" or "the students perform better" based on scientifically valid evaluation?

Another series of questions pertains to the possible infringement on copyrights in terms of user-interface design, content, or source code (see section 2.5).

4.8   When does ignorance become misconduct?

Science, by definition, must allow latitude for different opinions and interpretations, for fundamental disagreements, and even for honest errors. All of us would also agree that it is almost impossible to be aware of all the research done elsewhere on a particular subject. It can be invigorating or frustrating to discover, after having spent months on a particular question, that someone else has been studying the same problem. But isn't there a point where total ignorance of major achievements becomes unacceptable? Astronomers would never dare to announce now that they have discovered Pluto. We cannot imagine serious scientists declaring that they envision a unique way to fly that will replace the hot-air balloon—an invention they propose to call an airplane.

But cases just as blatant happen in research investigations, especially in new interdisciplinary fields. Some people enter such field as if it were a cheap marketplace, reinvent the wheel, make categorical statements without any knowledge of the preceding research, and expect to be recognized as experts. Though ignorance based on naïveté is not misconduct, it may become misbehavior if the person making preposterous assertions uses a position of academic authority or the framework of funded research to justify himself or herself or the results, rather than letting the research speak for itself and accepting the judgment of qualified peers.

In his 1998 dissertation, X2 states: "While, to our knowledge, no other AHS [adaptive hypermedia systems] formalism has, as yet, ever been applied to language tutoring, what ultimately makes the proposed CALLware [i.e., X2's system] unique in its genre, [is that] few, and mainly very recent, examples of CALL systems based on the communicative approach do actually exist" (X2, 141).

In section 3.7, I analyzed X2's proposed courseware, concluding that the program's blueprint is both primitive and defective. What is the appropriate response when such a program is presented as a "unique" system that, allegedly for the first time in the history of computer-assisted language learning, implements real adaptivity, is based on a sound learning theory, and even throws "a new light on the long-standing controversy within SLA [second-language acquisition] theorists" (X2, 144)?

4.9   Assessing hidden motives

Although research and publications must be judged on their merits, the question of hidden motives must also be considered in cases where the actual results are so anomalous. Why would a faculty member help, or even allow a colleague to cheat? Why would someone vote in favor of an obviously poorly qualified candidate? Why would a professor close his eyes when a student plagiarizes whole pages from one of his own publications? Why would members of a doctoral committee be willing to sustain their chair, when they acknowledge in private that they disagree with him?

The academic world is based, perhaps even more than other areas of the workplace, on a system of dependencies: nominations, elections, promotions, positions on committees and in scientific organizations, research and travel grants, prizes, and awards. It creates a network of fidelity and mutual obligations, sometimes reinforced by political and ideological allegiances.

These dynamics create a web of hidden motives behind decisions. Many know about these motives, but their impact can seldom be proven. In the realm of academic misconduct, each of the main contestants, whether whistle-blower or accused, has a lot to whisper about.

4.10   Conclusion

Assessment raises the fundamental question of unambiguous standards, as the result of professional agreement on norms and criteria.

The ambiguity of actual cases calls for the application of judgment based on the standards of ethical practice of the relevant community of scientists. Any definition that does not recognize the need for that kind of judgment in individual cases will in the end subject the accused scientist to legal standards taken from some other source. One of the major issues in defining misconduct in science is whether scientists can continue to be judged according to the scientific community's own standards of practice. (Buzzelli 1996:I)

At this point, it is important to reiterate that I have treated assessment as a phase between analysis and reporting. This sequence underlines the importance for the whistle-blower of assessing the apparent misconduct as carefully as possible before reporting. But, as is obvious from the description and context of some of the material covered in this chapter, a number of assessment elements pertain more, or even uniquely, to persons, committees, or official bodies after the whistle-blower's initial reporting.

5

Reporting and Handling

5.1 Introduction

Once the alleged research misconduct has been detected and, if possible, analyzed and carefully assessed as to its magnitude and provability, the whistle-blower—who is not actually a whistle-blower at this point—will face a major decision: Should he or she report it? It is essential to realize that such a decision can literally change the course of that person's life, as well as the life of the accused, for the way the matter is handled from that point on can have far-reaching implications, well beyond what one might expect.

5.2 Should one report misconduct?

Professional ethics would require a resounding "yes" to this seemingly rhetorical question. The reality is more complex.

5.2.1 Arguments against reporting

Whatever happens, whatever you see, don't file scientific misconduct charges. Don't even think about it. It's not worth it. Science isn't ready to deal with it. (Williams 1994:I)

Arguing against reporting is Jeff Williams, one of the most outspoken defenders of scientific ethics. His counsel not to report, from his testimony at the Ryan Congressional Commission on Research Integrity Hearing in 1994, is the result of his experience during a long ordeal of retaliation against him for whistle-blowing.

Even in the case of blatant cheating by students, many professors decide not to confront the student or report the cheating to university authorities, as various testimonies show (Schneider 1999). The reasons for this lack of action include unwillingness to devote time and energy to the issue, reluctance to undergo an emotional confrontation, and fear of retaliation by the student, of losing students, of being accused of harassment or discrimination, and even of being sued for these offenses and/or defamation of character.

Further, there is a widespread perception among faculty members that the university administration will not support them in such accusations: "A spate of cheating scandals has shaken professorial confidence in the effectiveness of university judicial panels. Scholars claim they're getting shafted by the system. Guilty verdicts are being overturned. Administrators, fearful of lawsuits or bad publicity, back down when challenged by litigious students. Professors who push to penalize cheaters somehow find themselves tied to the whipping post" (Schneider 1999:I).

One researcher has suggested that colleges and universities are reluctant to confront students about cheating because there has been a fundamental shift from a view that education is "enhancement" to the perspective that it is a consumer product, purchased by paying tuition:

If education is a product to be bought and sold, and each of us involved in the educational process, teachers and students alike, are construed simply as atomistic individuals following our own self-interest, then on this economic model cheating may indeed be an "efficient" way of the student attaining the best payoff, the highest grade, on his or her investment, while an instructor's "making waves" serves no one's interest and is counterproductive to maximizing the institution's profits. (Hawkins 1999)

If a professor who discovers plagiarism perceives that accusations directed at misbehaving students (on the lower end of the academic hierarchy) will not find administrative support, then accusations leveled at a faculty member (higher up in the hierarchy) become even more troublesome and hazardous. To accuse a colleague of academic misconduct goes against the unwritten law of collegiality and mutual protection. The whistle-blower will be suspected of other motives, such as professional jealousy or a conflict of interest. And, indeed, such motives have in some cases led to unfair accusations.

What sometimes begins as a simple critique becomes a long and lonesome crusade that turns into an emotional and professional nightmare. A whistle-blower may intend only to express concern or to warn, but academic misconduct is a hot topic, and the tone and the dimensions of the dispute may quickly rise to unwanted dramatic heights.

In a reaction to the National Academy of Sciences' standard that an observer has an "unmistakable obligation" to speak out against misconduct (see next section), Hoke (1995b:I) calls such counsel "facile, even irresponsible" when it is given to young researchers. Veteran whistle-blowers know the high price of following those moral maxims. As Bird and Hoffman-Kim (1998) put it: "Damned if you do, damned if you don't."

5.2.2   Arguments in favor of reporting

Someone who has witnessed misconduct has an unmistakable obligation to act. (National Academy of Sciences 1995:I)

The sentence above comes from one of the most widely used and most highly recommended booklets for beginning scientists, *On Being a Scientist: Responsible Conduct in Research*. The chapter on "Responding to Violations of Ethical Standards" makes it clear that not reporting misconduct is almost as serious as the misconduct itself.

The following, equally clear quotation comes from "a proposed policy that urges faculty members to take action if they believe that one of their colleagues has violated standards of professional conduct," by the American Association of University Professors:

The American Association of University Professors has long emphasized the obligations assumed by all members of the academic profession, including their responsibility to practice intellectual honesty in teaching and research and not to discriminate against or harass students, colleagues, or other members of the university community. Occasions arise, however, when professors have reason to believe that a faculty colleague has violated standards of professional behavior. When that occurs, professors should take the initiative to inquire about or to protest against apparently unethical conduct. (American Association of University Professors 1998:I)

We can only agree that integrity requires misconduct to be reported. It is an essential part of one's academic duty as described by Donald Kennedy (1997). Surely neither concern about personal convenience nor fear of libel suits should deter us. Yet some who have gone through the process warn potential whistle-blowers to report only if they have tenure and the highest rank and if they are close to retirement.

5.3   The whistle-blower

A key player in any occurrence of academic misconduct is the whistle-blower. The term has an unceremonious ring to it, but it has become, at least in the United States, an official expression for the informant of misbehavior in the public domain. Though the whistle-blower is usually an individual who happened to have witnessed wrongdoings and reports them on his own initiative, the term may also apply to inspectors or assessors whose professional duty it is to control procedures and expenditures. In the following sections I will concentrate on the nonprofessional whistle-blower—that is, the person who, usually unexpectedly and without preparation, is launched into this often grueling activity.

5.3.1   General profile

Some think of a whistle-blower as a chronic grumbler, or faultfinder, or even worse, a jealous individual who makes allegations in bad faith in order to destroy a competitor. However, according to Hoke (1995a:I), research indicates that academic whistle-blowers "are, in fact, people who believe in fairness and playing by the rules." In his article, Hoke interviewed Myron Glazer, coauthor of *The Whistleblowers* (1989), who declared: "The people we studied tended to be very strong-minded, committed people, and people who believed in the system, who believed that if they raised an issue, there would be a reasonable response. They were not alienated or radical or critics of the system, but rather true believers in the system" (Hoke 1995b:I).

Within the group of whistle-blowers, personalities will differ, from the apprehensive struggler with the inner voice that whispers "speak out," to the ethical knight who wishes to combat evil. But, in the latter case, at what point does the sincere feeling of obligation to speak up become a longing for more sensational revelations? The scientific community will accept a whistle-blower on the first occasion but may not accept subsequent or repeated accusations. In this sense Ned Feder and Walter W.

Stewart became controversial figures, viewed by some as brave watch-dogs protecting the whole of academia, by others as "self-serving science vigilantes" injuring the reputation of others (Hoke 1995a:1). A similar controversy swirls around Michael Burlingame, whose repeated criticism of plagiarized publications has led to negative reactions ("Not-So-Civil" 2000). It is also interesting to notice that such persons, once their involvement is publicly known, become lightning rods, attracting other cases. It did not take long before Burlingame was involved in a new case (Basinger 2000). Indeed, people who discover improprieties, and who are uncertain what to do with their discovery or who did not obtain a satisfactory response, sometimes send their information to a known whistle-blower. This person is drawn, perhaps unwittingly, into the role of misconduct expert.

Another group of whistle-blowers include the vindicators, who, out of professional jealousy or from an unworthy desire to hurt or to take revenge, will seize an opportunity to attack a colleague. Their favorite tactic is the immediate revelation of the charges, in a sensationalist or controversial paper or journal. Their preferred target is a top-profile person: a university president, dean, or prestigious scientist. The attack becomes all the more despicable when it is evident that the allegations are based on very few errors, on uncharacteristic slovenliness, or on genuinely ambiguous evidence. On top of that, the attacker sometimes chooses to remain anonymous. I remember a case in which a university president had failed, during a public speech later published and distributed to the faculty, to clearly delineate every quotation from an author, though he had indicated the general source of his inspiration. A professor at the same university documented the revelation of "plagiarism" in a contro-versial journal known for its antagonistic attitude toward that university. Such an approach lacks credibility.

Finally, there is the case of the bad-faith whistle-blower, who uses un-true or grossly exaggerated allegations to maliciously attack an opponent. Such instances, however, seem rare.

Once people become whistle-blowers, they seem to lose confidence in the academic environment. Disillusioned and wary, they may, even against their own better judgment, be perpetually on the lookout for new cases.

5.3.2   Personal and professional risks

What really happens when one does report is hardly encouraging. There are many more accounts of people claiming to have been harassed or punished for having reported misconduct than there are accounts with a happy ending for the whistle-blowers (see Basinger 1998; Duggins 1998; Elster 1998; Glazer and Glazer 1989; Gunsalus 1998a; Lubalin and Matheson 1999; Mangan 1997; Miceli and Near 1992; Reynolds 1998; Schmidt 1998; Schneider 1998).

McCutchen (1993:12) sums it up as follows: "Influence and fear permeate our profession. Disagree with a top figure in your field, and you may be unpublished and grantless. When someone blows a whistle, the truth of the charge comes second. What counts is whether it offends the powerful. The system sees the mere act of whistle-blowing as disrespect. The charge, whatever it is, will be found wanting, and the whistle-blower punished."

The negative consequences can be subsumed under three headings: the lingering controversy, a legal response in the form of a lawsuit, and indirect reactions in the form of underhanded retaliation.

The lingering controversy

Those accused of academic misconduct are entitled to defend themselves. One defense is denial of the allegations; another is to give justification for the occurrences, or to minimize them by claiming misunderstanding or oversight. Such responses by the accused bring the matter into the realm of interpretation of the facts and of subjective appraisal. The whistle-blower will feel obliged to react again, which starts a heated exchange of time-consuming replies and counterripostes. These exchanges become enmeshed in details focusing on issues outside the alleged misconduct itself. To outsiders, the battle looks like a personal academic feud, wearying and irrelevant to the nonparticipants. The institution will typically be willing to let the matter evolve in such a direction, for a collision between individual viewpoints requires no institutional investigation with its accompanying negative public attention.

Sometimes the personality of the whistle-blower, or the whistle-blower's motives in "attacking" a colleague, becomes the issue, instead of the allegation. Or the professional competence of the whistle-blower is questioned.

In these kinds of controversies, there is seldom a winner. The whistle-blower will feel abandoned, committed to conducting a long and lonely battle without the institutional support he or she expected. The accused person will feel unjustly assaulted and tarnished by the allegations.

Lawsuits

An allegation of academic misconduct is defamatory. One of the strongest answers of the accused—though emotional, unintelligent, and usually ill-advised—is immediately filing a civil suit for defamation, because the accused genuinely feels innocent and reacts in the most defensive way possible, or hopes to win the case against all odds, or wants to intimidate the whistle-blower into withdrawing the allegation, or wants to rechannel the whistle-blower's and the public's attention from the facts of the case into the expensive and emotionally erosive processes of lengthy legal proceedings.

If the whistle-blower has acted in good faith and has been careful in following recommended procedures (see section 5.4), a defamation claim normally has no chance of succeeding, even if the alleged misconduct ultimately proves untrue. First, whistle-blowers have a moral and professional obligation to speak out (see section 5.2.2). Second, whistle-blowers are considered to possess a "conditional privilege" to disclose information, which explicitly protects them from defamation claims. In countries using a Western legal code, the conditional privilege in a defamation suit is a privilege accorded by common law. However, this privilege may not constitute valid legal advice in all circumstances. Also, there are secondary consequences. For example, an appeals case in the United States has shown that a university can fire a faculty member believed to have falsely accused a colleague (Wilson 1999). In another case two professors won a defamation suit because the accusation of plagiarism was not handled appropriately (Yachnin 2001).

The whistle-blower who brings the matter to the attention of the media or to a broad range of outsiders loses this conditional privilege. However, such publicity still does not mean that a defamation suit against the whistle-blower will be successful. The whistle-blower who is certain of the case can make the matter public, even in a sensational way, without fear of losing a defamation suit, though such an action would be viewed as unprofessional. The whistle-blower can evoke his or her right of free speech, with the accused being expected to likewise answer publicly rather than resorting to legal action.

The whistle-blower who makes allegations in bad faith—that is knowing these allegations are false—also loses this conditional privilege. However, the burden of proof that the allegations are both false and were made in the knowledge that they are false normally falls on the person who claims that he or she has been defamed.

In spite of the legal protection the whistle-blower normally enjoys, the fear of a defamation suit no doubt deters potential whistle-blowers. Many find that even the threat of being sued is frightening, while the financial uncertainties related to a lawsuit give genuine pause to someone living on an academic salary. Moreover, changes in policies and the subsequent legal assessments seem to be creating more uncertainties and ambiguities. For the situation in the United States, I advise those interested in current developments to contact the ORI or the American Association for the Advancement of Science, which follow up on these issues through publications and conferences.

Underhanded retaliation

Accounts of academic misconduct cases often describe ways in which the accused, their allies, and even the institution itself retaliate against the whistle-blower, not as explicit punishment for the allegations, but indirectly.

The more serious consequences include loss of research funding, denial of tenure or promotion, and even the loss of academic position. Such repercussions do not come immediately. The problem is that a whistle-blower is led to begin a (hopeless) battle against the system after obtaining an initially unsatisfactory response to the allegations. Driven by indignation and a sense of justice, the whistle-blower intensifies the campaign, maneuvering into an impossible position. The actions taken against him or her will never be identified as retaliation, but will be explained on other grounds, justified or not: insufficient scholarly publication for advancement or tenure, insufficient student enrollment to justify continued funding of the position, a decline in financial resources for funding research, and so forth. Reports of such cases are given by Basinger 1998; Duggins 1998; Elster 1998.

Whistle-blowers also mention less identifiable punishments such as social shunning, lukewarm performance appraisals, delays in reviews and in approvals for proposals, and various forms of petty harassment.

In a study of underhanded retaliation in academia, Swazey, Anderson, and Louis (1993) canvassed 2,000 doctoral candidates and 2,000 graduate faculty. Fifty-three percent of the students and 26 percent of the faculty felt that reporting misconduct would result in retaliation. Not surprisingly, junior faculty members perceived themselves as more vulnerable to retaliation than senior members.

The ORI commissioned a study of the negative consequences for the whistle-blower (Research Triangle Institute 1995). Only 31 percent of the respondents reported no consequences for blowing the whistle, leaving more than two-thirds who felt that they had been the targets of retaliation. Some of the specific results that their respondents reported were:

Pressured to drop the allegation	43%
Subjected to counterallegations	40%
Ostracized by colleagues	25%
Research support reduced	21%
Fired	12%
Position not renewed	12%
Advancement denied	7%
Tenure denied	9%

When asked who was responsible for these actions, 37 percent of the respondents blamed the accused, 22 percent their colleagues, 14 percent the dean, 13 percent the department chair, and 10 percent administrators of the university.

5.3.3   Protection from retaliation

In 1977 the Government Accountability Project (GAP) was created in the United States to protect and provide legal counsel to employees who speak out on misconduct. Its booklet *Courage without Martyrdom: A Survival Guide for Whistleblowers* (Stewart, Devine, and Rasor 1989) is a functional guide, characterized by down-to-earth realism. Another landmark was the adoption of the Whistle-Blower Protection Act of 1989. After a number of dramatic academic misconduct cases in the 1980s and early 1990s, this act explicitly extended protection against retaliation to academic whistle-blowers. The 1993 Congress NIH Revitalization Act deals with retaliation in research institutions. As a result of this, but seven years later, the Department of Health and Human Services (DHHS) proposed new regulations to protect academic whistle-blowers from retaliation. These oblige universities to establish written procedures for handling allegations of retaliation (Department of Health and Human Services 2000). But already in 1995 the ORI had published its *Guidelines for Institutions and Whistleblowers*, which requires that institutions receiving research grants establish protections for whistle-blowers.

A similar concern for the whistle-blower is found in scientific organizations outside the United States, such as the Deutsche Forschungsgemeinschaft and Max-Planck-Gesellschaft in Germany, both of which suggest ways of keeping the whistle-blower's name confidential (Deutsche Forschungsgemeinschaft 1998:I; Max-Planck-Gesellschaft 1995:I).

In many instances, however, anonymity is impossible, as when the whistle-blower is the most obvious person to have noticed the incriminating data. Strict confidentiality is hard to preserve if more than one person is aware of a matter so prone to rumors. Underhanded retaliation, moreover, is by definition subtle. It evades clear identification and may occur months or even years after the whistle-blowing.

5.3.4   My experience as a whistle-blower

My reporting the cases of X1 and X2 led to different consequences, because the two cases were handled differently. The first case, though painful, was all in all a satisfying experience. The matter was handled with much care and even charity by those responsible for following up. At no point did I receive negative comments. On the contrary, X1 and I exchanged respectful notes while the assessment, reporting, and handling were going on, even counseling each other on the proper steps to take and publishing about the matter with each other's agreement. Two years after the events, we had the opportunity to meet in person. We reminisced about those difficult moments and confirmed our respect for each other.

The case of X2 was not so pleasantly resolved and provides telling illustrations of the reactions analyzed and described in the literature on misconduct. At first both X2 and the dissertation advisor reacted vehemently to my report. As is common in such cases, they immediately threatened a lawsuit for defamation, from which the university president successfully discouraged them, knowing such a step would be more detrimental to themselves and to the image of the institution. The vicepresident of the university, who had to fulfill the role of institutional shock absorber, tried to convince me that my allegation was unfounded, arguing that he had found no problem with the dissertation after a cursory reading. He also made sure that the case was quickly "closed" at the level of the Research Council.

Just before that meeting of the Research Council, the dissertation advisor sent an e-mail to its members impugning my motives by saying that I had opted "for a show and for sullying the scientific reputation of a young doctor" and suggesting that my accusations had made the university "an intimidating and menacing environment for world renowned scientists." Such rhetoric provides an example of how a whistle-blower can be misrepresented to the academic community. Such charges are, of course, a form of retaliation.

Indeed, subsequent to the advisor's letter, some members of the Research Council made similar derogatory comments. However, it had not been made clear to them that their own university had asked me to evaluate X2's dissertation and that I had done so discreetly. Nor did they see the text of my analysis. Some members of the council assumed that I had taken it on myself to "publicly accuse" one of theirs. I experienced a shift from "confidential evaluator upon invitation" to "allegation of plagiarism by Prof. Decoo," as the item was listed on the Research Council's agenda. Such a shift provided a distinct warning to any other potential whistle-blower about the probable negative consequences of such an action.

On the other hand, I honestly believe that the university president did what he thought was his duty. Some believe that an officer of the university must deflect scandal from the institution even if it inflicts professional embarrassment on one faculty member. I never felt any antagonism from him, and I should also concede that I have not suffered other retaliation, except possibly the denial of an application for major research funding from the allocation committee, on which the dissertation advisor served. At first there was also some uneasiness and slight ostracism from close colleagues of the dissertation advisor, which I understood to illustrate the threat I represented toward the social cohesion of their department. Such a reaction is a typical phenomenon in the case of a misconduct case against a colleague (Ellison et al. 1985).

But other colleagues called and congratulated me for my courage in reporting, admitting that the conclusion had been "a compromise" to save the institution's reputation. Their words meant a good deal to me in what was a distressing time. However, I cannot be certain that I will not experience some long-term retaliation from the dissertation advisor, an outcome that has occurred in the histories of many other whistle-blowers. My attempts to reach a reconciliation with him have not been successful.

X3's case, on the other hand, was again a positive experience, both for the perpetrator and me. A simple memo from me, genuine apologies from his side, and the case was closed within twenty-four hours (see section 5.4.1, part "Memo to the accused person").

5.4   Recommendations for reporting

Those who discover academic misconduct may react along a continuum depending on their personalities and circumstances. One person may feel extremely uneasy about the matter, pondering alone how and to whom it should be reported, struggling with the fear of the consequences, keeping silent for weeks or months. Another person might react indignantly, formulating an accusation in harsh, incriminating terms and immediately announcing it to others, even to the media. Those at both extremes, and all the variants in between, could profit from a number of recommendations.

5.4.1   Selection of the reporting form
The choice of the form for the initial reporting deserves careful consideration. Many whistle-blowers would have chosen a different form had

they known the consequences of their action and had they understood the alternatives in advance. It is also extremely important to realize that choosing the appropriate reporting form can invite disclosure and apologies from the accused (when guilty), a response that may avert major drama (see section 5.6.1).

The options discussed below are listed, more or less, in order of increasing severity and formality. Some steps can be taken simultaneously or subsequently.

Oral report to a superior

A safe way to report alleged misconduct is to discuss the problem orally and discreetly, in a nonaggressive way, with an academic superior, department chair, dean, or other administrator for academic affairs. This approach has some obvious advantages. No formal complaint is made in writing, and the whistle-blower can ask not to be named in subsequent discussions. It provides more time to evaluate the matter and usually yields advice for possible next steps. In this scenario, the whistle-blower remains in the role of a discreet messenger, leaves the whole affair in the hands of the superior or advisor, and thus shifts the actual complaint to another level. The disadvantage of this discreet-messenger approach is that the whistle-blower, while retaining confidentiality, loses control, and possibly even knowledge, of how the complaint is handled from that point on.

Depending on the nature of the case, written documentation probably must be provided as proof of the misconduct—for example, comparison between texts to show plagiarism. However, these documents need not identify the whistle-blower.

Informative exchange with the accused person

Another low-key approach is to bring the matter up in a private discussion with the person suspected of misconduct to the extent that hierarchical relations allow doing so. Here the whistle-blower can express concern, emphasize that a private approach will limit any personal and professional damage, and/or express the hope that the accused can make the necessary amends, for example, by pledging more care in the future, by withdrawing temporarily from a certain subfield, or by publishing a correction. Possibly such an exchange can take place at the initiative of a superior who has been informed by the whistle-blower and who can serve as mediator in the discussion. Of course, the nature of the offense must permit this approach. In serious cases of misconduct, with external consequences, such a low-key settlement would not be possible and could even be misinterpreted as a cover-up.

Professors who discover a student's misconduct may prefer this low-key approach as a more efficient way to help the student gain ethical insight and develop professional behavior, particularly if it is a first and minor offense and if circumstances warrant it. An agreement can be worked out for the student to make amends without being publicly reprimanded. At the same time professors themselves run less risk of getting involved in a public confrontation with the student or even with an educational system that would rather side with the student than with the professor.

Even if such an approach is not satisfactory because of a negative or combative attitude on the accused's part, it is still a valuable preparatory experience for the whistle-blower. With an eye to other steps, in particular the filing of a written complaint, the whistle-blower may become aware of weak spots in the allegations and aware of unforeseen defenses from the accused. A second conversation, after the emotional shock of the first conversation has waned, may reveal the accused's emerging attitude and possibly new arguments, thus providing valuable information to the whistle-blower in case he or she wants to pursue the matter further.

Moreover, the discussion with the accused allows the whistle-blower to later assure administrators and other university officers that he or she has made an amicable attempt to resolve the problem in private.

Memo to the accused person

If the matter needs to be put in writing, the simplest and most basic approach is a short and almost naïve memo that simply asks questions. I sent X3 (see section 2.3.3) a two-sentence letter that said I had found some interesting pages in his textbook and I wondered if there was any source for the information. The next day the man was in my office, acknowledging his impropriety and apologizing. He knew very well where he had taken the material from and gave the usual excuses: time pressure, loss of the original source, no real misdeed intended, and so on. He promised that the reference to my work would be added in the next edition, and we parted as friends.

The whistle-blower can also write a more substantial memo to the accused, stressing the same arguments used in the informal exchange (see the preceding section)—that is, that this approach is meant to avoid a broader confrontation involving outsiders.

For the whistle-blower the advantage of the memo approach is the creation of a paper trail, providing proof of the date and the content submitted, as well as of the constructive initial approach. This could be important should other developments follow.

Sending a copy of the memo to the appropriate academic superior makes the matter slightly more official and adds some pressure, while still keeping the discussion oriented primarily toward the accused person. However, the risk that the matter will leak out or that the superior will now feel obliged to take action become greater. If the whistle-blower wants a first-phrase approach that is strictly private and confidential, no copy should be sent to any third party.

Circumstances may encourage a whistle-blower to send this report anonymously in view of the risks involved with whistle-blowing (see section 5.3.2). If the tone of the report is basically one of genuine concern, rather than being threatening, and if the report is sent only to the accused, such a procedure can be acceptable, though less desirable. The disadvantage of anonymity is that the accused cannot respond to the whistle-blower or will suspect others of having sent the report. And the author of the memo, if later revealed, could suffer a loss of public esteem, because an anonymous memo may be understood by others as cowardice or even as a prelude to blackmail.

Written report to an institutional official

In submitting the matter in writing to an official party, one leaves the tentative or private realm for the formal arena. The value of this approach is that, from this point on, the institution and not the whistle-blower is obliged to deal with the matter. But in this arena, every word of the report will be scrutinized and every error will be used against the whistle-blower.

It is wise for the whistle-blower to mention explicitly in writing that the report is to be treated confidentially, with the whistle-blower's name left out of further proceedings. There is still a fair chance that the identity of the whistle-blower will leak out, but this explicit request provides a basis for a possible complaint against a breach of confidentiality at a later stage.

The identity of the person to whom the complaint is addressed depends on local circumstances. In the academic environment, it would normally be, as with the oral report, the direct superior, such as a department chair, faculty dean, or any appropriate administrator for academic affairs. Well-organized institutions should have an established protocol for filing complaints of academic misconduct (see section 5.5.2).

Whistle-blowers who feel too insecure or too vulnerable within an institution can consider reporting the matter to outside officials. Democratic countries usually have agencies providing direct help to citizens who want to report an allegation of misconduct, particularly if the case includes misuse of funding. Of course, much will depend on the authority and the experience of such an agency in handling allegations of academic misconduct. If the misconduct took place within the framework of funded research, the funding agency might be the entity to turn to, provided it has procedures for dealing with allegations and can guarantee confidential treatment. In the case of X2, his doctoral work was partly financed by the National Science Foundation of his country, as part of a project on multimedia applications in the modern-language curriculum. However, I did not report the problems to that foundation, because it lacked procedures for channeling allegations of this nature and because my personal experiences with the foundation gave me reason to doubt its objectivity and reliability.

Many people seem to feel that neither universities nor government agencies will ever succeed in providing proper and safe procedures for reporting and handling alleged misconduct. Important funding agencies, like the Deutsche Forschungsgemeinschaft, therefore recommend that the "learned societies" of each scientific field either start or continue the tradition of a "code of conduct" for their members. Though these societies have no legal standing, they can also provide structural opportunities for a whistle-blower to report alleged misconduct to a trustworthy and competent body of academic professionals. After proper investigation, such a group would be able to reprimand confirmed wrongdoers or expose them in a professional journal or on their Internet site. This exposure in itself would constitute professional punishment. For example, the Steering Committee of EURO-PAR conferences did not hesitate to put on the Internet the case of a person who had published seven plagiarized papers and who continued to submit plagiarized papers to conferences (EURO-PAR 1995). See also McKnight 1998 and section 6.2.11.

Published review

If the misconduct involves a recent publication, the whistle-blower may consider submitting a critical review of this publication to a professional journal. Obviously, this option is possible only in certain situations. The critical review brings the matter immediately before a national or even international forum of peers. It tackles more the content than the author. It may have a stronger effect on the overall professional reputation of the person whose work is thus analyzed than a lengthy and uncertain procedure within an institution is likely to have. The accused can respond through the same channel. These public exchanges should not only provide for lively debate but should also act as a warning to the whole profession: researchers must know that they are being watched and that misconduct can be publicized.

5.4.2   Precision in content and caution in tone

Whatever the form of reporting, the allegations must be carefully documented. As previously noted (see chapters 3 and 4), it is necessary to collect the relevant data as cautiously as possible and make a preliminary assessment. One should resist the temptation to make a case with peripheral arguments, engage in hyperbole, or use emotional language. The facts and only the facts, as the result of a conscientious analysis, should be sufficient.

Moreover, even facts can be presented with caution, by using the proper semantics: "In my opinion ...", "From the analysis it appears that ...", "Has the professional convention been respected that dictates that ...?" The whistle-blower should be careful not to accuse, but should try to leave the formulation of definitive conclusions to the readers of the report and to the actual evaluators. For example, in the case of plagiarism, it may be wise not to use that word (which entails a value judgment), but to speak of something like the "obvious resemblance to a source that the author does not quote." As noted (see section 4.3.1), the word *plagiarism* is also so ill defined that it can lead to exoneration, even if the misconduct is evident. A handy way is to use the very definition of the ORI—"substantial unattributed textual copying of another's work ... which materially misleads the ordinary reader regarding the contributions of the author" (see section 4.3.1), but again without using the word *plagiarism*. If the members of an evaluation committee have to concede that the definition is applicable to the case, they can hardly assert that it is not plagiarism.

5.4.3 Discretion

Indiscretion about the allegations weakens the position of the whistle-blower. Indeed, dwelling on the allegations of academic misconduct in conversations and publications is likely to create speculation about the whistle-blower's motives—most likely that he or she is acting out of professional envy or out of a desire to undermine the position of a competitor. This will be especially true if the whistle-blower and the accused are known to be long-time professional rivals or personal adversaries. Moreover, as discussed in the section on lawsuits (see section 5.3.2), the whistle-blower will lose some legal protection by needlessly informing outsiders or the media. Such reactions can greatly diminish the impact of the factual allegations, can shift the discussion from the merits of the case to the motives and personality of the whistle-blower, and can even bring harm to the whistle-blower.

But the basic reason for absolute discretion at the reporting stage is the seriousness of the consequences for the accused. A professional reputation is at stake. The matter can ruin a life. Strict discretion is therefore a key virtue for the whistle-blower. It requires much self-control in a matter that by its very nature is choice material for rumor and gossip. The entity that handles the allegation can decide, in a later step, how much publicity to give the case.

However, it is true that in some cases every other approach has failed and only the act of making a public announcement has been sufficient to trigger the necessary investigations. Goodman (1996) devoted an interesting press article to these "last-resort" reasons for going public and to the interaction between science and the media in misconduct cases.

5.4.4   Joint action

Discretion does not mean that the whistle-blower needs to report alone. The allegation will make a stronger impression if two or more people report it together. Such an approach requires not only a shared conviction about the precise nature and seriousness of the misconduct but also vigilant preparation to guarantee the necessary discretion on the part of several people.

In exceptional cases, a joint reaction may even take the form of a massive protest. In 1997, sixty-five scientists, most from the City University of New York (CUNY), signed a petition accusing a U.S. Public Interest Research Group of fabricating data (Friedly 1997b). Unfortunately, the conspicuousness of a large group of whistle-blowers taking action against a large group of defendants will all too easily be interpreted as a conflict over the interpretation of scientific data, rather than a case of deliberate misconduct.

5.5   The institutional response

Far too many cases of academic institutions that have responded to allegations of misconduct with inadequate and contrived responses are on record. In this section I will first discuss some of the damage-control tactics used by these institutions, then make some recommendations.

5.5.1   Damage control tactics

Administrators of institutions where a case of alleged misconduct becomes manifest usually react in immediate self-defense, as if such a case threatens their scientific reputation.

Tactic 1:   Appraising the odds rather than the case

The first reaction of the university administration will almost certainly be an immediate appraisal of the surrounding variables, rather than of the gravity of the facts. A dominant concern will be the extent of the publicity the case has already received. If the allegations are in the form of an internal confidential report, the administration has much more room to devise a strategy to minimize the effects than if the case is already widely known or has even been made public in the media.

Another important factor involves the stature of the whistle-blower versus that of the accused. An allegation made by a tenured professor with considerable professional prestige against a junior researcher is likely to be treated differently than an allegation made in the opposite direction. If the accusation involves people with some power (including outspoken students), administrators may weigh their range of possible actions against the risk of disturbances on campus, the impact on student enrollment, or the risk of litigation.

Various other factors, still completely independent of the substance of the allegations, also tend to play a role in the initial appraisal. These factors include the importance of the institution that funded the research in which the misconduct occurred, the relationship with private contractors that funded the research, the professional prestige of the department or faculty involved, and the perceived intentions of the whistle-blower and the accused to take further steps or to engage in legal disputation about the case. In the case of X2, I was told that the university administration was particularly interested in what my "next move" could be after I had submitted my report, as well as the possible "next move" of X2 and/or the dissertation advisor. These moves, more than the facts in the report, were to determine the strategy of the institution.

This appraisal by the university administration can be viewed only as a process of selecting the best damage-control strategy.

Tactic 2:   *Minimizing the seriousness of the offense*
Whistle-blowers may have written their report using official language like "research misconduct," "plagiarism," "significant misbehavior that fails to respect the intellectual contributions or property of others," and so on. However, whether the alleged facts fall under one of these categories is a matter of interpretation and assessment (see chapter 4) and opens a wide avenue for the minimization of the accusation. The accused may minimize accusations of plagiarism by referring to "some irregularity in the

citation," while the fabrication of data becomes "a few inaccuracies in recording results," and failure to respect the contribution of others becomes an "oversight." The administration may be willing to go along with these semantic minimizations to defuse the case.

Similarly, an institution may try to describe the complaint as involving a "difference of opinion" between two researchers. The institution may even make statements supporting such "healthy scientific contention," thus relocating the antagonists to the level of blunt but respectable contestants in the academic arena. Eventually the administration or well-meaning colleagues may even ask the whistle-blower to "bury the hatchet," thus totally altering the ethical perspective of the original predicament. Such an approach identifies the whistle-blower as the heart of the problem.

Tactic 3:   Keeping the matter internal

A university that solicits and welcomes external experts to sit on doctoral committees, on review panels for job applicants, or on evaluation boards for curricula and programs may be unwilling to invite outsiders to lead or sit in on an investigation of academic misconduct. However, such an approach lacks fairness toward the parties involved.

A common response is for the president of the institution (or a dean or a chair) to appoint a small committee of trusted members of the administration or the faculty to evaluate the allegations. The selection of these members can be read as an indication of the outcome. Sometimes the administration even requests evaluation from the very person accused of the misconduct or from the department or research group to which the accused belongs.

At some universities, more formal procedures have been established, and the matter is turned over to an appointed group, such as an ethical commission or an academic conduct council. Although this process is an improvement, it is still too likely that the underlying motivation will be to safeguard the reputation of the institution at any cost. Moreover, the outcome will almost certainly look unfair to one of the parties and sometimes to both. The dissatisfied party or parties will find it easy to blame improper internal connections for the outcome.

Tactic 4:   Dealing with the matter secretly

By keeping the handling and the outcome of a misconduct evaluation secret, an institution intends to protect both the whistle-blower and the accused. However, such a system also facilitates cover-ups. In contrast, the legal system is committed to public process and public trials, precisely to minimize the risk of covert manipulations. Moreover, creating a secret is one thing; maintaining it is another. In such a sensitive matter as academic misconduct, it is almost impossible to avoid leaks and rumors, almost always distorted and titillating by nature. Such reports can do more damage than making the deliberations and the outcome public (see for a discussion of this issue Wheeler 1992).

The principles of confidentiality and anonymity, certainly important in the early stages of an investigation, do not mean that the subsequent handling should become a secretive process. Williams (1994:I) argues:

I believe that secrecy is the enemy of truth. The shrouds of confidentiality that are wrapped around all aspects of these misconduct hearings are pernicious. The essence of any system of justice is its openness. Clandestine processes do not serve to protect the community from misinformation; they serve to prevent exposure of mistakes, blunders, and even well-intended errors of those who have the authority to impose the secrecy. Unless legally binding issues of confidentiality are at stake, such as patient records, I believe the hearings should be open.

Tactic 5:   Splitting up the problem to alter the focus

When cases of misconduct are reported, another common tactic is to split up the problem so that the focus can be placed on a debatable issue, while the essential problem is never really evaluated. This phenomenon occurred in the X2 case. My report first identified what I saw as the major issue—that is, that the dissertation lacked any personal research and that none of the announced original work had actually been carried out (see sections 3.4.2 and 3.6.2). The concern about possible plagiarism was a secondary issue in my report. But the university leadership focused exclusively on that issue and requested in writing only an evaluation of "a complaint regarding plagiarism," first from the original doctoral committee, and next from a three-member ad hoc committee. The fundamental problem—whether the dissertation was of sufficient quality to merit a doctoral degree and the resulting liability of the doctoral committee— was never at issue as events unfolded. The dissertation committee was reported to have "reconfirmed [its] decision." Whether only plagiarism or the quality of the dissertation as such was discussed is uncertain, but the official scope of their inquiry, as defined explicitly in the letter of request from the university president, pertained only to plagiarism.

The same limited focus was also assigned to the next group, the ad hoc committee. Responding to this mandate, the committee members began their report by stating that they had not evaluated the quality of the dissertation but only the question of plagiarism. It seemed clear that they explicitly excused themselves from dealing with the fundamental question. They invoked the limited scope of the assignment—to confirm or find against "plagiarism"—and succeeded in turning in an ambivalent report.

The most striking illustration of the usefulness of fragmenting and refocusing the issue came at the next step, when the conclusions were presented to the Research Council. According to the minutes, this council was led to believe that the investigation had actually been conducted on two levels, quality and plagiarism, the first being handled by the original doctoral committee and the second by the ad hoc committee. In fact the doctoral committee had only been asked to consider "a complaint regarding plagiarism."

The history of some famous misconduct cases shows that this shift in focus and the ensuing ambiguities make it possible to dodge the central issue, allowing secondary, debatable matters to take over. Whistle-blowers need to be careful not to get bogged down in arguing about these secondary matters, for it is exactly in such a swamp where, with the university administration's blessing, the case can quietly die.

Tactic 6: Uncovering the case to close it

A somewhat different tactic is to first have a small group, sworn to secrecy, prepare the evaluation, and then, in a rapid succession, submit the report and conclusions of this group to a major council, such as a faculty council, or research council, or the general board of the university. In the course of one large and formal meeting, sometimes taking only a few minutes during consideration of a long agenda of other items, this council or general board acknowledges the report and gives it a stamp of final approval. Although no genuine judgment was made, the apparent "action" of the large board gives the case an authoritative end result that is virtually beyond appeal.

5.5.2   Where and how should a case be handled?

There are those who strongly advocate handling cases of academic misconduct outside the walls of the concerned institution: "Many contemporary experiences emphasise that ad hoc institutional investigating bodies are inappropriate for handling cases of suspected fraud within an institution itself" (Riis 1999:114–115; see also Turner 1999). As Feder and Stewart (1994:I) point out: "If an institution conducts an investigation of wrongdoing within its own walls, a finding of no wrongdoing—even if valid—will often be unconvincing."

A common thread in the literature is that universities should learn to regulate themselves adequately in matters of alleged academic misconduct or outsiders will do it for them (see, e.g., Gunsalus 1993, 1997a; Ryan 1996). Overarching organizations, such as national funding agencies and professional societies, argue for the same principle (see, e.g., Office of Research Integrity 1995; Deutsche Forschungsgemeinschaft 1998). But it is not easy to convince some scientists to accept the necessity of institutionalized procedures within their own walls. Even if they support the principle of proper action against misconduct, scientists display vacillating attitudes and values when it comes to concrete cases. The research by Braxton (1999a) and by Braxton and Bayer (1999) reveals the complexities of individual reactions when it comes to self-regulating the profession.

For example, a Research Council meeting at my own Belgian university heard a proposal to elaborate a clear procedure for reporting and handling academic misconduct. According to the minutes, one of the members reacted by stating that there are not enough cases to justify such a procedure and that each case is so specific that a general procedure would have little value. Another member feared that such a procedure might bring unwelcome attention to misconduct cases and make an "amicable settlement" impossible.

Such individual reactions, no doubt representative of what other professors also think, need to be researched and analyzed because they are fundamental to a better understanding of the obstacles to self-regulation.

Here I will comment only briefly. If there "are not enough cases to justify such a procedure," it may be precisely because safe procedures for reporting are lacking. There are numerous indications that academic misconduct occurs more frequently than is commonly believed (see section 1.3). But even if there are very few cases, the seriousness of the matter when one does occur requires a formal procedure to safeguard all interests, including that of the general good of the institution.

Further, the idea that cases of academic misconduct can be solved by an "amicable settlement" reveals a confusion between academic misconduct and professional disagreements. Misconduct is an offense; because it involves falsification, deception, or misuse of funds, it can be subject to civil trial. In that context, "amicable settlements" are better described as obstruction of justice. Moreover, whistle-blowers, especially if they are at the lower end of the hierarchical ladder, are not in a position to negotiate an "amicable settlement" when they become aware of serious wrongdoings. They need a clear, secure, and confidential conduit within which they can report their concerns. Indeed, the "amicable settlement" will in many cases be another mechanism creating pressure on whistle-blowers to drop their report, thus complying with an administrative cover-up of the allegations.

Finally, keeping cases of academic misconduct secret means a lost opportunity to use them as a deterrent to similar wrongdoing and as an opportunity to educate the scholarly community about ethical problems (see also sections 6.2.1 and 6.3.1).

If institutions are to regulate themselves, the following frequently discussed principles, found in many already-existing procedures, are important:

• Protect the parties involved against unneeded publicity, the good-faith whistle-blower against retaliation, and the accused against a loss of reputation unless and until proven guilty.

• Ensure a swift procedure by setting a timetable.

• Let the matter be investigated and evaluated by a group of external, independent experts, without any personal or professional ties with the antagonists and without any conflict of interest. This item is no doubt the most difficult one for institutions to accept and implement correctly.

- Inform all parties involved of all the data available and keep them immediately informed of any new element.
- Provide all parties with the opportunity for appropriate reactions and hearings.

Still, in view of the botched handling of so many academic misconduct cases, there is serious reason to doubt that most academic institutions are capable of regulating themselves at this point. Furthermore, even if an institution decides to trust the evaluation of a case to an external committee, political maneuvering regarding the choice of the committee members usually predicts what the outcome will be. External arbitrators, if also selected by university administrators, are not necessarily impartial either. One possibility is to leave the choice to an overarching professional organization. Vital criteria in the selection of arbitrators are:

- They should have no ties to the institution involved or to the whistleblower, the accused, or any other person related to the case.
- They need sufficient familiarity with the subject, though not to the extent that they would know the protagonists personally.
- They should have a strong reputation for ethical firmness and evaluative clarity.

5.5.3   What sanctions are applied?

As far as I know, few efforts have been made to coordinate the determination of appropriate sanctions for academic misconduct on an inter-university and international scale. Guidelines and regulations on academic integrity do not include a list of recommended penalties tied to various offenses. If a person is found guilty, a local committee or a few members of the administration decide on a punishment, which is likely to be influenced by subjective factors such as the public visibility of the case, the status of the perpetrator, and the personal relations people have with him or her. This in turn leads to frustration and bitterness if an offender feels he has been treated too harshly in comparison with another or that he has been "sacrificed" because of the visibility of the case. Often the details of the misconduct and of the sanction are kept confidential, making it difficult to research the relation between misconduct and sanction on a wider scale (see also section 7.1.2).

Sanctions may include a warning, a transfer to another unit, denial of tenure or promotion, loss of rank, loss of funds, delayed salary increase, temporary prohibition to conduct new research, and dismissal. Sometimes sanctions are aberrant, like this decision by a university panel in a case of plagiarism: the perpetrator would have to teach undergraduate courses for five years (Cage 1996). Such a decision sends the message that teaching undergraduates is a disgrace. Perhaps more constructive methods could be found, like asking the perpetrator to develop and teach a course on academic ethics.

5.6   The accused

After the whistle-blower, the second key player to be intensely involved is the person charged with the wrongdoing.

5.6.1   Recommendations for the initial stage

Being accused of academic misconduct must be, for nearly everyone, a harrowing experience. Whether guilty or innocent, the defendant is likely to react with denial, anger, and indignation. Such a reaction sets a difficult tone for the rest of the unfolding drama. In an emotional and polarized atmosphere, a process is set in motion that involves more and more people, investigations, reports, and dreadful consequences that may ruin one's life and that of others. There are, no doubt, many perpetrators who deeply regret that they did not respond meekly and apologetically at the earliest stage of a case. They realize now that the matter could have stopped there, while their own emotional reaction and furious defense actually triggered much of the ensuing drama.

Even if they know that there is no real, intended misconduct in their work, accused individuals should realize that there is probably something wrong that needs to be assessed carefully, as long as they can still contain the case. Colleagues of mine who are familiar with the cases of X1 and X2 have commented that both matters could have been handled and closed within a day, had there been a different initial reaction from the accused. Had X1 reacted with sincere apologies and prompt action to provide proper citations to the Australian colleague who sent him a private letter with her concerns, not much more would have happened. Had X2 and his advisor, on receiving my confidential report through the university president, quickly recognized the weaknesses of the dissertation, explained the circumstances, and asked for understanding, the matter would have been handled very differently. Many whistle-blowers would be happy with a considerate response followed by professional corrections.

People who are justly accused of academic misconduct should therefore understand that it may be in their best interest to simply acknowledge the problem and apologize, in the hope that the matter will stop there. A person who honestly confesses and assumes responsibility can count on some sympathy and is less vulnerable to further action. An accused person who denies and fights back, particularly if the facts are undeniably problematic, draws much more attention than needed. And even if some form of fuzzy exoneration is the final outcome of a long procedure, the price paid along the way may have been too high.

Some try to mitigate culpability by pointing to circumstances and other people: time pressures, lack of proper equipment, defective data processing, changes in personnel, dependency on an inadequate researcher, and so on. Such problems are understandable, as long as they are not presented as justifications and as long as the final word is a genuine admission of liability.

It should be noted, however, that in the case of certain institutional procedures, even the accused's quick recognition of the problem and apologies will not automatically lead to a slap on the wrist and a closed case. The procedure may require the registration of definite findings of misconduct in a certain format, assessment by a proper investigative panel, and the implementation of appropriate action. Moreover, the law may require that the matter be reported to a higher authority, for instance, in the United States, on the basis of the Health Research Extension Act (Office of Research Integrity 1999). The subsequent oversight review of the ORI pertaining to misconduct cases in research programs of the Public Health Service may also require that the case be published and be available for consultation on its Internet site.

Of course, there are cases in which someone is totally innocent, not even responsible for an error. If the accusation is simply gratuitous, made in bad faith to harm an opponent, or as part of some form of retaliation, it is essential that such an injustice be countered by all the appropriate means. But even in such a case, the accused should take time to reflect and perhaps seek advice about how to limit the risk of needless controversy and escalating damage.

5.6.2 Protecting the rights of the accused

An allegation, even if proven untrue, can cost a graduate student or junior researcher a career. A scientist may see a reputation that has taken years to establish ruined in a matter of days. The case may even reach a civil court and result in a negative verdict (for examples, see Basinger 1997; Hoke 1995c; Van Kolfschooten 1993). In view of the seriousness of the consequences, it is obvious that the accused is entitled to a swift, fair, and independent investigation. It is also of the utmost importance that those who are informed observe the strictest confidentiality during the first phase of an allegation. Gillespie (1996) gives some pointed advice in this respect from a department chair's perspective. Lee (1999) provides essential background information for the legal protection of an accused academic. Such matters may go very far and take years to resolve as appeal follows appeal (see, e.g., Wilson 2000).

5.6.3 Coping with guilt and rancor

If sanctions have been imposed and if the matter has been made public, even a confession and an apology may not restore things to normal for the accused. A reputation—which is so sensitive in academia—has been damaged and will take a long time to rebuild. The accused may eventually reach the conclusion that regaining the respect of peers, students, or the general public is impossible. Feelings of vulnerability and judgment by others may be pervasive. On the other hand, as time changes the accused's perspective, he or she may become vulnerable to another reaction and begin minimizing the past misconduct, rationalizing the circumstances, dwelling on the harshness of the punishment, and indulging in feelings of increasing bitterness toward the whistle-blower or against the system that inflicted the sanctions. Calm and objective assessment of the past and the present, sustained by a compassionate and encouraging environment, should help overcome these diverse problems in time.

5.6.4   Exonerated, but not innocent

Except in the case of a bad-faith whistle-blower who viciously accuses without any grounds, an allegation of academic misconduct is sparked by something that seems irregular. This irregularity may be judged through further investigation to be a milder form of "unscientific behavior," due to sloppiness, incompetence, ignorance, uncollegiality, arrogance, time pressures, and so on. A statement of exoneration of misconduct is therefore seldom the same as a confirmation of total innocence. Goodman (1997:I), after reviewing the ORI's annual reports, concluded:

... of the 14 "no misconduct" cases summarized in the 1995 annual report, two respondents ... were completely vindicated. Respondents in the other 12 cases were guilty of sloppy science or a number of dubious behaviors even as they were cleared of official misconduct. One respondent, the report states, "lacked the skill and understanding to properly use experimental methods and to analyze data." Another "had failed to fulfill the responsibilities of a guest editor and had violated the faculty code of conduct by his uncollegial and unethical behavior toward his junior collaborators."

As this report shows, it is difficult for whistle-blowers and evaluators alike to assess the weight of facts situated on the borderline between real misconduct and lesser infractions. No doubt there are cases where, for exactly the same reprehensible actions, but in different places, one person is found guilty of misconduct and another is exonerated or given only a light reprimand.

5.6.5   Innocent, but suffering regardless

To be charged with scientific misconduct when you've spent a chunk of your life doing [research] and never did anything wrong—it hits you in the gut. Being cleared is like being exonerated of the charge of child molestation. (David Plotkin, cited in Goodman 1997:I)

In 1996 the ORI received from the Research Triangle Institute the results of a survey it had commissioned, similar to the survey of whistle-blowers the year before, but focused on "accused but exonerated individuals in research misconduct cases" (Research Triangle Institute 1996). Reportedly 60 percent of these persons suffered the same negative consequences as the whistle-blowers, including missed promotions, delayed salary increases, and even the loss of their position. Among the "less severe" consequences, the Research Triangle Institute report mentions "threatened lawsuits, additional allegations, ostracism, reduction in research or staff support, delays in processing manuscripts or grant applications, and pressure to admit misconduct."

5.7   The responsibility of editors and librarians

For the sake of completeness, I should mention a group that is normally not directly involved in reporting or assessing alleged academic misconduct but that has to deal with the long-term consequences. After false data or plagiarized material have been published, the publications become the purview of editors and librarians. They face difficult decisions with immediate bearing on their clients, sometimes with an impact on generations to come, because fraudulent material has been distributed far and wide and remains available to many who are not aware of the problems. For excellent treatments of this subject, I would refer readers to the book *Stealing into Print* by Marcel LaFollette (1992), to the collection of articles edited by Altman and Hernon (1997), and to Lock (1996b). The ORI also published a guidance document for editors who have to deal with allegations of misconduct (Office of Research Integrity 2000).

5.8   Conclusion

Reporting academic misconduct is not pleasant or thrilling but is a sad duty. In doing so we should, on the one hand, resist the temptation to become a detective in search of the convincing clue or a hunter tracking down quarry. On the other hand, we should not close our eyes but report what needs to be reported. However, it is a good idea to be aware beforehand of the possibilities and implications of our actions.

Looking back over this chapter on reporting and handling, with all the negative repercussions of this process, readers will sense that, even more important than pursuing accusations of misconduct, is avoiding or preventing academic misconduct in the first place. That topic will be the core issue of the next chapter.

6

Prevention

6.1 Introduction

How can scientific misconduct best be prevented: through information, education, and regulations, or through fear of detection and penalties? As far as I know, no experimental research (even if it were feasible) has been conducted to measure the effects of these alternatives. Common sense tells us that both are needed. The following discussion provides a number of suggestions from both approaches.

6.2 Constructive measures

Constructive measures are meant to send a positive signal to the members of the academic community, to raise awareness, and to give helpful hints. I recognize that some of those measures may also have a slightly deterrent dimension, depending on the perspective of who views them.

6.2.1 Providing ethical education

I have referred earlier (see section 5.2.1) to Jeff Williams, outspoken defender of scientific ethics. In his testimony at the Ryan Congressional Commission on Research Integrity Hearing in 1994, he said:

I regret that so much of the emphasis of what comes before hearings such as yours is focused on the downstream consequences of misconduct charges and the mismanagement of the procedures. I believe there is much room for improvement in the instillation of the underlying principles of scientific ethics and respect for the search for truth in the minds of young people coming into science. But that must go hand in hand with the generation of a reliable system that brings hope for justice, once breaches of integrity are encountered. (Williams 1994:I)

No doubt we can all agree with such a strong statement. After all, if academic misconduct occurs, shouldn't the whole academic environment be blamed for not having instilled the principles of ethical conduct?

The Deutsche Forschungsgemeinschaft adds an important element in its *Proposals for Safeguarding Good Scientific Practice*: "Young scientists and scholars can only acquire a firm foundation for assuming their personal responsibility if their more experienced superiors observe such rules of conduct in their own work that allow them to act as role models, and if they have sufficient opportunity to discuss the rules of good scientific practice including their ethical aspects in the widest sense" (Deutsche Forschungsgemeinschaft 1998). This remark reminds us that too often, guidelines for proper conduct are directed toward students and beginning researchers and seldom toward established faculty.

Major efforts to foster ethical education in academia have been undertaken by the Center for Academic Integrity (CAI), situated at Duke University, with a full-fledged program to promote values and behaviors reflecting academic integrity. Their approach is basically constructive, helping to develop appropriate pedagogies and showcasing positive initiatives. It can be seen as a more focused movement within the broader range of centers and organizations fostering ethical conduct, such as the Scientific Freedom, Responsibility and Law Program of the American Association for the Advancement of Science, the Josephson Institute of Ethics, the Centre for Applied Ethics of the University of British Columbia, the Association for Practical and Professional Ethics, the Institute for Global Ethics, the Center for the Teaching and Study of Applied Ethics at the University of Nebraska-Lincoln, the Center for Ethics at Loyola University Chicago, and many other comparable initiatives in various countries. For an excellent article on the inclusion of ethics in graduate education, see Bird 1999.

Though we have the sources, the criteria, and the material for ethical education, the principles must still be inculcated in students and others. An introductory lecture on norms that should be observed or a copy of the honor code at the time of registration is insufficient. Good practices are learned by exposure to role models. It seems, therefore, that the best center for ethical education remains the university department or research unit, provided it is a healthy, cohesive place. There professors, assistants, and students are confronted with daily challenges and decisions in concrete cases appropriate to their discipline. Formally or informally, proper research conduct can be taught on the basis of a coordinated effort by a collegial faculty making use of examples, of the codes of the profession, or of other appropriate publications and guidelines that are discussed and applied. Anderson, Louis, and Earle (1999) studied the effects of three variables—discipline, structure, and department climate—on graduate students' observations of misconduct. They discovered that "climate" is a most important variable: "Departments whose faculty give supportive attention and constructive, prompt, and detailed feedback tend to be places where ethical problems in research and employment are much less common" (Anderson, Louis, and Earle 1999).

McCabe and Pavela (2000) give a number of interesting recommendations to implement ethical education (geared toward students). These include surveying students anonymously to understand the nature and extent of academic dishonesty on campus, modifying honor codes to address the problems, having students play a major role on judicial bodies that assess cases, and letting student leaders raise their voice in favor of academic integrity. McCabe and Pavela (2000:38) adopt a constructive approach: "What students need is creative and courageous leadership, grounded in the belief that students—with proper guidance—should play a vital role in designing and enforcing standards of academic integrity."

6.2.2 Providing practical guidelines

It is one thing to know and articulate the ethical principles; it is sometimes quite another to apply them correctly in a concrete setting. Experience shows that seasoned practitioners as well as students can profit from practical guidelines. A number of professional organizations or public bodies, especially in medical and pharmaceutical research, have long since offered extensive regulations on "good practice." Such guidelines would be helpful in other disciplines as well. On all levels—local research units, laboratories, departments, universities, associations, journals—regular and sufficient attention needs to be paid to practical ways of implementing the standards of academic integrity.

Even so, sometimes the volume and detail of guidelines can be so overwhelming that they are never seriously read. A solution would be to rephrase the core guidelines as a set of questions presented to students and researchers for reflection and discussion. It would be more educational if people are encouraged to think seriously about personal answers rather than merely reading the guidelines. Such questions could include:

· In what form should I record and safeguard data so as to ensure strict objectivity?

· In what form and with what supporting information should I keep all the data for purposes of responding to audits or requirements for replication?

· How can I make sure that there is no ambiguity in my text as to the exact limits of citations and quotations?

· How will I handle the references when I include a source in my text?

And so on.

6.2.3   Providing alternatives to student plagiarism

Because plagiarism is the most common type of student academic misconduct, a few recommendations may be helpful. The primary focus seems to be on telling students how to avoid plagiarizing; more guidelines and training on how to create an acceptable text are needed. From an educational point of view, it may be that assignments to write papers and essays—a strong tradition in many courses—are too difficult and discouraging for the average student. Successfully completing a paper-writing assignment requires a sufficient content base, adequate personal involvement with the topic, and a number of skills that need to be acquired through careful training. These include source finding and source management, assessing the difference between available content and one's own potential input, structuring thought and argument, managing varied structures to express causes, consequences, and objectives, and so on. Many practical publications deal with these issues, but they need to be incorporated into the curriculum. Whenever the topic "no plagiarism" is handled, the positive alternatives need to be treated as well.

Moreover, depending on the discipline, professors could try to avoid assignments that foster plagiarism, such as papers on subjects that lend themselves easily to the collection of existing material. It is better to avoid traditional assignments, such as the evaluation of a book or a system, or a discussion of advantages and disadvantages of a certain approach, especially if those subjects have been amply treated in reviews and other publications. Assignments that require more personal efforts could include a number of precise questions to be answered, the pragmatic evaluation of a recent event or issue, or the elaboration of a personal outline. Pedagogical analysis of generating and implementing such alternatives would be good topics for departmental meeting and inservice training.

6.2.4   Requiring a declaration of intellectual honesty by submitters

Many publishers have a clause in their contract that obliges the author to state that the work is original and that the publisher bears no responsibility in the case of claims of fraud or plagiarism. Editors of journals and conveners of conferences could do more of the same by requiring the submitter to sign a formal declaration that the research on which the article or paper is based is authentic and original and that the text fully respects the ethical code of the profession. The prospect of signing such a commitment—which becomes a legal document—might encourage more authors to think twice before submitting an unethical paper.

6.2.5   Requiring homework from Internet surfers

I have referred earlier (see section 1.4.4) to the problem of academic juveniles who seize on a popular topic for a thesis or dissertation, then submit a speedy request for help on a listserve. The tone and content of such a request often make one suspect the lack of research that has preceded it. Instead of answering right away and providing the inquirer with vital information, bibliographical references, and Internet links, it might be better to first request the following from the person:

- A short overview of what he or she has already done on the topic.
- An overview of sources already explored.
- The name and address of his or her academic supervisor.

This could be standard policy for academic listserves. It would also address another problem: all too often the least specialized members of listserves seem eager to respond to such requests in order to show off a make-believe expertise.

6.2.6   Establishing high standards for accepting papers

The recent expansion of journals, symposia, and conferences provides many venues in which young researchers may submit their work. To the extent that these journals need articles and the conferences need paid participants, quality suffers and misconduct may easily go unnoticed. It is not a good sign when conferences have to extend their submission deadlines and send out urgent calls for papers. The problem is exacerbated by researchers' need to have a paper accepted in order to get funding to attend a conference. Such an environment invites a kind of collusion between inadequate gatekeeping and shoddy work.

This problem is especially obvious in the new interdisciplinary fields, because fresh academic organizations can easily pop up with impressive names and young researchers can enter these associations with little peer advice about and/or control over their work. While such fields reward creativity, ambition, and ingenuity, they may also tolerate charlatans.

A particular problem arises in connection with conference papers. Conferences require potential presenters to submit their proposals many months before the date of the conference. It is not uncommon to submit an abstract of a research effort still in progress (or even in a preliminary stage) at the time of the application. By the time of the conference, the project should have yielded concrete results. However, some research, especially when it deals with complex factors in the hands of less experienced persons, is so challenging and time consuming that the original deadlines cannot be met. The presenter thus has the unpleasant choice of presenting tentative and inconclusive but honest work in progress, withdrawing from the conference, or presenting results not yet obtained. If concrete results are to be shown, an incomplete or even fake demonstration might be used.

Both for conferences and for journals, review committees need to set high standards and act with scientific integrity. Critical questions must be asked. Do reviewers use the same, jointly developed criteria to evaluate an article or a paper? Are conferences set up to attract quality rather than a paying multitude? Can a reviewer judge the quality of a proposal of only a few hundred words? Should a complete copy of the paper be required before the conference?

The preceding remarks should not be misinterpreted. A number of excellent journals and conferences have been doing an admirable job for decades. Others are working hard to raise the standards. But a message must still be sent to the weaker groups that they need to meet higher professional standards.

6.2.7   Weighing authors coming from closed systems

As the field of computer-assisted language learning shows, an interdisciplinary field can be entered from various angles. In this case, ports of entry include language learning, literature, linguistics, pedagogy, psychology, sociology, human-computer interaction, and so on. It is precisely this variety that gives an interdisciplinary field its richness. As long as authors from each of these subfields try to foster mutual understanding, the interdisciplinary field will profit from their input. Of course, we expect them to have at least a minimal knowledge of that field's history and methodologies and to be sufficiently aware of what constitutes state-of-the-art knowledge in it. We would like them to articulate, as clearly as possible, their ideas and insights for moving the interdisciplinary field forward. But we should not be afraid to question authors who enter such a field from a "closed system"—that is, from a peculiar and isolated subfield and who are therefore unable to converse with outsiders because of limited perspectives and the use of specialized jargon.

6.2.8   Connecting interdisciplinary domains

In interdisciplinary fields, it would be helpful to have a semi-institutionalized network connecting a number of journals and organizations, enabling practitioners to refer interdisciplinary articles to specialists from all the relevant disciplines. For example, in the case of a conference on hypertext, a submission on the use of hypertext in language learning could also be evaluated by a reviewer with expertise in computer-assisted language learning. Or a journal on language learning could send a proposed article on human-computer interaction to a specialist in human-computer interaction. In this way, submissions deemed unacceptable in one discipline because of naïveté, errors, or even plagiarism will not be accepted in another, simply because they sound impressive to the uninitiated.

Building such a network is not difficult. An inventory of the disciplines from which an interdisciplinary branch draws, based on submissions as they come in, would provide the starting point; the Internet provides instant access to the main journals and organizations of these disciplines. Most have SIGs—special interest groups—able to provide adequate names. External scholars are normally willing to be included as "related specialists" on an official conference or journal list, presented as an interdisciplinary palette. The publication of such a list is also a deterrent for people looking for easy outlets, because they are made aware of the fact that expert control will check their eventual submissions.

6.2.9   Cataloging progress
In contrast to the natural sciences, where research and discoveries are better circumscribed, reported, and officially recorded, certain subfields in the social sciences and in the humanities are still heterogeneous and disparate. There is a need for strong standard works in these subfields that are updated at regular intervals, that summarize all research done previously within a vast taxonomy of subfields and branches, and that generate an annotated bibliography. Every researcher should be able to situate each submission in relation to the field's state of the art and to show the value added.

6.2.10   Establishing stricter standards for the evaluation of project proposals
Three decades of work in Belgian academia, including membership in research councils and on committees of scientific foundations, have shown me firsthand how sloppily, subjectively, or even dishonestly project proposals are sometimes handled. The same also seems true, to a certain extent, for research programs in the European Union. Major criteria for obtaining project funding seem to be personal or political connections, an eye-catching combination of marketable interdisciplinary novelties, and coincidental or strategic association with an entity that must be funded to maintain social or political balance. The intrinsic quality of the proposal is of less importance. If the proposals are judged by blind review (with the identity of the applicant concealed), subtle hints in project proposals help identify the applicant and may influence the decision. If the identity remains secret, clever make-believe in the proposal may lead to the granting of funds to persons or research units insufficiently qualified to carry out the program.

Naturally, such criticism should not be generalized to all cases. But overall a thorough review of existing evaluation procedures would be welcome. Where needed, stricter standards must be applied that will help committee members assess the value of a proposal in detail. After a first round of blind review, referees should be allowed to ask for more information, to call applicants and assess their true level of expertise, and to evaluate thoroughly the outcomes of previously funded research that the applicant has carried out. If a project is about to be approved for an unknown applicant, a visit and thorough review in loco of the person's facilities and current endeavors would provide better assessments of the likelihood that he or she will successfully complete the project. True, such a procedure requires extra time and money, but it is still cheaper than allocating funding for a lost cause. At the same time stricter norms could be imposed on referees themselves. They must be true experts in the precise field of the proposal's topic. Obligations could include filling out detailed review forms and making well-prepared oral comments on the proposal in committee meeting.

But even if committee members have done a thorough and fair analysis and rendered a truthful recommendation, their reports are usually summarized at a higher level. In some cases the "summary" provides an opportunity to highlight one or two positive or negative elements from an elaborate report and with a little manipulation give a completely different twist to the evaluation. Both on a European level and in national Belgian research programs, I have seen major projects rejected or approved in just that way, against the original recommendations of the experts. Such abuses should be eradicated.

6.2.11   Codes of conduct: making them work

Recommendation 10 of the Deutsche Forschungsgemeinschaft states:

Learned Societies should work out principles of good scientific practice for their area of work, make them binding for their members, and publish them. Learned societies play an important role in establishing common positions of their members, not least on questions of standards and norms of professional conduct in their disciplines, and on ethical guidelines for research.... Such efforts to develop codes of practice are an important element of quality assurance for research and deserve still wider attention. Since European learned societies now exist for many scientific disciplines, it is recommended to pursue discussions of good scientific practice at the European level as well as nationally. (Deutsche Forschungsgemeinschaft 1998)

Looking back over time, this recommendation has, to a certain extent, been implemented since the seventeenth century with the creation of the

royal scientific societies in England and France and the rules they have
established for proper conduct. A search of the Internet sites of many
learned societies today shows a prominent link to their codes of conduct.
The past few years have seen a surge in these kinds of "ethical protocols"
and "codes of conduct." In 2000 the American Association for the Advancement of Science (AAAS) surveyed scientific societies about their
approaches to research misconduct. About 75 percent of them had codes
of conduct; less encouragingly, few societies were apparently able to
specify to what extent the codes were working (Brainard 2000b; see also
DuMez 2000 for a report of the ORI/AAAS conference on this topic).

Indeed, many of these codes do not go beyond obvious suggestions.
Many fail to offer concrete strategies for improving research and safeguarding the profession from misconduct. Most lack useful information
on how alleged cases of misconduct can be reported and how they can be
handled swiftly and effectively.

6.3   Deterrent measures

For this "cynical generation" harsh realism suggests attaching sufficient
importance to deterrence: "... many young scientists we and our friends
have met recently view the required courses and lectures on scientific
conduct as exercises in hypocrisy. The plain fact is that cheating pays—
just don't get caught" (Feder and Stewart 1994).

6.3.1   Making academic misconduct visible

For years the virtual taboo surrounding discussions of child sexual abuse
resulted in continuing suffering for thousands, while allowing the perpetrators to go on exploiting children. When a new attitude of openness
developed, individual cases and population studies emerged, making it
possible to deal more frankly with the problem, to identify and penalize
offenders, and to work on solutions. Growing visibility, the pressure to
report cases, and the creation of laws to protect children, require reporting, and punish offenders no doubt have had some effect as deterrents.
When potential offenders know how much attention will be paid to their
misdeeds and what the consequences will be, it may cut down on the
number of offenses they commit.

In the realm of academic misconduct, a similar evolution seems necessary. It is irresponsible to pretend that such cases are so rare that the matter needs little attention. It is equally reprehensible to keep cases concealed out of fear of retaliation or libel lawsuits. We need to talk about this problem which, in all fields, is "reaching epidemic proportions worldwide" (Desruisseaux 1999).

This book provides an example of the struggle that it takes to even talk about the subject. When its topic was announced on a listserve, I received blunt reactions, one even from the executive board of a major professional organization in my field, that academic misconduct did not warrant a published study. None of the members of that board had seen my manuscript, but they felt that talking about academic misconduct, by drawing attention to practices that are "not widespread," would convey the impression to the uninitiated that the profession is "riddled with dishonesty." Others, however, confirmed a vital need for this kind of study.

6.3.2   Deterring student plagiarism

The following measures are purely deterrent. I have already emphasized the need for constructive solutions in order to prevent student plagiarism (see section 6.2.3).

• Students could be told in advance that plagiarism-detection systems may be applied to their work and that they may be requested to submit their work in digital format to facilitate the application of such detection mechanisms.

• If deemed desirable, the faculty member could demonstrate the result of a sample detection, including the power and speed of electronic exploration in identifying even altered sentences and determining the statistical improbability that such overlap could have occurred by chance.

For a general discussion of measures to deter student cheating as such, see Kerkvliet and Sigmund 1999.

6.3.3   Handling cases swiftly and effectively

If perpetrators know their actions are likely to be minimized or covered up and if previous cases have been suppressed out of fear of bad publicity or lawsuits, the institution has sent a signal that bad behavior pays.

Instead "what is needed is a prompt, fair and effective way to deal with cases of alleged misconduct when they occur" (Feder and Stewart 1994).

Investigative committees have a particular responsibility in taking action. Numerous cases in the literature document whistle-blowers' perceptions of spinelessness from those who were appointed to handle misconduct cases. True, part of the committee's role is to safeguard the rights of the accused, but there seems to be some justice in the view of many whistle-blowers that all too often, committee reports sidestep the crucial issues or obscure them, leaving the whistle-blowers vulnerable to retaliation and ultimately failing to address the ethical problems surrounding the misconduct.

6.3.4 Publishing proven cases

Institutions have a tendency to keep proven cases of misconduct internal. Professional organizations, journal editors, and conference organizers, however, should evaluate the need to publish proven cases of misconduct; certainly recidivism from the perpetrator could move them decisively toward publication. As an example, EURO-PAR '95 published on its Web site the full story of a repetitive plagiarist, with precise identification and references to his articles (EURO-PAR 1995). Evaluation is needed to see if such initiatives deter future plagiarists and also to assess the risks of litigation. On its Web site the ORI publishes the names of those found guilty as well as the details of their cases, under the heading "Findings of Scientific Misconduct." The publication of the case of X1, in which I happened to be involved (see Preface), sent a strong signal to the community of related scholars and, I believe, did some good in raising standards.

On the other hand, it is not so easy to decide when and how to publish misconduct cases. My experiences with X1 and X2 illustrate some of the quandaries. In the case of X1, the finding of plagiarism was definite, even though there were extenuating circumstances. In agreement with X1, the matter was published with his confession and apologies. The case was closed. But the long-term psychological effect of the publication was more devastating personally to X1 then he could have foreseen.

In X2's case, his university exonerated him from the allegations of plagiarism, but the fact remains that the analysis of his work raises serious questions about the standards applied. The private reactions of members of his doctoral committee confirmed the fundamental problem. Moreover, X2 had already been reprimanded by a major professional organization for his unacceptable citation habits, but without public disclosure. My anonymous discussion in this book of his case is a third expression of concern about his research practices. In similar cases, the published presentations identify the protagonists as part of a normal critical debate about professional standards and practices. This openness is painful for accused individuals, but it stirs up a vigorous exchange, allows these individuals to either confess or defend themselves, obliges them to improve future work, and persuades editors and conference committees to watch their proposals more closely. Because X2 remains unidentified, he can continue to use material from his dissertation in the form of conference papers or journal articles without anyone being aware of the questionable background of this material. During the writing of this book, I happened to come across a conference report in which X2 was praised for his "well structured paper" on language acquisition on the World Wide Web. The paper is a mere summary of the dissertation. However, one would hope that the past experience taught him "a good lesson," as one of the members of his own dissertation committee stated (see section 4.3.10) and that his future work will be characterized by improved quality.

As a final consideration in connection with publishing proven cases, I would recommend, if circumstances permit it, public recognition to the whistle-blower. "Thanks to the vigilance and ethical courage of so and so" is a sentence one seldom reads in an academic context.

6.3.5 Calling for help on listserves

Dear members, I found the following paragraphs in a term paper by one of my students. I suspect plagiarism. Does anyone recognize the possible origin of the text?

If students know that this kind of query can be placed on a professional list and sent to specialists all over the world in a matter of minutes, it should have a deterrent effect. Of course, lists could soon be swamped with scores of requests. But it remains to be seen how much such a strategy would catch on and how valuable it might be. If necessary, corrective measures could be taken—for example, lists solely for purposes of plagiarism identification within certain fields could be created, where questionable passages are sent only to professionals willing to look at them.

6.3.6   Revoking degrees

Since 1986, when the Ohio Supreme Court supported Kent State University in revoking the B.A. degrees of two former students, U.S. colleges and universities have become more aware of their power to nullify a diploma if they can prove it was obtained by fraud or deceit. The degree holder must, of course, have the right to a fair hearing. Similar provisions exist in other countries, but cases seem to be rare because they also bring disrepute to the institution and require that complex and sometimes unfamiliar procedures be followed. Moreover, in some countries, academic committees are the highest and only legal entity with the authority to decide on the granting of a diploma and no jurisdiction provides for appeal or reconsideration. It leads to the impression that once a diploma has been granted, nothing can happen any more, even if academic misconduct was involved in obtaining it.

Within an institution's proper legal framework, it might therefore be helpful as a deterrent to include in the academic regulations a provision asserting the institution's right to revoke a diploma at any stage after graduation, if it proves that fraud or error was involved in obtaining the degree. This information should be given adequate publicity so that students are aware of it. If the regulation is applied and a diploma is revoked, the case ought to receive considerable publicity so that it may have its full effect as a deterrent.

Care must be taken to make the relationship between the misconduct and the revoking of the diploma explicit. Otherwise, for example, plagiarism incidents could be confused with situations where a diploma is revoked for other serious misconduct, like a dangerous hazing incident, perpetrated while someone was a student and discovered after the degree had been granted. For a discussion of these issues, see Pavela 1999.

6.4   Conclusion

Obviously, preventive measures will never completely eradicate misconduct. But many steps can be taken to help reduce it. This chapter has outlined a number of suggestions, many of which are already being implemented in one form or another by individual professors, research units, departments, and universities. Still, such initiatives are often linked to specific and temporary circumstances like a misconduct case that suddenly attracts public attention, or they may depend on shifting interests and budgets. In an academic setting, prevention of misconduct should be part of the institution's fundamental mission, regularly discussed and evaluated, like fire prevention in buildings or other, more substantive goals.

7
General Conclusion

Looking back at the circumstances that led to the writing of this book, and at my experiences during the writing process, I must say that the whole endeavor was often painful but always fascinating.

7.1 My core issues

From the many facets of the problem that have been discussed, which ones would I emphasize as core issues?

7.1.1 The need for ethical firmness

Institutions need to realize that it is not detrimental to their reputation when a case of academic misconduct is discovered and handled appropriately. On the contrary, a correct approach and straightforward decisions will reverberate positively. They will act as deterrents and firmly establish the image of the institution as a place where foul play is not tolerated. But if university leaders, on whatever level, are convinced that minimization, exclusive internal handling, or blatant cover-ups are the best ways to safeguard the school's reputation, more harm is done in the long run. Therefore a culture of ethical firmness needs to be actively nurtured, both as a general atmosphere in the minds of all the participants and through explicit guidelines and clear procedures.

This is easier said than done. So many factors work against it—professional solidarity to hide improprieties, fear of retaliation, fear of stigmatization. Or one has an uneasy episode or two in one's own dark closet, so why call for integrity? It is amazing to see how scientists, eager to discover truth and willing to go to great lengths to publicize and defend it, shrug away the need for firmness when it comes to trouble-some cases involving people in their own circle. This attitude has been de-scribed more than once in the literature on misconduct. To quote only one source: "One of the most insidious features of science and academia, more broadly, is that the players show a preference for talking about, rather than action on, offense and offenders. Gossip about, rather than action on, fraud allows people to vent indignation or dissatisfaction yet avoid the due process and accountability of investigation" (Fox 1999:166).

Change must essentially come from the top levels of the institution, through example, messages, incentives, and support; furthermore, it must come in a regular flow. Certainly, our sympathy goes to the lone knights who, driven by a strong sense of justice, try to redress problems from their lower academic plateaus. But without strong institutional endorsement and proper action, they will remain the Don Quixotes of our profession.

7.1.2   The need for coherent and clear evaluations

In spite of firm criteria and standards that could and should be imposed in determining obvious misconduct, it is astonishing to see referees or committees of inquiry turning in a wide range of assessments and sanc-tions for similar or comparable offenses, even within the same discipline. In the case of alleged plagiarism, the very same textual material, copied without attribution, can yield results ranging from exoneration to the termination of employment, depending on the desires and dexterity of those conducting the investigation. This suggests another subject for fur-ther research—that is, comparing plagiarized texts and how they have been appraised for the purpose of identifying incongruities in assessment and making appropriate recommendations for normalizing evaluations. It is ironic that, when it comes to evaluating alleged misconduct, incon-sistencies in the norms applied continue to be rampant in what should be the most objective of environments: academia. Many scientists will do whatever they can to evade judging the conduct of their peers according to scientific norms.

For example, to return to the case of X2, the ad hoc committee came to a conclusion of nonplagiarism, while explicitly confirming that X2's work contained numerous offenses that would usually be thought of as plagiarism and fall under the ORI's definition of plagiarism. Such an evaluation is neither coherent nor clear; it certainly gives the wrong message to future offenders. On the other hand, I saw swift and straightforward action in the case of X1's plagiarism. What made the difference? Basically the climate of the respective institutions involved. Ethical firmness as part of the campus atmosphere will generally lead to coherent and clear evaluations of alleged misconduct.

7.1.3   Regrettable ingenuity in self-justification

From my experience, one of the most appalling aspects of academic misconduct is not that it occurs, but the postfactum ingenuity and rhetoric of the offenders in trivializing their misdeeds, altering the perspective on the problem, denying the facts at issue, and slandering the whistle-blower as a jealous and incompetent contender. Scientists are, for the most part, intelligent and clever. While these traits are definite strengths in their professions, they are less admirable when such inventiveness and rhetorical ingenuity are turned to the service of rationalization and justification.

This problem also seems compounded by the fact that professors, especially as I have witnessed the situation in the European system, are accustomed to privilege and power. They remain largely unchecked by any serious control system. Such autonomy fosters arrogance and sometimes even blindness to undeniable facts. If an atmosphere of integrity is not constantly infused in academia, pride and unscrupulousness are likely to take over.

7.1.4   A lesson applied to myself

I would be remiss if I left the impression in this book that I stand above reproach and speak from a position of pristine academic performance. As I dealt with cases of misconduct, studied the literature, and wrote this book, more than once I felt uneasy in looking back over my own career. I am confident I never indulged in the kind of academic misconduct that deserves whistle blowing, but for three decades I have been part of the system, with its traditions, pressures, and gray zones. Shouldn't I have made it clearer that I was reusing parts of a previous publication in a new one? Wasn't I at times a too-willing participant in creative accounting practices? In the case of coauthorships, shouldn't I have identified the respective input of each author? This book has had a purifying influence on my own professional efforts. We all need to look stringently at ourselves and dare to draw the necessary conclusions about our personal standards of integrity.

7.2   Final recommendations

For the whistle-blower:

- Don't talk openly about what you have discovered.
- Obtain definite evidence.
- Think three times before you blow the whistle.
- Choose the safest reporting channel and reporting form.
- Phrase your report in terms of questions rather than allegations.
- Report facts without emotion or judgment.
- Stick to the essence of the alleged misconduct.
- Request strict confidentiality.
- Give the perpetrator a chance to explain, confess, and apologize.
- Your duty done, do not pursue the matter against the system.

For the accused:

- Recognize why the allegations have been made.
- If you are guilty, even if only slightly, explain, confess, and apologize.
- Swallow your pride and contain the matter while you still can.
- Do not threaten a defamation suit.
- If you are totally innocent, reply in a dignified way.
- Once the matter is over, put it behind you.

For the institution:

- Set clear guidelines and procedures and articulate them frequently.
- Protect the rights of all parties involved.
- Address the problem itself rather than finding ways of defusing it.
- Let external, independent evaluators assess the case.
- In allegations of plagiarism, invite input from the plagiarized author.

· Inform the funding agency.

· After the preliminary investigation, do not keep the subsequent handling secret.

· Make the verdict in confirmed cases public so it can work as a deterrent.

· Help perpetrators make amends and help them restore their credibility.

· Congratulate and thank the whistle-blower.

To prevent academic misconduct in the first place:

· Never throw any of your research data away. Classify and store everything.

· When in doubt about research issues, consult a supervisor and record the answer.

· Whatever you copy-and-paste from whatever source, immediately enclose the material in quotation marks and add precise source references.

· It is safer to quote than to paraphrase in a citation.

· When you cite, make sure the boundaries of the citation are clear.

· Do not alter what your source said.

· If your author uses a quotation or citation from another author, check the original.

· If you are involved in coauthoring, clarify the input of each author.

· Never agree to deadlines you cannot meet.

· Do not give your students easily plagiarizable assignments.

· Do not pad or invent entries in your curriculum vitae.

· Stay away from gray zones—that is, avoid any arrangement you would not openly reveal to outsiders.

7.3   A never-ending story

Scientific researchers are human, faced with temptations, subject to fatigue and frustration, yielding to weaknesses, and struggling with emotions. At the same time the academic world is composed, for the most part, of strong and ambitious personalities working under significant pressure. The ingredients for misconduct will always be present, as much as, if not more so, than in any profession. Writing about academic misconduct will therefore be a never-ending story. When people became aware that I was working on this subject, they began telling me stories and asking questions. Each case has its own peculiarities because so many factual, methodological, social, judicial, and psychological variables can be involved. The realm of academic misconduct is extremely varied, cases will continue to emerge, and the need for practical answers will remain great.

To help prevent cases of misconduct and the dramas related to them, it seemed wise to bring the subject more explicitly to the attention of the profession. It is better to try to prevent misconduct than to cure it—especially because a case of academic misconduct is incurable when it happens. Even if a case is dismissed after an investigation, it usually leaves damage in its wake.

True, talking about academic misconduct seldom draws a sympathetic response. It is like revealing the ugly face of our beloved professional domain, which we would prefer to present as pure and uplifting. But we must learn to be conscious of the dangers and implications of academic misconduct and convey that awareness to others. It is my hope that this volume will help the academic profession better safeguard itself against problems that, when they occur, can be devastating.

Epilogue

In accounts of misconduct cases, listeners and readers are often genuinely interested in the later fate of the alleged perpetrators, not out of voyeurism, but out of a sense of personal projection: If I had been in this case, where would I stand now? Has justice been served? Has the process led to the improvement of the profession? Have tensions been ironed out and was peace restored? Though this book is not meant as a collection of case reports, X1 and especially X2 have been sufficiently present to say a word about their fate. These two cases, already different from the onset and exceedingly different in how they were handled and closed, also led to opposite personal and academic outcomes, at least at present.

X1, whose case was relatively minor, confessed courageously and received sanctions involving the publication of his case and a postponed promotion. The matter apparently has had a positive impact on the work quality of the related professional group. From comments made to me by X1's peers and many friends, the case was concluded honorably. All truly hoped X1 would resume his work and restore his credibility. No barriers were put in his path. In fact, requests to participate in conferences, invitations to submit work to the journal that had published the case, and personal expressions of esteem and confidence were extended to him. But now, several years after the events, it appears that he is still deeply conflicted over the episode, either unable to resolve it on an emotional level that will let him take up his original research again or unwilling to engage in his former specialty, although he has continued other professional activities.

X2, whose work the reader has been able to follow to some extent in this book, denied all charges. His own dissertation committee reconfirmed the summa cum laude designation for the dissertation, and the ad hoc evaluation committee exonerated him of plagiarism. X2, even before the alleged misconduct case was closed, accepted a lectureship at a university in another European country. Reportedly the very reason he completed his dissertation so quickly was the lectureship's application deadline. In his new position X2 deals with interdisciplinary topics in line with his dissertation. X2's dissertation advisor arranged for his protégé to continue a working relation with the original institution, where he is listed among the personnel. X2 probably has a long and prolific career ahead of him. Still the matter seemed to have some good effects. The university concerned, in the aftermath of the case, established a committee on ethics to recommend steps for good scientific procedures and correct citation practices.

Appendix: Cerberus

This more technical appendix is part of the contribution of Jozef Col-
paert dealing with a detection instrument for possible text plagiarism (see
sections 2.3.1 and 2.3.2).

Section A.1 tackles the problem of comparing texts. In section A.2 I
explain the text-comparison mechanisms used. Section A.3 explains the
use of the Cerberus program. Performance aspects are dealt with in section A.4. Because I would like any interested colleagues to continue this
effort, section A.5 presents the program structure.

A.1   Comparing texts

Before beginning to develop Cerberus, I had to conceptualize and specify
its design. Because the user interface had to be straightforward and because there were no other considerations in terms of data access or online
issues, I was able to focus on two topics: application requirements and
text-comparison algorithms.

A.1.1   Application requirements

An effective text-comparison program should comply with the following
input, output, and processing requirements:

· *Input:* The text-comparison program should allow easy conversion
from various formats used in text processing, scanning and OCR, Web
pages (HTML) or downloadable documents (DOC, TXT, PS, or PDF
format). The text-comparison-program interface should allow for typing,
drag and drop, copy-and-paste, and opening files through a common

dialog box. The program should be able to load a considerable amount of data such as a series of articles or entire books. Document preprocessing, frequently used with text indexing for information-retrieval purposes, should be avoided in plagiarism detection, because a text-comparison program should be able to quickly change documents.

• *Output:* The text-comparison program should permit saving the comparison results. The user should be able to filter the results according to relevant result length or matching level.

• *Processing:*

• The user should be able to choose between a fixed-length search string and a search string delimited by a set of characters, such as a space, comma, or period. Working with such delimiters allows definition of the search level.

• Two comparison mechanisms should be provided. On the one hand, a fast perfect-matching routine should allow the user to quickly identify common text clusters. On the other hand, a slower but accurate routine should be able to detect common text clusters that have been altered in some way. These alterations include involuntary typing or scanning errors, or voluntary morphological modifications (for example tense, number, gender, case), changes in word order, punctuation modifications, or sentence transformations as described in section 3.3.3.

• Not only running text, but also names and numbers should be recognizable.

In addition, the text-comparison program I had in mind had to be highly capable but not too sophisticated, in order to remain accessible to as many researchers as possible.

A.1.2   String-matching algorithms

Text comparison is based on search algorithms. Most documented search algorithms are "exact string-matching" or "perfect-matching" algorithms. With exact string-matching, a given search string or pattern (as text selected in document 1) is compared with a "scanning window" in document 2. A scanning window is a text sequence (selected in document 2) that is shifted to the right at every comparison.

The most important difference between search algorithms lies in the way documents are scanned.

The simplest algorithm is the brute-force algorithm: the scanning window is shifted to the right one character at a time. With normal documents, execution speed remains acceptable and the programmer's time is reduced to a minimum. When comparing larger documents or collections of documents, however, execution speed will increasingly hamper efficient text comparison.

The Boyer-Moore algorithm is a popular and perhaps the most efficient string-matching algorithm for common applications. Simplified or advanced versions of this algorithm are often implemented in text editors for the "search" and "replace" commands. It performs the comparison between search string and scanning window from right to left. When a mismatch occurs it shifts the scanning window to the right by the largest value produced by two functions: the bad-character shift (based on the position of c in the search string, c being the character in the scanning window that caused the mismatch) and the good-suffix shift (based on the number of matching characters at the end of the search string).

This algorithm has led to other more complex or advanced algorithms that I will not discuss here. For more information on exact string-matching algorithms, see the site of Christian Charras and Thierry Lecroq at the Université de Rouen.

Another type of string-comparison algorithms are the "approximate string matching algorithms," which look for occurrences of a particular search string or pattern, allowing a number of mismatches. This number is given in advance as comparison parameter. Comparison is done on the basis of binary tree structures or by using length tables (called *arrays* or *matrices*). So-called three-dimensional reconfigurable mesh architectures are frequently used. These and the "fuzzy algorithms" are rather complex routines that demand a strong mathematical background from the programmer. Finding the longest common subsequence between two strings has also become a popular area through new developments in DNA, chromosome, and music plagiarism research.

A brief exploration of string matching as an esoteric but challenging field has revealed the following:

• The Boyer-Moore algorithm is very powerful for perfect matching and can be implemented by any programmer. When programming in the Windows environment, the Windows "Find" function (reportedly based on the Boyer-Moore algorithm) can hardly be surpassed in execution speed and implementability.

• For approximate matching, complex mathematical routines do not always yield operational systems. Usefulness depends on programming effort, preprocessing time, and execution speed.

• In general, it seems that the structure of natural language as a redundant, multilayered, and stochastic organism has not yet been fully exploited. Many interesting linguistic research topics in this area still await investigation.

• The trade-off between programmer's time and performance (execution speed and quality) will determine the choice of an algorithm. The basic questions are:

• What amount of data do we want to compare?

• How long do we want to wait for the results?

• What is the desired degree of approximation (similarity) between two strings?

• What is the expected development and implementation time?

A.2   Cerberus text-comparison mechanisms

This section details the concept of the Cerberus application. It is based on two mechanisms: search string delimitation (fixed length or character set) and comparison mode (perfect or relative matching). I will also explain how the concept of matching degree function for relative matching should be interpreted.

A.2.1   Search-string delimitation

The search string or pattern, as a specific string selected in document 1, can be defined on the basis of fixed length or on the basis of a particular set of delimiters. Fixed-length delimitation offers the advantage of allowing both very short and very long search strings. Character delimitation, on the other hand, has more linguistic relevance: if spaces are used as delimiters, the comparison will be performed on the word level; if commas, semicolons, and colons, are used, the syntagm level will appear more in the results; and if periods become the delimiters, then only sentences will be compared.

The same delimitation is applied for document 1 and for target document 2.

A.2.2   Matching degree

For perfect matching, Cerberus uses the Windows "Find" function, because it is easily implemented and powerful. Its performance is explained in section A.3.

For approximate or "relative" matching, I developed a simple but robust routine, which describes string similarity using percentages.

The Cerberus routine measures string similarity, not as the longest common subsequence, but as the number of sequences of two characters they have in common divided by the length of the longest string minus 1.

Comparison in this case is performed by looking up the position in the scanning window of each sequence of two characters (pair) of search strings, shifting to the right one character at a time.

Consider search string SS taken from source document A. The scanning window SW in target document B is located at position x.

SS = "abcdefghijkl"

SW = "klopabhicdemo"

The first pair "ab" is found at position 5. Subsequent searches give the following results:

Pair in SS	Found position in SW
ab	5
bc	0 (not found)
cd	9
de	10
ef	0
fg	0
gh	0

hi	7
ij	0
jk	0
kl	1

The number of found positions is 5 and the matching degree is calculated as

$$(5/(13 - 1)) * 100 = 42\%$$

13 being the length of the longest string, in this case SW. Thirteen is decreased by 1 because the maximum number of pairs in a string is always the length of this string minus 1.

With identical strings, this matching degree function returns 100%:

SS = "abcdefghijkl"

SW = "abcdefghijkl"

Subsequent searches give the following results:

Pair in SS	Found position in SW
ab	1
bc	2
cd	3
de	4
ef	5
fg	6
gh	7
hi	8
ij	9
jk	10
kl	11

The result in this case is $(11/(12 - 1)) * 100 = 100\%$.

The comparison

SS = "abcdefghijkl"

SW = "mnopqrtsuvw"

returns $(0/(12 - 1)) * 100 = 0\%$.

A problem arises, however, with repeating pairs. The string comparison

SS = "ababababababab"

SW = "abcdefghijkl"

would return 100%.

This is why at each occurrence of a pair I include a special character (#) in the search window, so that this pair cannot be found again. If I return to the first example, the result is:

SS = "abcdefghijkl"

SW = "klopabhicdemo"

Pair in SS	Found position in SW	SW
ab	5	klopa # bhicdemo
bc	0 (not found)	klopa # bhicdemo
cd	9	klopa # bhic # demo
de	10	klopa # bhic # d # emo
ef	0	klopa # bhic # d # emo
fg	0	klopa # bhic # d # emo
gh	0	klopa # bhic # d # emo
hi	7	klopa # bh # ic # d # emo
ij	0	klopa # bh # ic # d # emo
jk	0	klopa # bh # ic # d # emo
kl	1	k # lopa # bh # ic # d # emo

This way, the comparison

SS = "ababababababab"

SW = "abcdefghijkl"

only returns 17%.

The source code in Visual Basic looks as follows:

```
Counter=0
For i = 1 To Len(SS) - 1
    p = InStr(SW, Mid$(SS, i, 2))
    If p > 0 Then
        Counter = Counter + 1
        SW = Left$(SW, p) & "#" & Mid$(SW, p + 1)
    End If
  Next i
FoundMatch = CInt((Counter / (MaxLength-1)) * 100)
```

MaxLength is defined as the longest string. SW and SS are always capitalized, so that this routine is not case sensitive.

This very simple routine tackles text alterations, which include typing or scanning errors, morphological modifications (tense, number, gender, case, and so on), changes in word order, punctuation modifications, or sentence transformations. The following examples give an idea of the results of the matching-degree function (MDF):

SS	SW	MDF Result
If the disk is identified as the original disk, the application will work normally.	The application will work normally, if the disk is identified as the original disk.	96%
If the disk is identified as the original disk, the application will work normally.	If the dist is identified as the original disk, the aplication will work normaly.	95%
If the disk is identified as the original disk, the application will work normally.	Normally the application on the disk will work as the original disk is identified.	91%

If the disk is identified as the original disk, the application will work normally.	If the disks are identified as the original disks, the applications will work normally.	90%

The problem with longer strings is that the natural distribution of character pairs, combined with the inevitable presence of frequent words (such as 'a', 'the', 'is', 'are') entails a relatively high matching-degree function result for texts that have nothing in common (example taken at random from the Web).

SS	SW	MDF Result
The little boy was only 9, and he had leukemia. To his parents he was one in a billion, a little charmer whose life was slipping away. But to the doctors at the Mayo Clinic in Rochester, Minn., he was one in 300: the child belonged to the .3 percent of the population who carry a gene leaving them unable to properly metabolize a whole family of drugs. One of the drugs, a member of a class of medications called thiopurines, is prescribed for childhood leukemia. But doctors at the boy's first hospital didn't check him for the gene.	Wisp Trail is another fabulous beginner trail that has a little more challenging grade than Possum, but not enough to scare off the new-comers. This trail is ideal for those who think they are ready for the intermediate trails, but want to be sure they are ready! The trail is long, covering 7.8 acres which allows for great skiing. I find myself on Wisp trail, carving on my board and enjoying the relaxing trip down the mountain. This trail is definitely one for all.	52%

A search for sequences of three (triplets) or four (quadruplets) characters (or more), instead of pairs reduces this "natural threshold level" considerably. For the above-mentioned example, the triplet matching-degree function returns 21% and the quadruplet matching-degree function 9%.

Strings that present some kind of relationship (using the same sequences "university," "learning," "technolog-," "nation-," "research") without obvious similarity return the following results:

SS	SW	MDF(2)	MDF(3)	MDF(4)
The Humanities Computing Facility of Duke University supports academic technology on campus and around the world. We seek out new resources and innovative ideas to maximize the effectiveness of teaching, learning and research. We work with Duke faculty, students, and staff, as well as with visitors from the U.S. and many foreign nations.	The Language Institute is a central support service available to all members of the University, and the focal point for research in language and linguistics. It has a national and international reputation for independent and open learning of languages, and is at the forefront of the application of new technologies to language learning.	59%	32%	21%

Let's now take a closer look at the examples mentioned earlier:

SS	SW	MDF(2)	MDF(3)	MDF(4)
If the disk is identified as the original disk, the application will work normally.	The application will work normally, if the disk is identified as the original disk.	96%	91%	91%
If the disk is identified as the original disk, the application will work normally.	If the dist is identified as the original disk, the aplication will work normaly.	95%	90%	85%

If the disk is identified as the original disk, the application will work normally.	Normally the application on the disk will work as the original disk is identified.	91%	84%	78%
If the disk is identified as the original disk, the application will work normally.	If the disks are identified as the original disks, the applications will work normally.	90%	85%	81%

The next step is to test these functions against the examples of text alterations cited in section 3.3.3 concerning replacing words with synonyms:

SS	SW	MDF(2)	MDF(3)	MDF(4)
Empirically, it has been **proven** that the **user's capacity** to understand and to remember a **document** depends on the document's degree of coherence.	**Empirical studies** have **shown** that a **reader's ability** to understand and remember a **text** depends on its degree of coherence.	64%	55%	49%
Even in small **documents** all this can **give rise to** a considerable memory load **insofar as** no external **help** is provided in the form of navigational cues. And such cues have to allow users to **grasp** the hyperdocument net-like structure by **providing** a visual **snapshot** of its information space.	Even for smaller **hyperdocuments** this can **result in** a considerable memory load **if** no external **orientation cues** are given. In order to provide cues that appropriately **capture** the net-like structure of most hyperdocuments, authors may employ graphical presentation formats that **give** a visual **impression** of the "information space."	66%	50%	41%

It seems indeed that memory for content and memory for spatial information **belong to the same** mental representation, i.e., the **user's** mental model.	**One interpretation of this result is** that memory for content and memory for spatial information **are different aspects of the same** mental representation, i.e., the **reader's** mental model.	68%	63%	62%

These examples are from section 3.3.3 (making syntactic permutations):

SS	SW	MDF(2)	MDF(3)	MDF(4)
Examples of instructional CALL programs **are** tutorials, drill and practice, holistic prac-tice, and several kinds of game software.	Tutorial, drill and practice, holistic practice, and many types of game software **are examples** of instructional programs.	82%	71%	71%
So, for each knowledge element, the overlay model stores a value **corresponding to the estimation** of the user's knowledge relative to that particular concept.	For each domain model concept, an individual overlay model stores some value **which is an estimation** of the user knowledge level of this concept.	62%	47%	41%
The effects of such features on users' performance **have been revealed by** several **empirical studies.**	A number of **empirical studies demonstrate the effects** of such features on various kinds of user performance.	63%	54%	52%

And in spatial hypertexts navigation actually becomes a mere matter of moving through several environments **where spatial proximity indicates** both the context and the relatedness between nodes.	Navigation in such systems becomes a matter of moving through the imagined environments **and spatial proximity indicates** context and geographic relatedness.	66%	57%	53%

The following examples are taken from section 3.3.3:

SS	SW	MDF(2)	MDF(3)	MDF(4)
MetaDoc [15], for instance, uses more sets of stereotypes (novice; beginner; intermediate; expert) and two classification dimensions, i.e., the user's knowledge of general computer science concepts and the user's knowledge of UNIX. Any user is modelled by assigning one stereotype for each classification dimension (e.g., novice for UNIX concepts).	For example, MetaDoc uses two dimensions of classification and two sets of stereotypes (novice —beginner— intermediate—expert: one) to represent user's knowledge of general computer concepts, another to represent user's knowledge of UNIX (which is the domain of the system). A particular user is usually modelled by assigning this user to one of stereotypes for each dimension of classification (for intermediate for general computer concepts, novice for UNIX).	66%	56%	51%

Therefore, the readability of a hyper-document can be enhanced by assisting users when constructing their mental models. This ultimately means that all factors fostering this process have to be increased, whereas those biasing it minimised.	If we want to increase the readability of a hyper-document we must assist readers in the construction of their mental models by strengthening factors that support this process and by weakening those that impede it.	69%	49%	42%
In order to give students some practical experience with hypertext while studying this course, **it was decided** to offer the course text in hypertext form, using World Wide Web technology. **It was as well decided** to offer the text as real hyperdocument, without having a linear or strictly hierarchical structure.	In order to give the students some hands-on experience with hypertext while studying this course **we decided** to offer the course text in hypertext form, using World Wide Web technology. **We also decided** to offer the text as a real hyperdocument, not having a linear or strictly hierarchical structure.	89%	85%	82%
In this chapter we focus on the use of World Wide Web technology to make one such course possible and on **the functionalities offered** by the courseware in the light of the theoretical proficiency-adapted framework discussed in Chapter 3.	**In this paper** we focus on the use of World Wide Web technology to make such a course possible, and on **the tools we developed** and/or used to help both the teacher and the student throughout the course.	60%	47%	43%

The following string comparison, taken from section 3.3.3 as an example of more complex transformations, returns the following results:

SS	SW	MDF(2)	MDF(3)	MDF(4)
In itself annotation is therefore not very dissimilar from hiding, although it is generally a more powerful technology than this latter one, since annotation supports a stable ordering of links and avoids incorrect mental maps formation …, though annotation can not reduce cognitive overload as much as hiding [62]. Hiding can nevertheless be simulated rather well by adaptive annotation by means of "dimming" (instead of just hiding) non-relevant links. To a certain extent, i.e., as long as the user can learn to ignore dimmed links, dimming can indeed limit cognitive overload, but can not eliminate it completely, since dimmed links are still visible, therefore also recognisable as such (links) and traversable. Still,	Annotation can be naturally used with all four possible forms of links. This technique supports stable order of links and avoids problems with incorrect mental maps. Annotation is generally a more powerful technology than hiding: hiding can distinguish only two states for the nodes—relevant and non relevant—while annotation, as mentioned above, up to six states, in particular, several levels of relevancy as implemented in Hypadapter (Hohl, Böcker & Gunzenhäuser, 1996). Annotations do not restrict cognitive overload as much as hiding does, but the hiding technology can be quite well simulated by the annotation technology using a kind of "dimming" instead of hiding for "not relevant" links.	76%	52%	44%

the fact that they are visible prevents users from forming wrong mental maps [191]. Finally, while hiding can only distinguish between just two node states, i.e., relevant or non-relevant nodes, annotation can recognise more levels in each node's relative relevance (see Section 2.3.4) [108].	Dimming can decrease cognitive overload in some extent (the user can learn to ignore dimmed links), but dimmed links are still visible (and traversable, if re-quired) which protects the user from forming wrong mental maps.			

A.2.3   Interpretation of matching-degree function results

Approximate or relative matching returns more results than perfect matching. The Cerberus routine is able to detect different forms of text reuse and sentence transformations that are sometimes almost invisible to the unsuspecting reader. It certainly confirms our previous findings in manual text-reuse detection (see section 2.3.1).

It is possible to define a *threshold for similarity relevance* (TSR). This TSR is about 60% for matching-degree function (MDF)(2), 40% for matching-degree function (3) and 30% for matching-degree function (4). The threshold for matching-degree function (2) is a little bit high and thus reduces its discriminating power for higher values.

Correlation of values for all examples given in the previous section are:

MDF(2) − MDF(3): 0.94

MDF(2) − MDF(4): 0.90

MDF(3) − MDF(4): 0.99

This means that differences between MDF(2), MDF(3), and MDF(4) are not really significant. MDF(3) and MDF(4) reduce not only the threshold for similarity relevance, but also the results of very similar strings. The difference between MDF(2), MDF(3), and MDF(4) looks more like a scaling problem than a matching difference. Therefore, it is important to include an output parameter, so that the user can easily adjust a minimum matching degree in order to filter relevant matches.

Pilot runs delivered no spectacular differences in execution speed. When comparing (on a Pentium 650 MHz) a document of 44 KB with a document of 72 KB on paragraph level (delimiter = CRLF), MDF(2) needed 110 seconds, MDF(3) 100 seconds, MDF(4) 96 seconds, and MDF(5) 93 seconds. Tests with longer sequences indicated that there was no real gain in execution speed (e.g. MDF(9): 89 seconds).

I could have left the choice of matching-degree function (sequence length) as a parameter to be defined by the user. Because consequences of this choice are rather difficult to assess, and because this choice does not entail significant changes in the results, I have included comparison sequence length as a constant (CompWidth) in the program. This means that in the compiled version it cannot be changed, but the source code can always be adapted and recompiled again.

Since I did not want the character sequence to be too long in order to be able to compare small fragments, I decided to define CompWidth as 3. The source code in Visual Basic now looks as follows:

```
Const CompWidth = 3
  Counter = 0
  For i = 1 To Len(SS) - (CompWidth - 1)
    p = InStr(SW, Mid$(SS, i, CompWidth))
    If p > 0 Then
       Counter = Counter + 1
       SW = Left$(SW, p) & "#" & Mid$(SW, p + 1)
    End If
  Next i
  FoundMatch = CInt((Counter / (MaxLength -
  (Comp-Width - 1))) * 100)
```

A.3   Using the Cerberus program

The startup screen of the Cerberus program displays a menu system, three text boxes, a progress bar, and an indicator of the estimated remaining time.

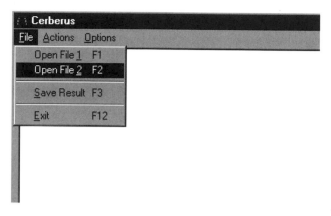

Figure 1

The texts to be compared can be inputted in three ways: by (1) typing in the text, (2) dragging or pasting the text in the corresponding text box, or (3) using the menu system and opening text in a particular folder or remote site. See figure 1.

When using the File menu, a standard dialog box allows loading of a source document as File 1 and a target document as File 2. Texts can be loaded both in Text Format and in Rich Text Format. Comparison parameters can be edited using the menu item Options—Modify Parameters. This opens the menu option shown in figure 2.

In the first frame "String definition," the user can determine the search string definition as based on a fixed length or delimited by a particular set of characters. Character delimitation allows different search levels.

Character set	Search level
empty (CRLF always included)	paragraph level
. (full stop)	sentence level
.;:,	syntagm level
.;:,(){}[]/ etc. + space	word level

The second frame "Comparison" contains option buttons for perfect or relative matching, as explained in the previous section.

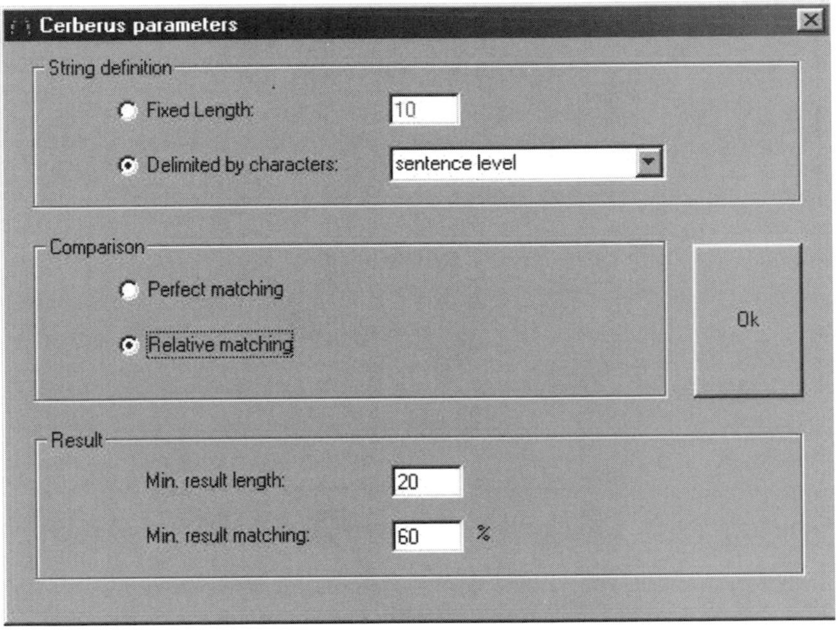

Figure 2

The "Result" frame allows the user to filter output according to length or relevance. Minimum result length (MRL) is the minimum length of the found similar string. Minimum result matching (MRM) is the minimum matching degree for output of relevant string similarity. MRM is only enabled with relative matching. MRL is only enabled with character delimitation.

	Perfect matching	Relative matching
Fixed length	MRL disabled MRM disabled	MRL disabled MRM enabled
Character delimitation	MRL enabled MRM disabled	MRL enabled MRM enabled

With the Actions—Compare menu item, see figure 3, comparison between the source document in the upper text box and the target document in the middle text box is started. As shown in figure 4, a string

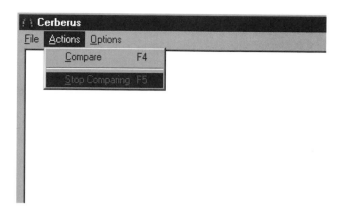

Figure 3

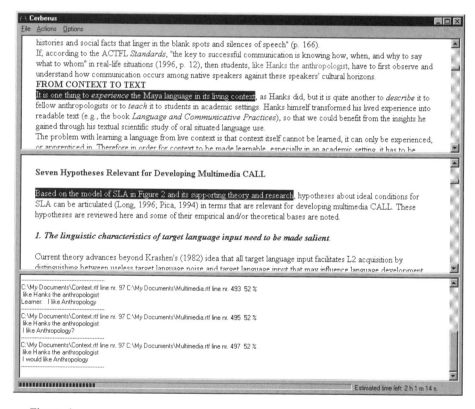

Figure 4

selected in the source document is used as search string (pattern) to scan the target document. Scanning is performed from left to right, using the same string definition. The text selected in the target document is the scanning window used for the matching-degree function with relative matching.

When a relevant match is found, the selected text in both text boxes is colored red, so that matches can easily be located and interpreted afterward.

The results of the comparison appear in the third text box, with their references to the documents and the matching result; they can be saved using the File—Save Result command, once the comparison is terminated.

A.4   Performance aspects

Cerberus can load several megabytes of data, depending on computer memory. Because documents are in Rich Text Format or in Text Format, they do not contain any pictures, so one megabyte means a lot of text. Books can be compared with articles or even with series of articles pasted together.

Rich Text Format and Text Format are universal formats that allow easy conversion from most text processors, Web browsers, and scanners. A lot of downloadable documents, however, are in PS (PostScript) or PDF (Portable Document) Format. They can be converted using Adobe Acrobat Reader or Acrobat Distiller.

The following tables show execution speed for several comparison tasks. The first test was carried out on a Pentium 650 MHz 128 MB, using a document 1 of 154 KB and a document 2 of 525 KB (MRL = 20; MRM = 60%).

	Perfect matching	Relative matching
Paragraph level	7 sec	35 min
Sentence level	28 sec	5 hrs 45 min
Syntagm level	75 sec	31 hrs 20 min
Fixed length 30	116 sec	approx. 80 hrs

A second test with smaller documents was carried out on the same Pentium 650 MHz 128 MB, using two documents of 45 KB (MRL = 20; MRM = 60%).

	Perfect matching	Relative matching
Paragraph level	2 sec	41 sec
Sentence level	5 sec	4 min 22 sec
Syntagm level	9 sec	11 min 35 sec
Fixed length 30	9 sec	25 min

The previously cited execution times may vary according to document type, number of matches, and so on. Not surprisingly, the perfect matching routine is very fast. The relative matching routine is rather slow. This is because every string from document 1 has to be compared with every string in document 2. This gives n(doc1) times n(doc2) string comparisons, n being the number of strings as defined. Each string comparison involves length(SS) − 2 sequence searches (if CompWidth = 3, cf. source code), which for the first test resulted in 1,294,867,672 triplet searches (fixed-length relative).

Because of execution speed, the use of perfect matching is recommended for quick identification of text overlap, especially in series of articles or books. Once a trace is found, comparison between articles or chapters with relative matching can deliver an accurate quantification and documentation of text reuse. Cerberus can also run in the background (while the user is continuing with other applications) or can run two or three comparisons at the same time (running two or three instances of the same program).

Execution speed in perfect matching also depends on the direction of the comparison. When document 2 is the larger document and document 1 the smaller one, Cerberus will profit maximally from the Windows "Find" function. This comparison direction influences not only speed, but also results. If in the following sentence (working on syntagm level)

"It elicits subsequent input from interlocutors, making new hypotheses, and producing more results." (document 1) the syntagm "making new hypotheses" can be found by perfect matching in the sentence

"It is improving its results by making new hypotheses at each step." (document 2)

but the inverse comparison (sentence 2 in document 1) does not lead to a perfect match.

Combining the two comparison parameters yields the following:

	Perfect matching	Relative matching
Fixed length	Every subsequent string of n characters in document 1 is searched in document 2.	Every subsequent string of n characters in document 1 is compared with subsequent strings of n characters in document 2.
	Very fast routine; length determines output relevance (depends on selected documents).	Slowest routine; not recommended as no extra relevant material is to be expected.
Delimited by characters	Every subsequent string delimited by a character belonging to the set of delimiters is searched in document 2.	Every subsequent string delimited by a character belonging to the set of delimiters is compared with all subsequent strings delimited in the same way in document 2.
	Fastest routines; choice of delimiters determines speed and output relevance.	Rather slow routine; very efficient for accurate quantification of common text clusters.

A.5   The Cerberus source code

The Cerberus program is a fairly simple program written in Visual Basic 6 (SP4). The following explanation should enable every novice to build this application. The complete source code and the compiled version 1.0 are available from the Didascalia site (www.didascalia.be).

The project CERBERUS.VBP contains two forms (frmMain and frmParameters) and a module mdGlobal.

MdGlobal contains the global variables and the error message procedure ErrorMessageBox. Main variables are:

VARIABLE	TYPE	FUNCTION
FixedStringLength	Integer	Length of Fixed Length String
MinResultLength	Integer	Minimum string length of comparison result
MinResultMatch	Integer	Minimum string resemblance
NegateCharString	String	Set of string delimiters
PerfectMatching	Boolean	Perfect Matching (TRUE) or Relative Matching (FALSE)
SS	String	Search String (string selected in document 1)
StringDelimitedByChar	Boolean	Fixed Length String (FALSE) or String Delimited by Char (TRUE)
SW	String	Search Window (string selected in document 2)

One constant CompWidth determines the length of the character sequence for the relative matching routine (default = 3).

The form frmMain contains three RTF-text boxes (RichtextBox1, RichTextBox2, RichTextBox3), a progressbar (ProgressBar1), a common dialog control (CommonDialog1), and a menu system. Initialization of forms and variables is performed in procedure InitMain (see complete code).

The menu system consists of three lists of menu items: File (mnFile), Actions (mnActions), and Options (mnOptions).

	Caption	Name Menu Item	Shortcut
File	Open File 1 Open File 2 Save Results Exit	mnFileOpen1 mnFileOpen2 mnFileSave mnFileExit	F1 F2 F3 F12
Actions	Compare Stop Comparing	mnActionsCompare mnActionsStop	F4 F5
Options	Modify Parameters	mnOptionsModifyParameters	F6

Opening File 1 or File 2 launches the procedure CommonDialog-LoadFile:

```
Private Sub CommonDialogLoadFile(ByRef rtBox As
RichTextBox)
        CommonDialog1.Filter = "Rich Text Format
        (*.rtf)|*.rtf|Text Format
(*.txt;*.asc)|*.txt;*.asc"
        CommonDialog1.ShowOpen
            If CommonDialog1.filename <> "" Then
            rtBox.Text = ""
            rtBox.LoadFile CommonDialog1.filename
            rtBox.ToolTipText = CommonDialog1.filename
        End If
End Sub
```

This procedure loads both Text and Rich Text Format files through a standard File Open dialog box. The chosen file is loaded into the Rich Text box; the file name is loaded in the tooltip text.

A similar mechanism is used for saving the comparison results:

```
Private Sub mnFileSave_Click()
 On Error GoTo eh
    CommonDialog1.DefaultExt = "*.rtf"
    CommonDialog1.filename = "Result.rtf"
    CommonDialog1.Filter = "Rich Text Format
    (*.rtf)|*.rtf"
    CommonDialog1.CancelError = True 'generates
```

```
      error on cancel
      CommonDialog1.ShowSave
      RichTextBox3.SaveFile CommonDialog1.filename,
      rtfRTF
 Exit Sub
 eh:
      'File was not saved
End Sub
```

When the menu item Compare is clicked, the procedure Loopfile1starts. It has the following structure (simplified code):

```
Private Sub LoopFile1()
  'variable initialization
  Do
      SS = SelectString(RichTextBox1)
      SearchFile2
      MoveInsertionPoint RichTextBox1, SelPos1
  Loop Until StopLoop1 'if at end of file or stopped
  by user
End Sub
```

The SelectString function looks as follows:

```
Private Function SelectString(ByRef rtBox As
Rich-TextBox) As String
    If StringDelimitedByChar Then
        rtBox.Span NegateCharString & vbCrLf, True,
        True
        SelectString = UCase(Trim(rtBox.SelText))
    Else
        rtBox.SelLength = FixedStringLength
        SelectString = UCase(rtBox.SelText)
    End If
End Function
```

If Fixed String Length is chosen, a fixed number of characters is selected in the first document. If not, the program selects a string up to the first character that belongs to the set NegateCharstring (hard return and line feed included).

To prepare for a new selection, the insertion point has to be moved. The MoveInsertionPoint procedure looks as follows:

```
Private Sub MoveInsertionPoint(ByRef rtBox As
Rich-TextBox, ByRef SelPos As Long)
    If StringDelimitedByChar Then
        rtBox.UpTo NegateCharString & vbCrLf, True,
        False
        rtBox.UpTo NegateCharString & vbCrLf, True,
        True
    Else
        SelPos = SelPos + FixedStringLength
        rtBox.SelStart = SelPos
    End If
End Sub
```

Once a search string defined, the second document has to be searched. The structure of the procedure SearchFile2 is slightly different from Loopfile1 and looks as follows (simplified code):

```
Private Sub SearchFile2()
  If PerfectMatching Then
    Do
     FoundPos = RichTextBox2.Find(SS, FoundPos, ,
     0)
     If FoundPos <> -1 Then
        FoundPos = FoundPos + 1
        OutputResult 100
     End If
    Loop Until FoundPos = -1
  Else
    RichTextBox2.SelStart = 0
    RichTextBox2.SelLength = 0
    StopLoop2 = False
    SelPos2 = 0
    Do
     SW = SelectString(RichTextBox2)
     i = FoundMatch
```

```
    If i > MinResultMatch Then
       OutputResult i
    End If
    MoveInsertionPoint RichTextBox2, SelPos2
    Loop Until StopLoop2 'if at end of file or
    stopped by user
  End If
End Sub
```

If the comparison is done through perfect matching, the standard Windows Find function can be used to scan the entire document 2 for perfect matches. In the case of relative matching, the second document is scanned by progressing n characters at a time, n depending on Fixed-StringLength or on String Delimiters, as defined in MoveInsertionPoint. The function FoundMatch compares two strings and returns a percentage of similarity, as described in section A.2.

The procedure OutputResult shows the found similar strings in the third text box, together with the comparison result as a percentage. Line numbers are given, so that these strings can easily be found again afterward. The results can be saved using the Save Result command in the menu system.

References

The references contain some sources not cited in the text.

I accessed a number of documents on the Internet, coding them with "(I)" after the citation. This explains the lack of a page reference for some documents, in particular those in html-formats. In the text such references are given with the year of publication, followed by "I," for example, (1996:I). If the Internet reference mentioned the page numbers of the original publication, they have been included in my reference as well. I do not give the URL because it may no longer be valid by the time the reader consults it. In many cases the reference points to well-known journals that can be consulted online. In other cases, an Internet search using key words from the reference's title should lead to the new URL if the material is still available online. In any case, the citation provides sufficient information about the original publication. In a few less obvious cases, I have included the general URL.

Academics in Australia blamed for student fraud. 1995. *Chronicle of Higher Education*, 24 February, A41. (I)

Altman, Ellen. 1997. The implications of research misconduct for libraries and librarians. In *Research misconduct: Issues, implications and strategies*, edited by Ellen Altman and Peter Hernon (113–123). London: Ablex.

Altman, Ellen, and Peter Hernon, eds. 1997. *Research misconduct: Issues, implications and strategies*. London: Ablex.

American Association of University Professors. 1998. On the duty of faculty members to speak out on misconduct. *Chronicle of Higher Education*, 24 November. Document. (I)

American Historical Association. 1986. *Statement on plagiarism and related misuses of the work of other authors*. Section of *Statement on standards of professional conduct*. May, amended May 1995. (I)

Andersen, Daniel. 2000. From case management to prevention of scientific dishonesty in Denmark. *Science and Engineering Ethics* 6, no. 1 (January): 25–34.

Andersen, Daniel, Lis Attrup, Nils Axelsen, and Povl Riis. 1992. *Scientific dishonesty and good scientific practice*. Copenhagen: Danish Medical Research Council.

Anderson, Judy. 1998. *Plagiarism, copyright violation, and other thefts of intellectual property: An annotated bibliography with a lengthy introduction.* Jefferson, NC: McFarland & Co.

Anderson, Melissa S. 1999. Uncovering the covert: Research on academic misconduct. In *Perspectives on scholarly misconduct in the sciences*, edited by John M. Braxton (283–307). Columbus: Ohio State University Press.

Anderson, Melissa S., and Karen Seashore Louis. 1994. The graduate student experience and subscription to the norms of science. *Research in Higher Education* 35: 273–299.

Anderson, Melissa S., Karen Seashore Louis, and Jason Earle. 1999. Disciplinary and departmental effects on observations of faculty and graduate student misconduct. In John M. Braxton, ed., *Perspectives on scholarly misconduct in the sciences* (213–235). Columbus: Ohio State University Press, 1999.

Arnau, Frank. 1961. *The art of the faker: 3,000 years of deception.* Boston: Little, Brown.

Atwal, Sandy. 1996. New Web page aids plagiarism, claim professors. *Imprint News (University of Waterloo)* 19, no. 9 (13 September).

Babbage, Charles. 1830. *Reflections on the decline of science in England and some of its causes.* Viewable as Gutenberg E-text. (I)

Baines, Lawrence. 1997. Future schlock: Using fabricated data and politically correct platitudes in the name of education reform. *Phi Delta Kappan: The Professional Journal for Education* 78, no. 7 (March). (I)

Basinger, Julianne. 1997. Court finds that professor plagiarized term paper. *Chronicle of Higher Education*, 3 October, A61. (I)

Basinger, Julianne. 1998. Professor accuses Naval Postgraduate School of cover-up. *Chronicle of Higher Education*, 6 February, A12. (I)

Basinger, Julianne. 1999. Questions raised about academic credentials of Albright College's president. *Chronicle of Higher Education*, 15 October. (I)

Basinger, Julianne. 2000. Wesley College president's papers mirrors passages from speech by another. *Chronicle of Higher Education*, 4 May. (I)

Basinger, Julianne, and Kelly McCollum. 1997. Boston U. sues companies for selling term papers over the Internet. *Chronicle of Higher Education*, 31 October, A34. (I)

Bell, Robert. 1992. *Impure science: Fraud, compromise, and political influence in scientific research.* New York: Wiley.

Bell, Robert. 1997. How to define misconduct in science. *Chronicle of Higher Education*, 16 May, B11. (I)

Ben-David, Joseph. 1991. *Scientific growth: Essays on the social organization and ethos of science.* Vol. 8 of California Studies in the History of Science, edited by Gad Freudenthal. Berkeley: University of California Press.

Bennington, Harold. 1952. *The detection of frauds*. Chicago: LaSalle Extension University.

Best, Joel. 2001. *Damned lies and statistics: Untangling numbers from the media, politicians, and activists*. Berkeley, CA: University of California Press.

Birchard, Karen. 2000. British medical establishment ignores research fraud, journal editors charge. *Chronicle of Higher Education*, 15 December. (I)

Bird, Stephanie J. 1999. Including ethics in graduate education in scientific research. In *Perspectives on scholarly misconduct in the sciences*, edited by John M. Braxton (174–188). Columbus: Ohio State University Press.

Bird, Stephanie J., and Alicia K. Dustira. 1999. Misconduct in science: Controversy and progress. *Science and Engineering Ethics 5*, no. 2 (April): 131–136.

Bird, Stephanie J., and Alicia K. Dustira. 2000. New common federal definition of research misconduct in the United States. *Science and Engineering Ethics 6*, no. 1 (January): 123–130.

Bird, Stephanie J., and Diane Hoffman-Kim. 1998. Damned if you do, damned if you don't: The scientific community's responses to whistleblowing. *Science and Engineering Ethics 4*, no. 1 (January): 3–6.

Bloomfield, H. 1994. Links in hypertext: An investigation into how they can provide information on inter-node relationships. Ph.D. thesis, Queen Mary and Westfield College, University of London. (I)

Blumenstyk, Goldie. 2001. New database seeks to illuminate researchers' ties to industry, *Chronicle of Higher Education*, 17 May. (I)

Blumenthal, David. 1992. Academic-industry relationships in the life sciences. *Journal of the American Medical Association 268*, no. 23: 3344–3349.

Bollag, Burton. 1993. American academics are drawn to the Czech Republic: Visitors help to revitalize universities that suffered under Nazi and Communist regimes. *Chronicle of Higher Education*, 27 January, A40.

Bonekemp, L. 1994. Courseware evaluation activities in Europe, *Journal of Educational Computing Research 11*, no. 1: 73–89.

Brainard, Jeffrey. 2000a. As U.S. releases new rules on scientific fraud, scholars debate how much and why it occurs. *Chronicle of Higher Education*, 8 December, A26. (I)

Brainard, Jeffrey. 2000b. Science societies are called upon to bolster efforts to ensure research integrity. *Chronicle of Higher Education*, 12 April. (I)

Braxton, John M. 1991. The influence of graduate department quality on the sanctioning of scientific misconduct. *Journal of Higher Education 62*, no. 1: 87–108.

Braxton, John M. 1999a. Toward a guiding framework for self-regulation in the community of the academic profession. In *Perspectives on scholarly misconduct in the sciences*, edited by John M. Braxton (139–161). Columbus: Ohio State University Press.

Braxton, John M., ed. 1999b. *Perspectives on scholarly misconduct in the sciences*. Columbus: Ohio State University Press.

Braxton, John M., and Alan E. Bayer. 1999. Perceptions of research misconduct and an analysis of their correlates. In *Perspectives on scholarly misconduct in the sciences*, edited by John M. Braxton (236–258). Columbus: Ohio State University Press.

Breittmayer, Jean-Philippe, a.o. 2000. Responding to allegations of scientific misconduct: The procedure at the French national medical and health research institute. *Science and Engineering Ethics* 6, no. 1 (January): 41–48.

Broad, William J., and Nicholas Wade. 1982. *Betrayers of the truth: Fraud and deceit in the halls of science*. New York: Simon and Schuster.

Brown, A. S., and D. R. Murphy. 1989. Cryptomnesia: Delineating inadvertent plagiarism. *Journal of Experimental Psychology* 15: 432–442.

Brusilovsky, P. 1996. Methods and techniques of adaptive hypermedia. *User Modeling and User-Adapted Interaction* 6: 87–129. (I)

Brydensholt, H. 2000. The legal basis for the Danish committee on scientific dishonesty. *Science and Engineering Ethics* 6, no. 1 (January): 11–24.

Buranen, Lise, and Alice M. Roy, eds. 1999. *Perspectives on plagiarism and intellectual property in a postmodern world*. Albany: State University of New York Press.

Burbules, N. C., and T. A. Callister. 1996. Knowledge at the crossroads: Some alternative futures of hypertext learning environments. *Educational Theory* 46, no. 1, 23–50.

Burd, Stephen. 1995. Federal panel will seek tougher rules on scientific misconduct. *Chronicle of Higher Education*, 3 November, A42. (I)

Burk, Dan L. 1995. Research misconduct: Deviance, due process, and the disestablishment of science, *George Mason Independent Law Review* 3 (summer): 305–350.

Buzzelli, Donald E. 1993. The definition of misconduct in science: A view from NSF. *Science* 259 (29 January): 584–648.

Buzzelli, Donald E. 1994. NSF's definition of misconduct in science, *Centennial Review* 38: 273–296.

Buzzelli, Donald E. 1996. Letter to the editor. Misconduct: Judgment called for. *Science* 272, no. 5264 (17 May). (I)

Buzzelli, Donald E. 1999. "Serious deviation from accepted practices". *Science and Engineering Ethics* 5, no. 2 (April): 275–282.

Byrd, Robert C. 1998. Pulling the plug on term-paper mills. U.S. Senate Document. 7 January. (I)

Cage, Mary Crystal. 1996. U. of Chicago panel finds history professor guilty of plagiarism. *The Chronicle of Higher Education* 9 August, A18. (I)

Campbell, Teresa, Isabelle Daza, and Sheila Slaughter. 1999. Understanding the potential for misconduct in university-industry relationships: An empirical view. In *Perspectives on scholarly misconduct in the sciences*, edited by John M. Braxton (259–282). Columbus: Ohio State University Press.

Carlson, Scott. 1999. "Ref in your head" campaign seeks to discourage classroom cheating. *Chronicle of Higher Education*, 9 September. (I)

Carnevale, Dan. 1999. Web services help professors detect plagiarism. *Chronicle of Higher Education*, 12 November, A49. (I)

Chalk, Rosemary, and Patricia Woolf. 1989. Regulating a "knowledge business": The research community must better investigate—and prevent—scientific misconduct, lest others fill the breach. *Issues in Science and Technology* 5, no. 2: 33.

Chalmers, Iain. 1990. Underreporting research is scientific misconduct. *Journal of the American Medical Association* 263, no. 10: 1405–1408.

Chapelle, Carol. 1989. Using intelligent computer-assisted language learning. *Computers and the Humanities* 23, no. 1 (January): 59–70.

Chapelle, Carol. 1997. CALL in the year 2000: Still in search of research paradigms? *Language Learning and Technology* 1, no. 1: 19–43.

Cho, Mildred K. 1997. University-industry research must get closer scrutiny. *Chronicle of Higher Education*, 1 August, B4. (I)

Cohen, V. B. 1983. Criteria for the evaluation of microcomputer courseware. *Educational Technology* 23, no. 1: 9–14.

Committee on Science, Engineering, and Public Policy (COSEPUP). 2000. *Enhancing the postdoctoral experience for scientists and engineers: A guide for postdoctoral scholars, advisors, institutions, funding organizations, and disciplinary societies*. Washington, DC: National Academy Press.

Cong, Cao. 1996. Plagiarism in China. *Science* 274, no. 5294 (13 December): 1820a–1825a. (I)

Cook, V. J. 1985. Bridging the gap between computers and language teaching. In *Computers in English Language Teaching* (13–24). ELT Documents 122. Oxford: Oxford University Press.

Cooper, Alan. 1999. *The inmates are running the asylum: Why high-tech products drive us crazy and how to restore the sanity*. Indianapolis: Sams.

Counelis, James Steve. 1993. Toward empirical studies on university ethics: A new role for institutional research. *Journal of Higher Education* 64, no. 1: 74–92.

Crews, Frederick, and Ann Jessie Vansant. 1984. *The Random House Handbook*. 4th ed. New York: Random House.

Daniloff, Nicholas. 1993. Teaching democracy in an authoritarian country. *Chronicle of Higher Education*, 31 March, B5. (I)

Davis, Michael. 1993. Of Babbage and kings: A study of a plagiarism complaint. *Accountability in Research* 2 (spring): 273–286.

Davis, Randall. 1999. The digital dilemma: Intellectual property in the information age. *Public Briefing of the National Research Council.* 3 November. National Academy of Sciences Web site. (I)

De Bra, Paul M. E. 1996. Teaching hypertext and hypermedia through the Web. In *Proceedings of the WebNet '96 Conference.* (I)

Decoo, W. 1984. An application of didactic criteria to courseware evaluation. *Calico-Journal* 2, no. 2 (December): 42–46.

Decoo, W. 1986. Informatique et linguistique appliquée: La dimension humanisante. *Bulletin of the Canadian Association of Applied Linguistics* 8, no. 2: 7–23.

Department of Health and Human Services. 2000. Public Health Service Standards for the Protection of Research. *Federal Register* 65 (28 November): 70830–70841.

Desruisseaux, Paul. 1999. Cheating is reaching epidemic proportions worldwide, researchers say. *Chronicle of Higher Education*, 30 April, A45. (I)

Deutsche Forschungsgemeinschaft. 1998. *Proposals for safeguarding good scientific practice.* (I)

Devine, Tom. n.d. A whistleblower's checklist. Government Accountability Project. (I)

Dieberger, A., and J. D. Bolter. 1995. On the design of hyper "spaces." *Communications of the ACM* 38, no. 8 (August): 98. (I)

Dobrow, Julia R. 1993. Letters to the editor: The problem of plagiarism on campus. *Chronicle of Higher Education*, 15 August, B6. (I)

Donner, Irah H. 1994. Intellectual property protection: Everything you've always wanted to know. *Computer* 27, no. 10: 74–75.

Dresser, Rebecca. 1993. Defining scientific misconduct: The relevance of mental state. *Journal of the American Medical Association* no. 269 (17 February): 895–897.

Duggins, Kamilah. 1998. Governors State U. president draws fire for suspending scholar. *Chronicle of Higher Education*, 24 July, A10. (I)

DuMez, Elizabeth. 2000. The role and activities of scientific societies in promoting research integrity. *Professional Ethics Report* 13, no. 3. (I)

Edwards, William Allen. 1933. *Plagiarism: An essay on good and bad borrowing.* Cambridge, Mass.: Minority Press.

Eklund, J. 1996. Cognitive models for structuring hypermedia and implications for learning from the World-Wide Web. In *Proceedings of the First Australian WWW Conference.* (I)

Ellison, F., J. Keenan, P. Lockhart, and J. Van Schaick. 1985. *Whistleblowing research: Methodological and moral issues.* New York: Praeger.

Elster, Richard S. 1998. Letters to the editor: Tenure procedures at postgraduate school. *Chronicle of Higher Education*, 27 March, B11. (I)

England, Elaine. 1984. Design and evaluation issues in CAL materials. *CALICO Journal* 2, no. 1: 11–13, 27.

EURO-PAR. 1995. *The plagiarism story.* 6 January. (I)

Evans, Stephen. 1996. Statistical aspects of the detection of fraud. In *Fraud and misconduct in medical research*, edited by Stephen Lock and Frank Wells (226–239). 2nd ed. London: BMJ Publishing Group.

Falzone, Nick. 1998. U. Michigan utilizes Web service to curb plagiarism. *U-Wire Today*, 12 September, 1. (I)

Fassin, Y. 1991. Academic ethos versus business ethics. *International Journal of Technology Management* 6: 533–546.

Feder, Ned, and Walter W. Stewart. 1994. Testimony before the Commission on Research Integrity II. *Reports: Commission on Research Integrity II.* 7 November. (I)

Feder, Ned, and Walter W. Stewart. n.d. Material on plagiarism. (I)

Fetter, W. R. 1984. Guidelines for evaluation of computer software (with an evaluation form). *Educational Technology* 24, no. 3: 19–21.

Foreign students at Southern Cal. found disproportionately among cheaters. 1998. *Chronicle of Higher Education*, 11 December, A61. (I)

Forester, Tom. 1990. Software theft and the problem of intellectual property rights. *Computers and Society* 20, no. 1: 2–11.

Fowler, H. Ramsey, and Jane Aaron. 1989. *The Little Brown Handbook.* Glenview, IL: Scott, Foresman.

Fox, Mary Frank. 1999. Scientific misconduct and editorial and peer review processes. In *Perspectives on scholarly misconduct in the sciences*, edited by John M. Braxton (162–173). Columbus: Ohio State University Press.

Fox, Mary Frank, and John M. Braxton. 1994. Misconduct and social control in science: Issues, problems, solutions. *Journal of Higher Education* 65, no. 3: 373–383.

Francis, Sybil. 1999. Developing a federal policy on research misconduct. *Science and Engineering Ethics* 5, no. 2 (April): 261–272.

Friedly, Jock. 1997a. Scientific misconduct: ORI's self-assessment: A batting average of .920? *Science* 275, no. 5304 (28 February): 1255–1260. (I)

Friedly, Jock. 1997b. Scientific misconduct: Charges fly over advocacy research. *Science* 275, no. 5305 (7 March): 1411–1412. (I)

Friedman, P. J. 1996. Advice to individuals involved in misconduct accusations. *Academic Medicine* 71, no. 7: 716–723.

Gillespie, Iain E. 1996. A head of department's view. In *Fraud and misconduct in medical research*, edited by Stephen Lock and Frank Wells (257–266). 2nd ed. London: BMJ Publishing Group.

Glatt. Glatt Plagiarism Services. http://www.plagiarism.com. (I)

Glazer, Myron Peretz, and Penina Migdal Glazer. 1989. *The whistleblowers: Exposing corruption in government and industry.* New York: Basic Books.

GLIMPSE: A tool to search entire file systems, http://glimpse.cs.arizona.edu. Updated 6 January 1998. (I)

Goldman Herman, Karen, Philip L. Sunshine, Montgomery K. Fisher, James J. Zwolenik, and Charles H. Herz. 1994. Investigating misconduct in science: The National Science Foundation model. *Journal of Higher Education* 65, no. 3: 384–400.

Goodman, Billy. 1996. Scientific whistleblowers stress that the media are a last resort. *The Scientist* 10, no. 6 (18 March): 1, 4. (I)

Goodman, Billy. 1997. Scientists exonerated by ORI report lingering wounds. *The Scientist* 11, no. 12 (9 June): 1, 3. (I)

Goodnough, Abby. 1999. Answers allegedly supplied in effort to raise test scores. *New York Times*, 8 December. (I)

Goodstein, D. 1991. Scientific fraud. *American Scholar* 60: 505–515.

Government Accountability Project. 1995. Striking a blow for scientific integrity. (I)

Government Accountability Project. n.d. Survival tips for whistleblowers. (I)

Gray, A. R., P. J. Sallis, and S. G. MacDonell. 1997. Software forensics: Extending authorship analysis techniques to computer programs. In *Proceedings of the 3rd Biannual Conference of the International Association of Forensic Linguists* (IAFL) (1–8). Durham, NC: International Association of Forensic Linguists. (I)

Gray, Rachel J. 1999. New plans to investigate research misconduct and improve research integrity. *Professional Ethics Report* 12, no. 4 (Fall). (I)

Grayson, Lesley. 1995. *Scientific deception: An overview and guide to the literature of misconduct and fraud in scientific research.* London: British Library, Science Reference and Information Service.

Grinnell, Frederick. 1999. Ambiguity, trust, and the responsible conduct of research. *Science and Engineering Ethics* 5, no. 2 (April): 205–214.

Guernsey, Lisa. 1998a. Judge dismisses Boston U.'s suit against on-line term-paper companies. *Chronicle of Higher Education*, 18 December, A23. (I)

Guernsey, Lisa. 1998b. Web site will check students' papers against data base to detect plagiarism. *Chronicle of Higher Education*, 11 December, A38. (I)

Gunsalus, C. K. 1993. Institutional structure to ensure research integrity. *Academic Medicine* 68 (September): 33–38. (I)

Gunsalus, C. K. 1997a. Ethics: Sending out the message. *Science* 276, no. 5311 (18 April): 335. (I)

Gunsalus, C. K. 1997b. Rethinking unscientific attitudes about scientific misconduct. *Chronicle of Higher Education*, 28 March, B4. (I)

Gunsalus, C. K. 1998a. How to blow the whistle and still have a career afterwards. *Science and Engineering Ethics* 4, no. 1 (January): 51–64. (I)

Gunsalus, C. K. 1998b. Preventing the need for whistleblowing: Practical advice for university administrators. *Science and Engineering Ethics* 4, no. 1 (January): 75–94. (I)

Guston, David H. 1994. The demise of the social contract for science: Misconduct in science and the nonmodern world. *Centennial Review* 38: 215–248.

Guston, David H. 1999. Changing explanatory frameworks in the U.S. government's attempt to define research misconduct. *Science and Engineering Ethics* 5, no. 2 (April): 137–154.

Guterman, Lila, and Scott Heller. 2000. Yale professor attacks history-department over book on David Baltimore case. *Chronicle of Higher Education*, 11 February, A14. (I)

Hacker, Diana. 1991. *The Bedford handbook for writers.* Boston: St. Martin's Press.

Hacker, Diana. 1993. *A pocket style manual.* New York: Bedford Books of St. Martin's Press.

Hackett, Edward J. 1999. A social control perspective on scientific misconduct. In *Perspectives on scholarly misconduct in the sciences*, edited by John M. Braxton (99–115). Columbus: Ohio State University Press.

Hansson, Mats G. 2000. Protecting research integrity. *Science and Engineering Ethics* 6, no. 1 (January): 79–90.

Harrison, Wilson R. 1958. *Suspect documents: Their scientific examination.* New York: Praeger.

Hartocollis, Anemona. 1999. Liar, liar, pants on fire. *New York Times*, 9 December. (I)

Hawkins, Ronnie. 1999. Response to colloquy "why professors don't do more to stop students who cheat." *Chronicle of Higher Education*, 18 January. (I)

Heller, Scott. 1997. Russian immigrants change a campus as they become Americans. *Chronicle of Higher Education*, 14 March, A36. (I)

Hering, Daniel Webster. 1924. *Foibles and fallacies of science: An account of celebrated scientific vagaries.* New York: Van Nostrand.

Hertling, James. 1995. Embarrassment in Hong Kong: Colony's efforts to produce better scholarship are marred by charges of plagiarism. *Chronicle of Higher Education*, 24 March, A43. (I)

Hixson, Joseph. 1976. *The patchwork mouse.* Garden City, NY: Anchor Press/ Doubleday.

Hodges, Christopher. 1996. Investigating, reporting, and pursuing fraud in clinical research: Legal aspects and options in England and Wales. In *Fraud and misconduct in medical research*, edited by Stephen Lock and Frank Wells (74–89). 2nd ed. London: BMJ Publishing Group.

Hoke, Franklin. 1995a. On their own: Stewart and Feder persist with misconduct inquiries. *The Scientist* 9, no. 3 (6 February). (I)

Hoke, Franklin. 1995b. Prevailing misperceptions. *The Scientist* 9, no. 10 (15 May). (I)

Hoke, Franklin. 1995c. Novel application of federal law to scientific fraud worries universities and reinvigorates whistleblowers. *The Scientist* 9, no. 17 (4 September). (I)

Holton, Gerald, and Frederick Grinnell. 1996. Letter to the editor. Defining misconduct. *Science* 273, no. 5277 (16 August). (I)

Home, Stewart. 1995. *Neoism, plagiarism and praxis*. Edinburgh: AK Press.

Hopkin, Karen. 1993. Scientific plagiarism and the theft of ideas, *Science*, no. 261 (30 July): 631.

Horowitz, Arthur M. 1996. Fraud and scientific misconduct in the United States. In *Fraud and misconduct in medical research*, edited by Stephen Lock and Frank Wells (144–165). 2nd ed. London: BMJ Publishing Group.

Hosie, James. 1996. Fraud in general practice research: Intention to cheat. In *Fraud and misconduct in medical research*, edited by Stephen Lock and Frank Wells (40–62). 2nd ed. London: BMJ Publishing Group.

Hubbard, Philip L. 1987. Language teaching approaches: The evaluation of CALL software and design implications. In *Modern media in foreign language education: Theory and implementation*, edited by Wm. Flint Smith (227–254). Lincolnwood, IL: National Textbook Company.

Hubbard, Philip L. 1988. An integrated framework for CALL courseware evaluation. *CALICO Journal* 6, no. 2: 51–72.

Hudgins, Sharon. 1997. Letters to the editor: Cultural differences in the classroom. *Chronicle of Higher Education*, 2 May, B11. (I)

Hugenholtz, B. 1996. *The future of copyright in a digital environment*. The Hague: Kluwer International.

Husson, J. M., Y. Bogaievsky, E. Hvidberg, J. Schwarz, and D. Chadha. 1996. Fraud in clinical research on medicines in the European Union: Facts and proposals. In *Fraud and misconduct in medical research*, edited by Stephen Lock and Frank Wells (206–225). 2nd ed. London: BMJ Publishing Group.

IntegriGuard. 1998. http://www.integriguard.com. (I)

iThenticate® n.d. http://www.plagiarism.org. (I)

Jacobsen, G., and A. Hals. 1996. *Medical investigators' views about ethics and fraud in medical research*. London: J. R. Coll.

Jansen, Kees. 1996. Grensverleggende stijlen van citeren in ontwikkelingsstudies. *Facta* 4, no. 5: 2–8.

Johnson, David. 1999. From denial to action: Academic and scientific societies grapple with misconduct. In *Perspectives on scholarly misconduct in the sciences*, edited by John M. Braxton (42–74). Columbus: Ohio State University Press.

Kaiser, Jocelyn. 1996. Scientific misconduct: HHS is still looking for a definition. *Science*, no. 272 (21 June): 1735b.

Kantrowitz, Barbara, and Daniel McGinn. 2000. When teachers are cheaters. *Newsweek*, 11 June. (I)

Kendall, Robert. 1996. Hypertextual dynamics in "A Life Set for Two." In *Proceedings of the Seventh ACM Conference on Hypertext* (74–83). Washington, DC: Association for Computer Machinery. (I)

Kennedy, Donald. 1997. *Academic duty*. Cambridge, MA.: Harvard University Press.

Kenning, Marie-Madeleine. 1991. CALL evaluation. The learner's view. *Computer Assisted Language Learning* 4, no. 1: 21–27.

Kerkvliet, Joe, and Charles L. Sigmund. 1999. Can we control cheating in the classroom? *Journal of Economic Education* 30, no. 4 (Fall): 331–343. (I)

Kevles, Daniel J. 1998. *The Baltimore case: A trial of politics, science, and character*. New York: Norton.

Kilgour, R. I., A. R. Gray, P. J. Sallis, and S. G. MacDonell. 1997. A fuzzy logic approach to computer software source code authorship analysis. In *Proceedings of the 1997 international conference on neural information processing and intelligent information systems* (865–868). Dunedin, New Zealand: Springer-Verlag. (I)

Knowles, S. 1992. Evaluation of CALL software: A checklist of criteria for evaluation. *ON-CALL* 6, no. 2: 9–20.

Koenig, Robert. 1997. Panel calls falsification in German case "unprecedented." *Science* 277, no. 5328 (15 August): 894. (I)

Korenman, Stanley G., Richard Berk, Neil S. Wenger, and Vivian Lew. 1996. Evaluation of the research norms of scientists and administrators responsible for academic research integrity. *Journal of the American Medical Association* 279 (7 January): 41–47.

LaFollette, Marcel C. 1988–89. Beyond plagiarism: Ethical misconduct in scientific and technical publishing. *Book Research Quarterly* 4: 65–73.

LaFollette, Marcel C. 1992. *Stealing into print: Fraud, plagiarism, and misconduct in scientific publishing*. Berkeley: University of California Press.

LaFollette, Marcel C. 1996. Paycheques on a Saturday night: A brief history and analysis of the politics of integrity in the United States. In *Fraud and misconduct in medical research*, edited by Stephen Lock and Frank Wells (1–13). 2nd ed. London: BMJ Publishing Group.

LaFollette, Marcel C. 1999. A foundation of trust: Scientific misconduct, Congressional oversight, and the regulatory response. In *Perspectives on scholarly misconduct in the sciences*, edited by John M. Braxton (11–41). Columbus: Ohio State University Press.

Lagarde, D., and H. Maisonneuve. 1996. Fraud in clinical research from the original idea to publication: The French scene. In *Fraud and misconduct in medical research*, edited by Stephen Lock and Frank Wells (180–188). 2nd ed. London: BMJ Publishing Group.

Leatherman, Courtney. 1999a. At Texas A&M, Conflicting charges of misconduct tear a program apart. *Chronicle of Higher Education*, 5 November, A18. (I)

Leatherman, Courtney. 1999b. Boston U. professor voluntarily resigns his chairmanship over an omitted attribution. *Chronicle of Higher Education*, 9 December. (I)

Lee, Barbara A. 1999. Legal aspects of scholarship misconduct. In *Perspectives on scholarly misconduct in the sciences*, edited by John M. Braxton (189–210). Columbus: Ohio State University Press.

Leibowitz, Wendy R. 1999. Council's report on copyright discusses issues without settling any. *Chronicle of Higher Education*, 4 November. (I)

Levy, Mike, and Dennis Farrugia. 1988. Evaluation of new software packages. In Mike Levy and Dennis Farrugia. *Computers in language teaching: Analysis, research and reviews* (57–60). Melbourne: Footscray College of Technical & Further Education.

L'Huillier, M. 1990. Evaluation of CALL programs for grammar. *Computer Assisted Language Learning* 1, no. 1: 79–86.

Lindey, Alexander. 1952. *Plagiarism and originality*. New York: Harper.

Lippert, Bernhard M. 1999. Dealing with academic misconduct in Germany. *Professional Ethics Report* 12, no. 2 (Spring). (I)

Lock, Stephen. 1996a. Research misconduct: A résumé of recent events. In *Fraud and misconduct in medical research*, edited by Stephen Lock and Frank Wells (14–39). 2nd ed. London: BMJ Publishing Group.

Lock, Stephen. 1996b. Fraud and the editor. In *Fraud and misconduct in medical research*, edited by Stephen Lock and Frank Wells (240–256). 2nd ed. London: BMJ Publishing Group.

Lock, Stephen, and Frank Wells, eds. 1996. *Fraud and misconduct in medical research*. 2nd ed. London: BMJ Publishing Group.

Lubalin, James S., and Jennifer L. Matheson. 1999. The fallout: What happens to whistleblowers and those accused but exonerated of scientific misconduct? *Science and Engineering Ethics* 5, no. 2 (April): 229–250.

Magner, Denise K. 1995. Law professor at Drake U. is accused of plagiarism. *Chronicle of Higher Education*, 24 November, A16. (I)

Mallon, Thomas. 1989. *Stolen words: Forays into the origins and ravages of plagiarism*. New York: Ticknor and Fields.

Malpohl, Guido, and Lutz Prechelt. 1999. Web page on *JPlag*. (I)

Mangan, Katherine S. 1997. Plagiarism case at St. Thomas U. Law School angers professors. *Chronicle of Higher Education*, 21 February, A11. (I)

Marshall, Eliot. 1998a. The Internet: A powerful tool for plagiarism sleuths. *Science* 279, no. 5350 (23 January): 474.

Marshall, Eliot. 1998b. Medline searches turn up cases of suspected plagiarism. *Science* 279, no. 5350 (23 January): 473–474.

Martin, Brian. 1992. Scientific fraud and the power structure of science. *Prometheus* 10, no. 1 (June): 83–98. (I)

Mawdsley, Ralph D. 1994. *Academic misconduct: Cheating and plagiarism.* NOLPE Monograph Series, no. 51. Topeka, KS: National Organization on Legal Problems of Education.

Max-Planck-Gesellschaft. 1997. *Procedure in cases of suspected scientific misconduct: Rules of procedure adopted by the Max-Planck-Gesellschaft on 14 November 1997.* Max-Planck-Gesellschaft zur Förderung der Wissenschaften. (I)

McCabe, Donald L., and Patrick Drinan. 1999. Toward a culture of academic integrity. *Chronicle of Higher Education*, 15 October, B7. (I)

McCabe, Donald L., and Gary Pavela. 2000. Some good news about academic integrity. *Change*, September–October, 32–38.

McCabe, Donald L., and Linda Klebe Trevino. 1993. Academic Dishonesty: Honor Codes and Other Contextual Influences. *Journal of Higher Education* 64, 5: 522–538.

McCollum, Kelly. 1996. Term-paper Web site has professors worried about plagiarism. *Chronicle of Higher Education*, 2 August, A28. (I)

McCollum, Kelly. 1999. On line, ways to misbehave can outpace college rules. *Chronicle of Higher Education*, 17 September, A35. (I)

McCutchen, Charles W. 1993. Support for Stewart, Feder. Letter. *The Scientist* 7, no. 13 (28 June): 12.

McKnight, Diane M. 1998. Scientific societies and whistleblowers: The relationship between the community and the individual. *Science and Engineering Ethics* 4, no. 1 (January): 97–113.

McLeod, Ramon G. 1997. Students look to Internet for new ways to cheat. *San Francisco Chronicle*, 16 December, A1. (I)

Meese, Jennifer. 1998. Web site used to detect cheating. *State News*, 10 December, 1.

Miceli, Marcia P., and Janet P. Near. 1992. *Blowing the whistle.* New York: Lexington Books.

Mishkin, Barbara. 1999. Scientific misconduct: Present problems and future trends. *Science and Engineering Ethics* 5, no. 2 (April): 283–292.

Mooney, Carolyn J. 1992. Critics question higher education's commitment and effectiveness in dealing with plagiarism. *Chronicle of Higher Education*, 12 February, A13, A18. (I)

MOSS. 1999. Measure Of Software Similarity. (I)

Murray, Liam, and Ann Barnes. 1998. Beyond the "wow" factor: Evaluating multimedia language learning software from a pedagogical viewpoint. *System* 26: 249–259.

National Academy of Sciences. 1992. *Responsible science: Ensuring the integrity of the research process.* Washington, DC: National Academy of Sciences.

National Academy of Sciences. 1995. *On being a scientist: Responsible conduct in research*. Washington, DC: National Academy Press. (I)

National Science Foundation. 1998. FY 1999 GPRA Performance Plan, March. (I)

National Science Foundation. n.d. *Code of Federal Regulations*. Title 45: Public welfare, chap. VI, pt. 689: Misconduct in science and engineering. (I)

Nissenbaum, Stephen. 1990. The plagiarists in academe must face formal sanctions. *Chronicle of Higher Education*, 28 March, A52. (I)

Noah, Harold J., and Max A. Eckstein. 2001. *Fraud and education: The worm in the apple*. Lanham, MD: Rowman & Littlefield.

Not-so-civil war among Lincoln scholars includes accusation of plagiarism. 2000. *Chronicle of Higher Education*, 18 February, A23. (I)

Office of Research Integrity. 1994. ORI provides working definition of plagiarism. *ORI Newsletter* 3, no. 1 (December). (I)

Office of Research Integrity. 1995. Guidelines for institutions and whistleblowers: Responding to possible retaliation against whistleblowers in extramural research. Document. 20 November. (I)

Office of Research Integrity. 1999. *HHS Fact Sheet*. 22 October. (I)

Office of Research Integrity. 2000. Managing allegation of scientific misconduct: A guidance document for editors. January. (I)

Office of Research Integrity. n.d. *Scientific misconduct regulations, 50.102: Definitions*. (I)

Office of Science and Technology Policy. 2000. Federal policy on research misconduct. *Federal Register* 65, no. 235 (6 December): 76260–76264. (I)

Parini, Jay. 2000. Living up to the meaning of "emeritus." *Chronicle of Higher Education*, 12 May, A68. (I)

Parrish, Deborah. 1996. The scientific misconduct definition and falsification of credentials. *Professional Ethics Report* 9, no. 4 (Fall). (I).

Pascal, Chris B. 1999. The history and future of the Office of Research Integrity: Scientific misconduct and beyond. *Science and Engineering Ethics* 5, no. 2 (April): 183–198.

Pavela, Gary. 1999. For the same reasons that students can be expelled, degrees ought to be revocable. *Chronicle of Higher Education*, 22 October, B6. (I)

Peters, L. S., and H. Etzkowitz. 1990. University-industry connections and academic values. *Technology in Society* 12: 427–440.

Phinney, Carolyn. 1991. Toward some scientific objectivity in the investigation of scientific misconduct. *DPR symposium: Whistleblowers, advocates and the law*. ACS meeting, New York, 27 August. (I)

Poulsen, E. 1990. Evaluation of CALL from a classroom perspective. *Computer Assisted Language Learning* 1, no. 1: 73–78.

Price, Alan R. 1994a. Definitions and boundaries of research misconduct. Perspectives from a federal government viewpoint. *Journal of Higher Education 65*, no. 3: 286–297.

Price, Alan R. 1994b. The 1993 ORI/AAAS conference on plagiarism and theft of ideas, *Journal of Information Ethics* 3: 54–63.

Price, Alan R. 1996. Federal actions against plagiarism in research. *Journal of Information Ethics* 5, no. 1: 34–51.

Price, Alan R. 1998. Anonymity and pseudonymity in whistleblowing to ORI about misconduct in biomedical research. *Academic Medicine* 73: 467–472.

Research Triangle Institute. 1995. *Consequences of whistleblowing for the whistleblower in misconduct in science cases: Final report submitted to the Office of Research Integrity.* Washington, DC: Research Triangle Institute. (I)

Research Triangle Institute. 1996. *Survey of accused but exonerated individuals in research misconduct cases: Final report submitted to the Office of Research Integrity.* Washington, DC: Research Triangle Institute. (I)

Reynolds, Jason. 1998. Cornell Ph.D. charges her professor with copying from her dissertation. *Chronicle of Higher Education*, 13 March, A16. (I)

Rhoades, Lawrence J. 1996. Whistleblower protection. *Science* 272, no. 5263 (10 May): 793. (I)

Rhoades, Lawrence J. 2000. The American experience: Lessons learned. *Science and Engineering Ethics* 6, no. 1 (January): 95–107.

Rhoades, Lawrence J., and Andrzej Górski. 2000. Scientific misconduct: An international perspective. *Science and Engineering Ethics* 6, no. 1 (January): 5–10.

Riis, Povl. 1996. Creating a national control system on scientific dishonesty within the health sciences. In *Fraud and misconduct in medical research*, edited by Stephen Lock and Frank Wells (114–127). 2nd ed. London: BMJ Publishing Group.

Riis, Povl. 2000. Sociology and psychology within the scope of scientific dishonesty. *Science and Engineering Ethics* 6, no. 1 (January): 35–39.

Rodgers, John. n.d. Introduction to graduate research: Plagiary and the art of skillful citation: Why and how people commit plagiarism. Webpage of the Department of Microbiology and Immunology, Baylor College of Medicine. (I)

Rothenberg, David. 1997. How the Web destroys the quality of students' research papers. *Chronicle of Higher Education*, 15 August, A44. (I)

Ryan, Kenneth J. 1996. Scientific imagination and integrity. *Science* 273, no. 5272 (12 July): 163.

Sallis, J., S. G. MacDonell, G. MaClennan, A. R. Gray, and R. I. Kilgour. 1997. IDENTIFIED: Software authorship analysis with case-based reasoning. In *Proceedings of the Addendum Session of the 1997 International Conference on Neural Information Processing and Intelligent Information Systems* (53–56). Dunedin, New Zealand: University of Otago.

Salzman, Maurice. 1931. *Plagiarism: The art of stealing literary material.* Los Angeles: Parker, Stone and Baird.

Samuelson, Pamela. 1993. The ups and downs of look and feel. *Communication of the ACM* 36, no. 4: 29–35.

Samuelson, Pamela. 1994. Copyright's fair use doctrine and digital data. *Communications of the ACM* 37, no. 1: 21–27.

Samuelson, Pamela, and Robert Glushko. 1990. Survey on the look and feel of lawsuits. *Communications of the ACM* 33, no. 5: 483–87.

Savan, Beth. 1988. *Science under siege: The myth of objectivity in scientific research.* Montreal, Quebec: CBC Entreprises.

Schmidt, Peter. 1998. U. of Arizona fires prominent researcher over charges of scientific misconduct. *Chronicle of Higher Education*, 14 August, A12. (I)

Schneider, Alison. 1998. Adjunct says pursuit of alleged plagiarist cost him his job at Fordham U. *Chronicle of Higher Education*, 12 June, A14. (I)

Schneider, Alison. 1999. Why professors don't do more to stop students who cheat. *Chronicle of Higher Education*, 22 January, A8. (I)

Schneider, Alison. 2000. Report calls postdocs "neglected" and proposes a series of reforms to the system. *Chronicle of Higher Education*, 12 September. (I)

Schneider, Christoph. 2000. Safeguarding good scientific practice: New institutional approaches in Germany. *Science and Engineering Ethics* 6, no. 1 (January): 49–56.

Schneiderman, Ben. 1990. Protecting rights in user interface designs. *SIGCHI Bulletin*, 22, no. 3: 18–19.

Schultz, John S., and Steven Windsor, eds. and comps. 1994. *International intellectual property protection for computer software: A research guide and annotated bibliography* Littleton, CO: Fred B. Rothman.

Scollon, Ron. 1995. Plagiarism and ideology: Identity in intercultural discourse. *Language in Society*, 24, no. 1: 1–28.

Shapiro, Martin F. 1996. Data audits in investigational drug trials and their implications for detection of misconduct in science. In *Fraud and misconduct in medical research*, edited by Stephen Lock and Frank Wells (166–179). 2nd ed. London: BMJ Publishing Group.

Shea, Christopher. 2000. Don't talk to humans. *Linguafranca* 10, no. 6 (September): 26–35.

Shivakumar, Narayanan, and Hector Garcia-Molina. 1995. The SCAM approach to copy detection in digital libraries. *D-Lib magazine*, November. (I)

Shore, Eleanor. 1995. Effectiveness of research guidelines in prevention of scientific misconduct. *Science and Engineering Ethics* 1, no. 4 (October): 383.

Sieber, Joan E. 1998. The psychology of whistleblowing. *Science and Engineering Ethics* 4, no. 1 (January): 7–23.

Sokal, Alan. 1996. Transgressing the boundaries: Toward a transformative hermeneutics of quantum gravity. *Social Text* 46/47: 217–252.

Sokal, Alan, and Jean Bricmont. 1998. *Impostures Intellectuelles*. Paris: Éditions Odile Jacob. A revised edition in French was published in 1999 by Livre de Poche. The English edition is titled *Intellectual impostures* (London: Profile Books, 1998), the American edition *Fashionable nonsense* (New York: St. Martin's Press, 1998).

Southwick, Ron. 2000. Final federal rules on research ethics offer more flexibility than did earlier draft. *Chronicle of Higher Education*, 4 December. (I)

Spier, Raymond, and Stephanie J. Bird. 2000. Scientific misconduct: Ongoing developments. *Science and Engineering Ethics* 6, no. 1 (January): 3–4.

Sprague, Robert. 1989. A case of whistleblowing in research. *Perspectives On the Professions* 8: 4–5.

Sprague, Robert. 1991. From doubts to conviction of fraud: Tales of trauma. In *Proceedings of the American Chemical Society fourth chemical congress of North America*. New York: American Chemical Society.

Sprague, Robert L. 1998. The voice of experience. *Science and Engineering Ethics* 4, no. 1 (January): 33–44.

Stegemann-Boehl, Stefanie. 1996. Some legal aspects of misconduct in science: A German view. In *Fraud and misconduct in medical research*, edited by Stephen Lock and Frank Wells (189–205). 2nd ed. London: BMJ Publishing Group.

Stegemann-Boehl, Stefanie. 2000. Misconduct in science and the German law. *Science and Engineering Ethics* 6, no. 1 (January): 57–62.

Steneck, Nicholas H. 1999a. Confronting misconduct in science in the 1980s and 1990s: What has and has not been accomplished? *Science and Engineering Ethics* 5, no. 2 (April): 161–176.

Steneck, Nicholas H. 1999b. Research universities and scientific misconduct: History, policies, and the future. In *Perspectives on scholarly misconduct in the sciences*, edited by John M. Braxton (75–95). Columbus: Ohio State University Press.

Stewart, Julie, Thomas Devine, and Dina Rasor. 1989. *Courage without martyrdom: A survival guide for whistleblowers*. Washington, DC: Government Accountability Project. (I)

St. Onge, K. R. 1988. *The melancholy anatomy of plagiarism*. Lanham, MD: University Press of America.

Strowel, A., and J. P. Triaille. 1997. *Le droit d'auteur: Du logiciel au multimedia*. Brussels: Larcier.

Suggs, Welch. 2001. Berkeley professor cheated for athletes. *Chronicle of Higher Education*, 16 March, A44. (I)

Swan, Norman. 1996. Baron Munchhausen at the lab bench. In *Fraud and misconduct in medical research*, edited by Stephen Lock and Frank Wells (128–43). 2nd ed. London: BMJ Publishing Group.

Swazey, J. P., M. S. Anderson, and K. S. Louis. 1993. Ethical problems in academic research. *American Scientist* 81 (November–December): 542–553.

Switula, Dorota. 2000. Principles of good clinical practice (GCP) in clinical research. *Science and Engineering Ethics* 6, no. 1 (January): 71–77.

Taubes, Gary. 1995. Plagiarism suit wins; experts hope it won't set a trend. *Science* 268 (26 May): 1125.

Teich, Albert, and Mark Frankel. 1992. *Good science and responsible scientists: Meeting the challenge of fraud and misconduct in science.* Washington, DC: American Association for the Advancement of Science.

Thüring, M., J. Haake, and J. Hannemann. 1995. Hypermedia and cognition: Designing for comprehension. *Communications of the ACM* 38, no. 8 (August): 57–66. (I)

Tolloczko, Tadeusz. 2000. Ethical implications in the allocation of scarce medical resources in Poland. *Science and Engineering Ethics* 6, no. 1 (January): 63–70.

Trimmer, Joseph. 1989. *A guide to MLA documentation.* Boston: Houghton Mifflin.

Tsou, Chen-Lu. 1998. Science and scientists in China. *Science* 280 (24 April): 528–529. (I)

Turner, Stephen. 1999. Universities and the regulation of scientific morals. In *Perspectives on scholarly misconduct in the sciences*, edited by John M. Braxton (116–36). Columbus: Ohio State University Press.

University of Kentucky, Department of Chemistry. n.d. *Plagiarism: Definitions, examples and penalties.* (I)

Van Kolfschooten, Frank. 1993. *Valse vooruitgang: Bedrog in de Nederlandse wetenschap.* Amsterdam/Antwerp: L. J. Veen.

Walfish, Daniel. 2001. Chinese applicants to U.S. universities often resort to shortcuts or dishonesty. *Chronicle of Higher Education*, 5 January, A52. (I)

Walker, Janice R., and Todd Taylor. 1998. *The Columbia guide to on-line style.* New York: Columbia University Press.

Watkins, Elizabeth W. Plagiarism. In *Don't Perish—Publish! Faculty Notebook*, edited by Howard A. Christy, Jennifer S. Harrison, and Elizabeth W. Watkins (25–35). Provo, Utah: Scholarly Publications, Brigham Young University, 1994.

Weiner, J. S. 1955. *The Piltdown forgery.* New York: Oxford University Press.

West, Adrian. n.d. Webpage on *Bandit.* (I)

Wheeler, David L. 1992. Scientists question secret fraud investigations. *Chronicle of Higher Education*, 29 April. (I)

Wheeler, David L. 1993. Is technology a new venue for plagiarists? *Chronicle of Higher Education*, 30 June, A17. (I)

Wilkinson, S., Crerar, A., and N. Falchikov. 1997. Book versus hypertext: Exploring the association between usability and cognitive style, 1997. (I)

Williams, Jeff. 1994. Williams's Testimony at the Ryan Congressional Commission on Research Integrity Hearing, 1 December. (I)

Williams, Nigel. 1997. Editors seek ways to cope with fraud. *Science* 278, no. 5341 (14 November): 1221. (I)

Williams, Nigel. 1998. Editors call for misconduct watchdog. *Science* 280, no. 5370 (12 June): 1685–1686. (I)

Wilson, Robin. 1999. Appeals court says colleges may oust scholars who falsely accuse their colleagues. *Chronicle of Higher Education*, 25 March. (I)

Wilson, Robin. 2000. Judge has authority to reinstate fired U. of Arizona professor, State Appeals Court rules. *Chronicle of Higher Education*, 27 July. (I)

Wise, Michael J. 1996. YAP3: Improved detection of similarities in computer program and other texts. In *Twenty-Seventh SIGCSE Technical Symposium* (130–134). Philadelphia: ACM Special Interest Group on Computer Science Education.

Wissoker, Ken. 2000. Negotiating a passage between disciplinary borders. *Chronicle of Higher Education*, 14 April, B4. (I)

Woolf, Patricia K. 1988. Deception in scientific research. *AAAS-ABA National Conference of Lawyers and Scientists, Project on scientific fraud and misconduct. Report on workshop number one* (37–86). Washington, DC: American Association for the Advancement of Science.

Wright, David E. 1994. The federal research misconduct regulations as viewed from the research universities. *Centennial Review* 38: 249–272.

Wyatt, David H. 1987. Applying pedagogical principles to CALL courseware development. In *Modern media in foreign language education: Theory and implementation*, edited by William Flint Smith (85–98). Lincolnwood, Ill.: National Textbook Company.

Xiguang, Li, and Xiong Lei. 1996. Scientific misconduct: Chinese researchers debate rash of plagiarism cases. *Science* 274 (18 October): 337–340.

Yachnin, Jennifer. 2001. Two professors at Columbia College Chicago win $250,000 judgment in defamation suit. *Chronicle of Higher Education*, 24 April. (I)

Ziman, John. 1998. Why must scientists become more ethically sensitive than they used to be? *Science* 282, no. 5395 (4 December): 1813–1814. (I)

Index

AAAS. *See* American Association for the Advancement of Science
Aaron, Jane, 121
Accounting as fraudulent environment, 33–34
Accused
  protecting the rights of, 179–181
  recommendations for, 177–179
Advertising Council, 23
Advies Commissie Wetenschap en Ethiek, 35
AHA. *See* American Historical Association
Altman, Ellen, 181
American Association for the Advancement of Science, 31, 184
American Association of University Professors, 1, 153
American Committee on Science, 16
American Historical Association, 126–128
American Psychological Association, 128
Amicable settlement, 174–175
Analysis
  of connections, 99–103
  of courseware, 112–115
  of fabrication and falsification, 62–63
  of make-believe, 105–112
  of plagiarism, 63–99
  of plagiarism of ideas, 115–116
Andersen, Daniel, 7, 57
Anderson, Judy, 136

Anderson, Melissa S., 2, 15, 25, 159, 185
Anonymity
  of the accused, x, xiv, 62, 66, 195
  of the whistle-blower, 160, 165, 172
Arnau, Frank, 3
Assessment
  of fabrication and falsification, 118–119
  of plagiarism, 119–139
Association for Practical and Professional Ethics, 184
Atwal, Sandy, 30
Australia, 7, 19, 177
Authorship disputes, 55

Babbage, Charles, 2–3
Baines, Lawrence, 38
Baltimore, David, 42, 119
Bandit, 54
Barnes, Ann, 146
Basinger, Julianne, 31, 58, 155, 156, 159, 179
Bayer, Alan E., 174
Belgium, 53, 174, 190, 191
Bell, Robert, 3, 5–6, 8
Ben-David, Joseph, 17
Bennington, Harold, 3
Berkeley, University of California at, 45
Best, Joel, 38
Birchard, Karen, 16
Bird, Stephanie J., 153, 184